MYSTERIES
of the
UNEXPLAINED

A modern myth, or evidence of life on other planets?
Sightings of U.F.O.s (Unidentified Flying Objects) are
reported worldwide.

For many years scholars did not believe the enigmatic giant statues of Easter Island in the Pacific were the work of the islanders, but ascribed them to visitors from other cultures – or even outer space.

MYSTERIES
of the
UNEXPLAINED

by Richard and Amanda O'Neill

DreamHouse

Dream House is a trademark of
Ottenheimer Publishers, Inc.
10 Church Lane
Baltimore, Maryland 21208

The Authors

Richard O'Neill, the English-born author of the "Strange World" and "Men and Monsters" chapters of this book, has had a varied and exciting career as a soldier, professional boxer, actor, and writer – both nonfiction, especially historical works, and fiction, including plays for stage and television. In recent years, he has concentrated on historical nonfiction, particularly military subjects. He is the author of *Suicide Squads: Special Attack Weapons of World War II*, and he has contributed to many books on military history and weapons.

Amanda O'Neill, the author of the "Gods and Demons" chapter of *Mysteries of the Unexplained*, was educated and has worked at the university level in her native England. A specialist in early English literature, her primary field of interest is in the Celtic myths and the medieval romances of King Arthur.

Credits

Editor: Philip de Ste. Croix
Designer: Jill Coote
Picture research: Leora Kahn
Typesetting: SX Composing Ltd.

Voodoo rites in Haiti: these worshipers have made a pilgrimage to offer up their prayers to Erzulie, goddess of love and bringer of good health and prosperity.

C O N T E N T S

CHAPTER 1 – STRANGE WORLD

INTRODUCTION 12

Searchlight on U.F.O.s	16	England's holy hills	62
Natural Wonders	18	Giants on the Earth	64
Improbable: impossible?	20	The cursed seas	66
Visitors from space?	22	Lands beneath the oceans	68
The Martians are coming!	24	Lure of the "Money Pit"	70
Close encounters	26	Stately homes: stately ghosts	72
Mistaken identity?	28	Curse, jinx, or hex?	74
Is anyone out there?	30	Curse of the boy king	76
Aliens under water	32	Doomed giants of the oceans	78
The Earth is flat . . .	34	Accursed autos and luckless locos	80
. . . or is it hollow?	36	Curse or coincidence?	82
Riddles in rocks	38	Hexes and hoaxes	84
Signs of ill omen?	40	Lucky for some?	86
Corpse-candles, goblins, and Merry Dancers	42	Doomsday!	88
Fire from Heaven	44	The Devil's footprints	90
Cereal stories	46	Into thin air	92
Strange rains	48	From out of nowhere	94
Wild children	50	What happened at Philadelphia?	96
Numerate nags and complaining cats	52	Invasion of the body snatchers	98
Nazca Lines: art for aeronauts	54	Trial by fire	100
Monuments of the Mound Builders	56	Food for thought!	102
Secrets of ancient stones	58	Hit or myth?	104
Riddle of the stone giants	60		

C O N T E N T S

CHAPTER 2 – MEN AND MONSTERS

Men of mystery and magic	108	Written in the stars	152
New sciences and old oracles	110	Hands of fate	154
Monsters in fact and fiction	112	Oracles of east and west	156
The secret art of alchemy	114	Cards of destiny	158
The immortal St. Germain	116	Body language	160
Houdini: trickster against trickery	118	Nostradamus: prophet of doom?	162
The holy terror	120	From crystal ball to computer	164
Wickedest man in the world?	122	Monsters of olden times	166
Jack the Ripper: black magician?	124	Lucky dragons and loathsome worms	168
Mind over matter	126	Virgins' prey: the unicorn	170
Mesmer the magnetic man	128	Terrors of the deep	172
Psychic detectives: hit and miss?	130	Lure of the mermaid	174
Mental radio: extrasensory perception	132	Nessie and her cousins	176
Kirlian photography: pictures of the unseen	134	Giants of the snows	178
The twitching twig	136	Missing link in the American wilderness?	180
Defying the law of gravity	138	Do dinosaurs walk the Earth?	182
Talking with the dead	140	New wild beasts and undiscovered animals	184
R101: the medium and the messages	142	Giants in the sky	186
Voices from beyond the grave	144	Werewolves and their kin	188
In touch with genius?	146	Risen from the tomb	190
Travelers through time	148	Zombie: the walking dead	192
More lives than one?	150	Man-made monsters	194

C O N T E N T S

CHAPTER 3 – GODS AND DEMONS

Religious mysteries and miracles	198
Wise folk and witches	200
Fairies, sprites, and spooks	202
God the Father: God the Mother	204
The life everlasting	206
Angelic hosts of Heaven	208
The legions of the damned	210
The terrors of Hell	212
Holy Mother and Holy Son	214
Gods of ancient empires	216
Gilgamesh, the first superhero	218
Egypt's cult of the dead	220
Soap opera on Mount Olympus	222
The bull as god and monster	224
Hercules: Superman of the ancient world	226
Good versus evil – the cosmic battle	228
Priests of the sacred grove	230
Ax age, sword age	232
Arthur: once and future king	234
Shinto: way of the gods	236
Lord Jaguar and the Long Count	238
Golden hoard and green hell	240
Native American dreamers and dancers	242
Shamans of the north	244
Dreaming down under	246
Killers for faith: Assassins and Thugs	248
Ancient wisdom of Africa	250
Miracle men of Tibet	252
The man who talked with Angels	254
The witches of the West	256
Matthew Hopkins, Witch-finder General	258
Witch mania in Massachusetts	260
White witches and black magic	262
Magic and the Third Reich	264
Fairy tales	266
Sherlock Holmes in Fairyland	268
Doctor Johnson's strangest case	270
The real ghostbusters	272
Harry Price, ghost-hunter	274
Poltergeists, the unquiet spirits	276
England's screaming skulls	278
No earthly harbor: ghost ships old and new	280
The haunted White House	282
Victims of violence	284
Stranger than truth	286
SUPERFACTS	288
INDEX	306
PICTURE CREDITS	312

Introduction

M ysteries – the strange, the inexplicable, the unknowable – fascinate people. From the earliest civilizations, human beings have tried to discover the meanings – "the facts" – behind events for which there is no logical explanation. When the answers have not been found easily, people have crafted explanations that made them comfortable, or at least allowed them to sleep at night.

For our earliest ancestors, these mysteries were invested with great powers, so they worshiped sun and sea gods, among many others. Later societies looked for solutions to practical problems (such as whether alchemists could really turn lead into gold) and developed theories about why werewolves and vampires existed. For modern men and women, the mysteries of space – Are there aliens? Are they friendly? Is time travel possible? – draw the most attention.

Almost all of these topics, however, have existed in one form or another – sometimes simple, sometimes sophisticated – since humankind's earliest days. These very real concerns endure *because they are mysteries.*

Mysteries of the Unexplained presents the most intriguing, the most perplexing, and the most terrifying of the mysteries that people have encountered from antiquity to the last years of the 20th century. There are three primary chapters in the book: "Strange World," "Men and Monsters," and "Gods and Demons." "Strange World" is an exploration of terrestrial and extraterrestrial enigmas, while "Men and Monsters" looks into whether amazing humans and incredible beasts are myth or reality. "Gods and Demons" profiles a gallery of unearthly beings and fantastic beliefs. The topics in each chapter include a fact file with a miscellany of further information, much of it humorous. In the final section of the book, "Superfacts," strange and unforgettable tidbits are collected – ideal for browsing.

Strange World
A collection of natural and unnatural phenomena – both weird and wonderful – this chapter starts in space and returns to Earth to look at some of its meteorological marvels, from the Tunguska meteor to crop circles, and to tour its most mysterious places, from the lost Atlantis to the Bermuda Triangle. U.F.O.s were once scoffed at, but now NASA has mounted a multibillion-dollar scan of space to search for extraterrestrial intelligences.

Men and Monsters

Whether they are real or unreal, or somewhere in between, strange humans and beasts occupy a prominent place in the world's societies. In this chapter, readers will encounter some of the most controversial beings that have inhabited (or have been rumored to inhabit) the Earth: magicians, psychics, prophets, mermaids, unicorns, zombies, and water monsters.

Gods and Demons

In ancient times, "mysteries" were directly connected to religion – the gods and goddesses of Egypt, Greece, Rome, and other societies. These associations with religion have continued into more modern eras, with detours that involved ordinary people, such as the witch hunts in Massachusetts. Many famous intellects, including Dr. Samuel Johnson and Sir Arthur Conan Doyle, creator of Sherlock Holmes, believed in supernatural forces, sometimes to their regret.

A demon from the East: this fearsome figure may represent Hayagriva, enemy of the gods in both Buddhist and Hindu mythology and known to Tibetan Buddhists as the "Lord of Wrath."

Moonrise over Callanish, a stone circle on the Isle of Lewis, Scotland, regarded as a sacred site by some occultists.

CHAPTER 1
STRANGE WORLD

Searchlight on U.F.O.s

Like its companion chapters *Men and Monsters* and *Gods and Demons*, this chapter celebrates the mysterious, odd, bizarre and sometimes, macabre. The greater part of this chapter deals with the natural (or unnatural) wonders of Earth. In it we scan the planet's skies and oceans for space ships; wonder whether it is really flat – or hollow; consider some of its meteorological and biological marvels, from Northern Lights to talking animals; and pry into the secrets of its strangest places. Finally, some of the strange beliefs and even stranger behavior of the world's peoples are examined, and sometimes questioned.

The COMING of the SAUCERS

By Kenneth Arnold & Ray Palmer

The modern rash of U.F.O. sightings began with Kenneth Arnold's 1947 encounter, which he put into print in 1952 in his book *The Coming of the Saucers*.

In 1967 a Colorado weather station technician took an ordinary landscape photo – and discovered this flying saucer image only when the picture was developed.

Unlike former President Jimmy Carter, many people have never seen an Unidentified Flying Object (U.F.O.) and are by no means convinced of the existence of the alien craft described in the first part of this book. But it seems that if the U.S. electorate voted the straight U.F.O. ticket, Carter would have remained in office in perpetuity. In 1991 a Gallup poll revealed that about 50 percent of Americans believe there is some form of extraterrestrial life. Fair enough, so do many scientists – in 1992 NASA's radio telescopes began a 10-year scan through the Milky Way galaxy for extraterrestrial intelligences (E.T.I.s) – neither they nor ordinary believers expect to find a message from "E.T." on their answering machines. But the same poll revealed that 47 percent of

ranged from *The Coming of the Saucers* (1952) by Kenneth Arnold – whose sighting of nine flying saucers on June 24, 1947, began the U.F.O. mania – to Timothy Good's bestselling *Alien Liaison* (1991), which has an approving commentary by Admiral of the Fleet, Lord Hill-Norton, Britain's former defense chief. Some were out to lunch: others, like Good's work, sober and well argued. But one disturbing element was how speculations and rumors printed by Ufologists in the 1950s-60s somehow became established facts in the books of some of their successors in the 1970s-80s. Nor is it a valid argument that if a government agency or other official body has "no comment" on a supposed marvel, then there must be something in it – and if it issues a flat denial, then what is denied must be true, or why should they bother to deny it?

A sense of wonder is a fine thing. But then so is common sense.

Today scientists explain away eerie Northern Lights as a matter of electrically charged solar particles; in earlier times they seemed as unearthly as any U.F.O.

This photograph purports to show an alien corpse in the wreckage of a flying saucer that crashed in New Mexico in 1948 – but many find it unconvincing.

Americans believe U.F.O.s are real – and 14 percent claim to have seen one.

Reluctance to go all the way with U.F.O. believers may some day put skeptics in the company of those who advised the Wright Brothers to stick with repairing bicycles, or rank them with former British Astronomer Royal Sir Richard Woolley, who in 1956 announced: "Space travel is utter bilge." And if you believe in U.F.O.s – or the Hollow Earth, or King Tut's curse, or any other of the beliefs examined in this book – then your right to do so should be respected and your arguments listened to. Provided they are convincing ones.

Sources consulted in researching U.F.O.s

Natural wonders

In 1992 Dr. Ari Ben-Menahem of Israel's Weizmann Institute of Science theorized that some miraculous happenings detailed in the *Old Testament* could be attributed to natural phenomena. The destruction of Sodom and Gomorrah, he believes, may have been caused by a well-authenticated earthquake in c.1560 B.C. King David's vision of "the Angel of the Lord with a sword in his hand" (*Chronicles I*: Chapter 21; Verse 16) may refer to the appearance in 986 B.C. of what we now know as Halley's Comet. The *Book of Joshua* (Chapter 10; Verse 13) tells how Joshua successfully commanded the Sun to stand still over Gibeon, so daylight lasted until the Amorites were defeated. A few verses earlier we are told that "the Lord cast down great stones from Heaven." Dr. Ben-Menahem thinks this may refer to a meteor shower, pointing out that reports of the Tunguska meteor of 1908 say that after its explosion night

Today we know who carved the Easter Island statues, and how – but whether they represent gods or chieftains remains a mystery.

The Andes Candelabrum drawn in the desert of Paracas, Peru. Why, and how, did ancient peoples create such giant landscape drawings visible only to the gods – and to modern airplanes?

was turned into bright daylight for several hours.

The Tunguska meteor is one of several natural wonders examined later in this chapter. Some are spectacular, like the comets that our ancestors looked on as signs and omens. Some are still unexplained, like the footprints of humans in ancient rocks where, according to science, no human could have walked. Some, like the strange rains of frogs and other creatures and the appearance of "crop circles," may have a simple explanation.

There follows a tour of some of Earth's most mysterious places. They range from the very real and impressive remains of northern and southern Native American civilizations to more controversial locations such as the Bermuda Triangle and other cursed seas, and the fabled Atlantis and other lost continents. It is unfortunate that so many able and interesting writers have chosen to concentrate on the latter, when so many real places of mystery remain underexplored. To many, the origin of things such as Britain's chalk giants is of more interest than speculation as to whether the inhabitants of Shangri-La knew the secret of negative gravity. And let us solve the real mysteries surrounding the Easter Island stone heads before we begin conjecturing about whether they were erected by supermen or by alien gods from outer space.

This chapter ends with a look at curses, jinxes, and hexes. Although certain famous curses have gained weight with each retelling (such as the curse of Tutankhamun's tomb or that of the Bermuda Triangle), it cannot be denied that even ordinary artifacts such as warships, automobiles, and locomotives seem sometimes to act as a focus for bad luck. The chain of unpleasant circumstances that binds them cannot be wholly ascribed to what has been named "synchronicity," a succession of seemingly meaningful coincidences. A personal curse is rather different: rather than attribute its working to some supernatural power wielded by the curser, many believe that it will work only to the extent that the victim believes it will.

A modern puzzle: are the widely reported "crop circles" in wheat fields created by freak weather conditions, visitors from outer space, or hoaxers?

Modern popular tradition associates the treasures of ancient Egypt with sinister tales of cursed tombs and murderous mummies.

Improbable: impossible?

The final chapter of this book is given over to a miscellany of mysteries and oddities, ranging from prophets of doom to raisers of the dead – even eaters of the dead; taking in a selection of unexplained appearances and disappearances, including the alleged teleportation of a World War II destroyer escort; and ending with a look at popular superstitions and urban legends.

These latter – the one about the microwaved cat (always the pet of a friend of a friend of the raconteur) is perhaps the archetype – are truly strange and fascinating. Also useful – as many

The late ex-King Zog I haunted his Rolls Royce – or so the scent of cigarettes persuaded its new owner. Smells – from mystery fragrance to grave-stench – often suggest ghosts.

aspects of the mysterious, however intriguing, are not. Some of the urban legends collected here are really moral fables for our time, illustrating the dangers of drug taking and other excesses.

Readers may think the text is overly skeptical about some aspects of "the unexplained" that are examined in this book's various sections. One example is of a gentleman who owned for a time an armored Rolls Royce automobile (he was a dealer in such exotica) that had belonged to Albania's ex-King Zog I (1895-1961). It was, he claimed, haunted: often, the distinctive smell of the monarch's Turkish cigarettes filled its interior. Skeptics might comment that unless he had had the upholstery thoroughly cleaned this was not surprising: Zog was one of the world's champion smokers, lighting up more than 200 per day.

Although it is easy to be skeptical when it comes to U.F.O.s, space gods, and lost continents, there is much in this world

By prayer and fasting the human body can apparently break natural laws: this Muslim ascetic endures weighted daggers through his flesh without pain or even bleeding.

Prehistoric monuments were long thought to have healing powers. Until recent times sick people crawled through the holed stone of the Men-an-tol in England to seek a cure.

that we do not, and perhaps never shall, understand. In investigating mysterious facts please bear in mind the advice of the immortal detective Sherlock Holmes: " . . . when you have eliminated the impossible, whatever remains, however improbable, must be the truth." (And do not forget that Holmes's literary creator, Sir Arthur Conan Doyle, who is greatly admired for his intellect, was himself a true believer in the supernatural.)

But who is to say what "the impossible" is? Perhaps the true *guru* of all lovers of the mysterious fact – all those who would like to able to believe, like the Duchess in *Alice in Wonderland*, in two or three impossible things before breakfast; and that is most of us, including this writer – is the German physicist Werner Karl Heisenberg (1901-76). In the late 1920s his studies led him to the conclusion that it was impossible to know everything there was

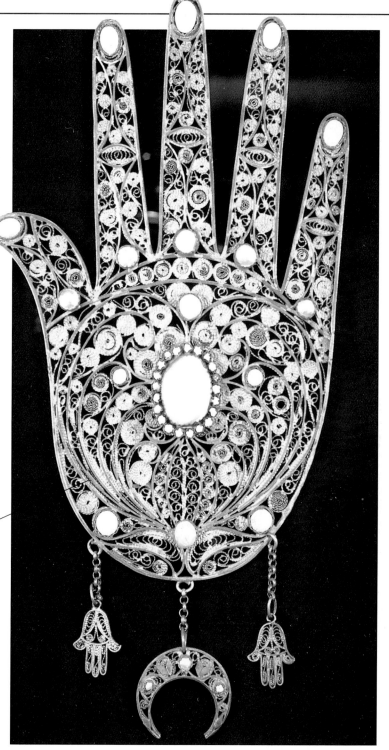

Amulets to ward off evil date back to ancient times and range from natural objects like a holed pebble to this Turkish "hand of Fatima."

to know about a subatomic particle at any given moment. His formulation of this Uncertainty Principle was bitterly opposed by Einstein, among others, but is now accepted by many scientists, some of whom speak of an "unseen world" below the threshold of observed reality. Its relevance to the "strange world" of this book is obvious.

Visitors from space?

A number of N.A.S.A. astronauts have reported sighting – and, as seen here, have even photographed – Unidentified Flying Objects in space.

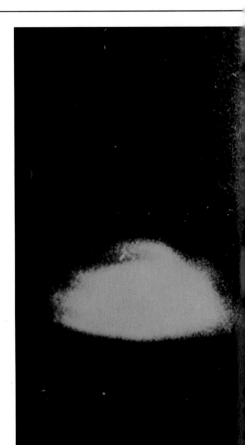

On June 24, 1947, Idaho businessman Kenneth Arnold, flying his private plane near Mount Rainier, Wash., sighted 9 disks, each about 100ft (30m) in diameter, flying in formation at about 1,700mph (2,735kmh). Soon, many similar reports were made worldwide – but it was Arnold's description of how they "skipped like saucers across water" that gave the world's press a name for them: "flying saucers." Today we call them Unidentified Flying Objects (U.F.O.s), and those who study them "Ufologists." Many believe they are visitors from outer space, crewed by extraterrestrial beings (E.T.s). Scientists attributed Arnold's sighting, and many others, to unusual atmospheric conditions, but the U.S. Air Force – in Cold War days, perhaps fearing a Soviet secret weapon – made a long study of U.F.O.s. Its *Project Blue Book* (1950-69) examined some 12,000 sightings, concluding that most were of mundane objects and denying there was any evidence that U.F.O.s were craft from another planet. Recent polls show that nearly 50 percent of Americans (and similarly large minorities in other countries) disagree. Some Ufologists say these craft have been with us since the beginning of time: that our ideas of gods are based on E.T.s who sowed the seeds of civilization on Earth. Some say they come from within our Hollow Earth or from beneath our oceans. Perhaps they are the craft of benevolent aliens who protect us from some extraterrestrial threat – or perhaps their crews are carrying out reconnaissance for a coming invasion. Psychiatrist Carl Jung theorized that U.F.O.s filled a religious vacuum for modern humanity, representing "a hope . . . the expectation of a savior." A recent view is that U.F.O.s exist not in reality, but as paranormal phenomena – ghosts for our troubled times.

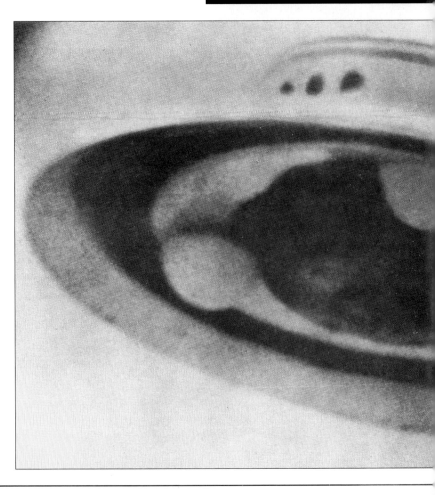

This photograph was taken through the window of a Parisian building: the Eiffel Tower U.F.O. is the reflection of an electric light and shade on the window pane.

The U.S. Air Force released this photograph of a glowing disk, brighter than the Moon (on right of picture), but did not say it was a U.F.O.

George Adamski's famous photograph, taken at Palomar Gardens, California, in December 1952, is said to show a spacecraft from Venus.

Another of Adamski's California photographs: this is claimed to show an interplanetary carrier ship and two scout craft.

FACT FILE

❑ Reports of strange craft in Earth's skies date back some 3,000 years: some exponents of "the gods were astronauts" theories say that the Old Testament prophet Ezekiel's vision of four living creatures and a wheel (*Ezekiel*: Chapter 1; Verses 4-28) describes an encounter with space gods and their craft. The great Sanskrit epic *Mahabharata*, probably composed c.300 B.C., tells of gods fighting in the sky in aircraft (*vimanas*) with laser-like weapons.

❑ In 1968 a University of Colorado team headed by Dr. Edward U. Condon (above), Professor of Astrophysics, produced a 1,465-page report based on data from the U.S.A.F.'s *Project Blue Book*. The *Condon Report*, seen as authoritative by skeptics of U.F.O.s, said at least 90 percent of U.F.O. sightings were caused by ordinary objects and that most of the others were of dubious worth. It concluded that the study of U.F.O.s had not added to scientific knowledge.

The Martians are coming!

Makers of fictions favor the "red planet," Mars, as a likely source of alien invasion. This owes much to U.S. astronomer Percival Lowell (1855-1916), whose many real accomplishments (including prediction of the existence of the planet Pluto, confirmed in 1930) are shadowed by his "discovery" of life on Mars. In 1894, after observing channels (Italian: canali) there noted by Italian astronomer Giovanni Schiaparelli, Lowell pronounced them "canals," built by Martians struggling to irrigate their desert planet by channeling water from its ice-caps. Some believed in the Martians and their canals until photographs taken by Mariner space probes in the 1960s-70s showed they did not exist. Lowell's speculations triggered the U.S. airship scare of 1896-97. Rumor said a large, cigar-shaped, propeller-driven dirigible (no dirigible nor aircraft would fly in the United States until 1903), perhaps from Mars, was making a west-to-east transcontinental journey. Letters to prominent Americans were produced, said to have been dropped by the Martians: one to the great inventor Thomas Edison, who denounced the affair as a hoax. Britain's scareships of 1909-13 were a product of war fears. The night-flying dirigibles, about 230ft (70m) long and very fast, were said to be crewed not by Martians but Germans (whose Zeppelin airships would attack Britain in reality after war came in 1914). War rumors also helped fuel the U.S. Martian scare of October 30, 1938, when actor Orson Welles's Mercury Theater of the Air broadcast a dramatization of *The War of the Worlds* by H.G. Wells. It was so realistic that many persons believed Martians had landed in Princeton, N.J., and were slaughtering with death rays all who opposed them. Across the nation, police and military posts were deluged with calls for help.

The "red planet," Mars, as seen from a Viking orbiter spacecraft. No signs of life were found on the planet at the sites examined by the Viking missions' lander spacecraft.

Martian fighting machines ravage Earth – in the movie *The War of the Worlds* (1952). Some radio listeners in 1938 believed they really faced this peril.

Dirigible airships, like this visionary steam carriage of 1863, were a mainstay of science fiction – and a source of many popular scare stories – until the early 20th century.

Many early sci-fi tales told of Moon men: but the first living beings to imprint the ancient dust of the Moon's Sea of Tranquillity were the astronauts of the *Apollo 11* landing in 1969.

❑ Some astronomers suggest that Lowell (below) was misled by huge dust storms that periodically sweep the arid surface of Mars. They say the storms occasionally create an effect resembling the "network of straight lines" seen by Schiaparelli and Lowell.

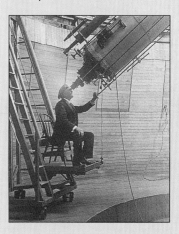

❑ The airship scare of 1896-97 produced tales as bizarre as any reported by Ufologists. A farmer in Sioux City, Ia., claimed he had been caught by a grappling hook from an airship and dragged some distance before struggling free. A Michigan man claimed a voice "from above the clouds" had ordered him to fetch 48 egg salad sandwiches and a pot of coffee – and had let down a basket to receive them.

❑ A wave of airship sightings hit Texas in April 1897, when it was said "Mr. Wilson of Illinois" was chugging around the state in an advanced airship of his own design. Several Texans claimed to have spoken to him when he dropped in on their properties.

Close encounters

Dr. J. Allen Hynek, an astronomer who became convinced of the reality of U.F.O.s while working on *Project Blue Book*, divided sightings into three classes. "Close encounters of the first kind" are when a U.F.O. is seen aloft or on the ground. In "second kind" encounters it leaves behind evidence of its presence, such as marks on the ground. "Third kind" encounters are when alien beings are sighted. These are the most controversial. Most scientists say that if E.T.s exist it is most unlikely they would look like humans, having evolved very differently. Yet about 90 percent of those claiming to have met with aliens describe them as humanoid, ranging from tiny goblins to handsome supermen. Skeptics point out that, from George Adamski's famous encounter with a Venusian in 1952 onward, most people have described encounters in standard sci-fi terms: the aliens wear "metallic space suits," often carry "ray guns," and, surprisingly, are fluent in the language of those they meet. Even those who do not conform to such patterns are B-movie characters: hulking robots or bug-eyed monsters. Some Ufologists add to Hynek's classifications "close encounters of the fourth kind": when humans are abducted by aliens, who may take them into their craft for examination or experimentation, sometimes using hypnotic or telepathic powers to take over their minds. An added peril of a fourth kind encounter is that the human subject may later be visited by "Men in Black" (M.I.B.s). These sinister persons (very occasionally women) typically arrive in black Cadillacs (outdated models, but apparently brand new), produce U.S.A.F. or C.I.A. type identity documents (although some say the M.I.B.s themselves are E.T.s), and warn fourth kind encounterers that to speak of their experiences could have unpleasant consequences.

From information given by Betty and Barney Hill during deep trance therapy, an artist produced portraits of the aliens who abducted the New Hampshire couple in 1961.

Pancake Joe Simonton displays a cookie given to him by aliens whose U.F.O. made a stop for water at his Wisconsin chicken farm in 1961. Analysis showed it was made of corn and wheat flours of unknown origin.

Travis Walton claimed to have been taken up by a U.F.O. (seen also by five of his workmates) in a National Forest near Heber, Ariz., on November 5, 1975. Missing for five days, he reappeared in a telephone booth 15mi (24km) away.

Police patrolman Lonnie Zamora saw an oval U.F.O. about 16ft (5m) long land near Soccoro, N. Mex., in April 1964. Two small aliens briefly exited the craft.

Apparently alarmed by Zamora's approach, the aliens reentered their craft and blasted off. He immediately examined the site, placing stones to outline marks left by the U.F.O.'s "landing legs."

❏ A fairly high proportion of "fourth kind" encounters seem to relate to sexual fantasies: many men and women claim to have had sexual intercourse, either forced or voluntary, with E.T.s. In 1966 a Melbourne, Australia, woman claimed to be pregnant after rape by a handsome alien. Most reports of sexual encounters of the fourth kind seem to originate from South America. Perhaps stories about the superiority of Latin lovers have spread through space.

❏ Many cases of cattle mutilation (above) throughout the United States from c.1963 to the present have been blamed on E.T.s "taking samples." Mysterious lights in the sky, or unidentified aircraft, have been reported by police patrols and ranchers who have lost stock. Other suspects include Satanic cultists – even the U.S. military or C.I.A., supposedly using the unfortunate animals in secret weaponry experiments. But after a particularly severe outbreak of mutilations in New Mexico in 1979, a government funded inquiry reported that all were "consistent with . . . normal predation, scavenger activity, and normal decomposition. . . ."

Mistaken identity?

Many reports of U.F.O. sightings stem from strange lights in the sky, like this striking example. Skeptics attribute most to meteorological phenomena.

Although some say the "aliens among us" have sinister motives, only one person has died as a direct result of alleged U.F.O. activity. On January 7, 1948, when a saucer was reported over Kentucky, Capt. Thomas Mantell, U.S.A.F., pursued it in a P-51 Mustang. He radioed from about 20,000ft (6,100m): "[the craft] appears metallic . . . tremendous size . . . following up." His wrecked plane was found later that day. Some claimed it had exploded in midair; there were rumors that no body was found, or that the corpse bore marks of a "death ray." The U.S.A.F. believes the U.F.O. was a huge U.S. Navy Skyhook balloon (then semi-secret) used to carry scientific instruments into the upper atmosphere, its aluminized fabric catching sunlight to give a saucer effect. At 30,000ft (9,000m) in an aircraft without oxygen equipment, Mantell lost consciousness and crashed.

Hannah McRoberts was intent on a landscape photograph on Canada's Vancouver Island, October 1981. Neither she nor her husband spotted the U.F.O. until the film was developed.

Skeptics think almost all U.F.O. sightings, and most photographs that are not faked, are cases of mistaken identity. Although very few aircraft are actually saucer shaped (exceptions include experimental models like the U.S. Navy's Chance Vought Flying Flapjack and U.S. Army's Avro-Canada Avrocar), mis-identifications of low flying aircraft are said to account for 17 percent of all U.F.O.s; aircraft vapor trails that break up into strange shapes are another source. Many U.F.O.s prove to be as ordinary as the reflections of automobile or street lights from low cloud or fog. Natural phenomena such as ball lightning and lenticular (lens shaped) cloud formations account for a few sightings, but experts say that nearly one third of all U.F.O.s prove to be sightings of the planet Venus – exceeded in brightness only by the Sun and Moon – other astronomical objects, and man-made satellite debris reentering Earth's atmosphere.

After computer analysis, U.F.O. experts said Villa's picture was probably faked.

Lenticular clouds like this, usually formed by rising air currents in hilly country, may seem to be convincing saucers. Further, they often appear to move in regular formations.

Paul Villa claimed this shot taken near Albuquerque, N. Mex., in 1963 showed a star ship whose nine-being crew spoke with him for about 90 minutes.

FACT FILE

❏ In 1944-45 Allied night fighter pilots over Germany reported trouble with red or silver balls of fire, apparently in controlled flight, that flew alongside and buzzed them, sometimes causing instruments to malfunction. Some suggested they were alien craft, but official sources, having at first suspected a radio-controlled psychological weapon, later attributed the ''Foo Fighters'' (below), as the pilots named them, to hallucination under combat stress.

❏ In October 1973 Governor James Earl ''Jimmy'' Carter of Georgia, later U.S. president, filed an official report on a U.F.O. he sighted, in company with 20 other persons, in Leary, Ga., on January 6, 1969. Experts believe that the object he viewed (''the darndest thing I've ever seen'') – described as being about 30 degrees above the horizon and a little smaller than the Moon – was the planet Venus, but in 1976 President Carter still insisted: ''I am convinced that U.F.O.s exist because I've seen one.''

Is anyone out there?

Scientists estimate that the Milky Way galaxy, in which Earth lies, contains about 100 billion stars, of which 10 percent may have habitable planets. Some hope that contact with extra-terrestrial intelligences (E.T.I.s) may soon be achieved. The first practical steps were taken by U.S. Mariner space probes which flew by Venus, Mars, and Mercury in the 1960s-70s, and by the Viking unmanned landings on Mars in 1976. In 1992 N.A.S.A. announced a $120,000,000, 10-year "alien hunt." In an attempt to detect radio signals from 1,000 stars within 100 light years of Earth, the huge Arecibo, Puerto Rico, radio telescope will examine each one for about 17 minutes. The movable Goldstone radio dish in California's Mojave Desert will make unlimited sweeps through the galaxy. Some hold that E.T.I.s have already attempted radio contact with us. Around 1900, radio pioneers Nikola Tesla (1856-1943) and Guglielmo Marconi (1874-1937) claimed to have received recognizable signals from space. It is claimed that "voices in an unknown language" interrupted astronaut Gordon Cooper's conversation with mission control from a Mercury spacecraft on May 15-16, 1963, and that similar alien voices, speaking clearly in what appeared to be a structured language, were picked up by Apollo 8 astronauts orbiting the Moon in December 1968. But it is hard to take seriously those who claim to be in regular touch with E.T.I.s by radio, telepathy, or direct personal contact. One of the largest and best known of such organizations is the London-based Aetherius Society, founded in 1955 by George King. King and his followers claim to guard Earth against evil E.T.I.s with the aid of the Cosmic Masters (who include Jesus, the Buddha, and a Martian scientist) and the Saturn-based Interplanetary Parliament.

American astronaut Gordon Cooper: some claim voices that broke in on his talk with mission control while orbiting Earth in a Mercury spacecraft were those of the crew of an alien spaceship from the constellation of Boötes.

While circling the Moon, the Apollo 8 astronauts are also said to have heard alien voices.

Built by Cornell University in association with the Department of Defense, the world's most powerful radio telescope at Arecibo, Puerto Rico, will play a major part in N.A.S.A.'s "alien hunt" of the 1990s.

Ancient astronomers quite accurately estimated inter-planetary distances. Like scientists today, some believed intelligent life might exist on other planets.

❑ In the 19th century believers in E.T.I.s suggested it might be possible to communicate with them via the Sahara. It was proposed that enormous geometrical figures be dug in the desert – but to be visible from Mars, even with modern telescopes, they would have needed to be some 400mi (645km) across. Some suggested that huge fires in the shape of universal geometric concepts such as the Pythagorean theorem might be lit in the Sahara. French inventor Charles Cros (1842-88) advocated construction of a giant mirror to flash messages to Mars.

❑ In November 1974 scientists at Arecibo Observatory, Puerto Rico, used the world's most powerful radio telescope, with a 1000ft (305m) bowl, to beam a 3-minute message a distance of 22,500 light years to the globular star cluster Messier 13 in the constellation of Hercules. But even if alien beings there are capable of decoding the signal, no one expects an early reply: the message will not arrive until about A.D. 25,000.

❑ There have been reports of U.F.O.s seen by astronauts in space. Orbiting Earth in Gemini 4 in 1965, James McDivitt saw an object "with big arms" about 25mi (15km) away. The photographs he took were unaccountably lost, and McDivitt claimed that some later published were fakes. N.A.S.A. attributed the sighting to optical illusion.

Aliens under water

Skeptics say that many "alien craft" are in reality military missiles being tested secretly.

Ufologists are undecided whether Unidentified Submarine Objects (U.S.O.s) – strange craft seen in or above the waters covering nearly three-quarters of Earth's surface – are U.F.O.s with submarine capabilities, or separate phenomena. Some suggest they may be from an unknown, undersea civilization, even from lost Atlantis. Some say extraterrestrials have undersea bases in the South Atlantic off Argentina, where there have been so many U.S.O. reports since 1959, when an "enormous, fish-shaped craft" was spotted in Buenos Aires harbor, that local people refer to "Martian bases" as established fact. Earlier U.S.O.s favored the Persian Gulf, where in c.1840-1910 there were a dozen well-attested sightings of silent, luminous, revolving wheels, up to 130ft (40m) in diameter. In 1946 there were more than 1,000 reports of craft entering or leaving Scandinavian lakes. It was suggested the "ghost rockets" were Soviet test missiles – but the missile program was then in its infancy, and no wreckage was found to support the view. Common sense says craft seen entering the water may be crashing aircraft or mis-sightings of heavenly bodies low on the horizon. Those seen emerging may be submarine-launched missiles – or simply flocks of seabirds taking off. Many U.S.O.s located underwater by electronic means are likely to be mundane submarines on clandestine missions – like the 50 or more contacts a year made up to the 1990s by the Swedish military with what were almost certainly Soviet submarines. But not all: off Puerto Rico in 1963 the carrier *Wasp* and 12 other U.S. warships tracked an underwater contact for four days, registering speeds of up to 175mph (280kmh) and depths exceeding 27,000ft (8,230m) – some four times the capabilities of any terrestrial submersible.

A chance witness of the launching of a submarine missile like Trident might well think it a U.S.O.

A scientist investigates the bottom of Lake Kölmjärv, northern Sweden, one of the many sites of reported "ghost rocket" or U.S.O. "landings" or "take-offs" in Scandinavia in 1946.

Discreet testing of equipment meant for clandestine warfare is a possible source of U.S.O. reports. Here, members of a U.S. Navy SEALs underwater demolition team ride a swimmer delivery vehicle.

French novelist Jules Verne anticipated modern U.S.O. scares – and the powers of today's submarines – in Captain Nemo's sinister *Nautilus* of *Twenty Thousand Leagues Under the Sea* (1870).

The Earth is flat . . .

Most ancient peoples assumed that Earth was a flat disk, floating on a great ocean or supported by gigantic beings, such as Atlas of Greek myth. Early Christians accepted Flat Earthism: some fundamentalists still do, arguing that the books of *Isaiah* and *Revelations* refer to "the four corners of the Earth." From the 6th century A.D., when the *Christian Topography* of Cosmas of Alexandria said that Earth was a rectangular plane centered on Jerusalem and separated from Paradise by a surrounding ocean, Flat Earthism was an article of faith, unquestioned by theologians from St. Augustine to Luther. By the 17th century scientists had convinced most people that Earth was spherical. But some disagree. In Britain the Zetetic Society (Greek: *zeteo*; "I find out for myself") flourished in the 19th century, "proving" Flat Earthism by complex measurement experiments in Eastern England. The leading U.S. Flat Earthists belonged to the Christian Apostolic Church founded by John Dowie, who in 1895 set up a fundamentalist settlement at Zion, Ill. From 1905, under Glenn Wilbur Voliva, Zion was a strictly-ruled and prosperous community, supporting publications and radio stations through which Voliva spread his beliefs. He taught that the North Pole is the central point of Earth's disk; its circumference is the South Pole, a wall of ice, beyond which lies Hell. Earth is stationary in space; the Sun and Moon are small and only a few hundred miles away. Faced with evidence derived from the space program, his remaining disciples say the program is a hoax – set up by the British government, agreed to by President Kennedy and Soviet leader Khruschev at a secret summit, scripted by sci-fi eminence Arthur C. Clarke, and with visual effects faked by Hollywood.

Like others of its kind, the 13th century *Mappa Mundi* (World Map) now in Hereford Cathedral, England, portrays Earth as a flat disk surrounded by water.

It was axiomatic to mapmakers of the medieval Christian era that Jerusalem, Holy City of the faith, must be situated at the very center of the Earth.

A sphere in space: Earth as most people now accept it to be. Some Flat Earthists say such evidence from the space program is faked.

Galileo's perfection of the astronomical telescope in c.1610 enormously advanced humanity's knowledge of the universe.

Galileo (1564-1642) was one of many scientists persecuted for questioning then orthodox religious teachings on the nature of the universe.

FACT FILE

❑ Martin Luther (1483-1546), father of Protestantism, produced a telling argument against those who said Earth was a sphere. It could not be, he said, for if it were, people living "underneath" would not be able to witness Christ's Second Coming.

❑ Paul Kruger (1825-1904), pillar of the fundamentalist Dutch Reformed Church and leader of South Africa's Transvaal Republic against the British in the Boer War (1899-1902), sailed to Europe to seek support. On the way, the ship's captain, with sextant and telescope, convinced him of Earth's curvature. Kruger, it is said, then threw his *Bible* into the ocean: proved untrue, he declared, it was no longer any use to him.

❑ Glenn Wilbur Voliva became a millionaire from the manufacture of chocolate-covered cookies – but showed little sweetness in his rule over Zion, Illinois. Its c.16,000 inhabitants were subjected to a 10 p.m. curfew and forbidden to whistle or sing in public or drive at more than 5mph (8kmh). Alcohol, cigarettes, and, for women, makeup, high heels, swimsuits and other immodest dress were banned. The rules were enforced by Voliva's private police force, whose badge was a Dove of Peace with the word "Patience." Voliva's reign ended in the late 1930s, after he lost most of his wealth in the Depression.

. . . or is it hollow?

Flat Earthism is of ancient origin; Hollow Earthism dates from the time most people accepted that Earth was spherical. Astronomer Edmond Halley (1656-1742) was among the first to theorize that Earth might consist of two or more concentric spheres. Fantasies soon arose about unknown lands peopled by strange races in Earth's interior. In the 1820s, John Symmes, a U.S. Army officer, came close to persuading Congress to fund an expedition to the North Pole where, he said, lay an entrance to five inner spheres. His son Americus claimed that one "gate" had been found in ancient times by the lost tribes of Israel: hence their disappearance. Later disciples claimed that the aurorae seen in polar regions were reflections of an inner Earth's Sun on our clouds. In 1909, Admiral Peary reached the North Pole – and, like later Arctic (and Antarctic) travelers, failed to notice a large hole. But Hollow Earthists say no one has ever really been to either pole – they may think they have, but are misled because compasses go haywire within a 150mi (240km) radius of the poles – and claim that dark patches on satellite photographs clearly show large holes in polar regions. Others believe we live not on Earth's surface, but inside it. This was the view of Cyrus Reed Teed ("Koresh") (1839-1908), American healer and alchemist, who from 1894 established a New Jerusalem at Estero, Fla., where he planned a great Koreshan city. He built a Rectilineator apparatus to prove that Earth's surface slopes upward, showing we live within a hollow sphere. Estero declined after his death, but revived after 1945 when its land holdings in coastal Florida soared in value. Today it is reported to be a flourishing community dedicated to "green" principles – reflecting Teed's own pioneer interest in magnetic Earth energy.

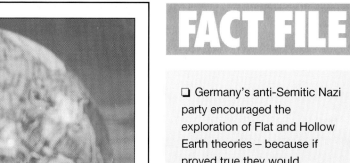

A projection based on satellite photography shows the Antarctic ozone hole. Hollow Earthists say a real hole (gate) opens there too.

In the 1930s Hollow Earthists hoped pioneer rocket engineer Wernher von Braun would aid their cause – but he appears to be seeing through it in 1958!

Cyrus Reed Teed (Koresh: Hebrew for Cyrus) and his helpmate Annie Ordway (Victoria Gratia) relax in the luxurious surroundings of the Founder's House at his New Jerusalem at Estero, Fla., in the late 1890s.

37

Riddles in rocks

Science has solved prehistoric puzzles once thought supernatural. We now know "dragons' bones" for dinosaur fossils, "elfshot" for Stone Age weapons, and "giants' graves" for ancient human burial chambers. But some mysteries – such as human footprints in stones much older than the first humans – remain. In rocks at Glen Rose, Tex., tracks of humans and dinosaurs (extinct more than 60,000,000 years before humans evolved) run side by side. Some are fakes, made for sale in the Depression: but locals swear they were inspired by real ones – and researchers in 1976 found more, in inaccessible underwater sites. Humans have existed for fewer than 2,000,000 years and have worn shoes for a fraction of that time – but in 1927 a fossil hunter in Nevada found the print of a leather shoe (with stitching finer than the average modern shoemaker's) in limestone c.180-225,000,000 years old. In 1968 Antelope Spring, Utah, yielded a similar puzzle: a trilobite (a small marine species extinct for 280,000,000 years) embedded in the print of a sandaled foot. Human artifacts have been found embedded in solid rock: nails, gold thread, tools, and an 18th century French stonemason's complete kit. Blasting work at Dorchester, Mass., in 1851 freed a rockbound, fragile metal vase – so fine it was said to be the work of Tubal-cain, Biblical father of metallurgy. In 1969 a geode (hollow stone) said to be 500,000 years old was cut open to reveal a metal shaft with white ceramic casing that looked like a modern spark plug. There are hundreds of reports of people breaking open stones to find a live toad in a snug, toad-shaped cavity. No one has explained how they get there, or how they survive without air, food, or water. Scientists no longer think they were trapped in mud at the time of the Flood or even the Creation – but have yet to produce a better explanation.

19th century quarry workers break open a stone and find a live toad within. Many such cases are reported; scientists disagree about whether they are folklore, hoaxes, or baffling fact.

Perhaps entombed toads get air or moisture through cracks in the rock; or perhaps they survive in suspended animation. But how does a toad get into its rocky hole in the first place?

Fossil tracks by the Paluxy River near Glen Rose, Tex., look very human – though one theory ascribes them to a small, two-legged dinosaur trailing its toes in the mud.

Alongside run the larger tracks of a three-toed dinosaur. If the small tracks are accepted as human, then geologists have a major problem – or time travel is a reality.

FACT FILE

❏ The puzzle of entombed toads has inspired some cruel experiments. One subject, a horned toad nicknamed Old Rip, was walled up in a cavity in a new courthouse at Eastland, Tex., in 1897. When the building was demolished in 1928 crowds came to see if the toad had survived. It had – but died a year later, worn out perhaps by the demands of fame and a nationwide tour, including a visit to the White House to meet President Coolidge.

❏ In 1932 gold prospectors in the Pedro Mountains of Wyoming found a human mummy only 14in (36cm) tall (above). X-rays proved that it was a real human body, apparently of advanced age. Speculation sprang up of a lost tribe of miniature Native Americans. In 1979 new studies of the X-rays led to a reassessment that "Pedro" was a prehistoric infant or fetus. Further study is frustrated: the mummy disappeared in 1950.

Signs of ill omen?

To our ancestors, who saw signs from Heaven in the sky, comets foretold "famine or pestilence or war or the destruction of the Earth by fearful means." Halley's Comet, seen every 76 years, was blamed for all manner of disasters, and in 1456 was condemned by Pope Callixtus as an agent of the Devil. But omens can be read two ways. A visit from Halley's Comet before the battle of Hastings in 1066 heralded English defeat – but for victor William the Conqueror it was a case of "A new star: a new king." That same belief inspired the Wise Men, who, St. Matthew says, followed a star to the Holy Child in Bethlehem. The Star in the East remains a mystery to astronomers, though it too may have been a comet – or a nova, aurora, or planetary conjunction. Another comet may have caused the Tunguska Event, a mystery explosion that shook the world on June 30, 1908. At Tunguska, Siberia, peasants saw the sky "open to the ground and fire pour out," devastating an area of c.770sq mi (2,000sq km), killing livestock, and flattening forests and buildings. The blast was heard 500mi (800km) away; shock waves registered as far off as Washington, D.C.; and over Europe a burning crimson sky made midnight as bright as noon. Tunguska's remoteness delayed serious investigation until 1927, when Soviet scientist Leonid Kulik began a 20-year inquiry that raised more questions than it answered. Whatever hit Tunguska left no material traces such as craters or meteorite fragments, but caused radiation burns on livestock and genetic mutations in local plants and animals – suggesting an atomic blast on a scale far beyond that seen 37 years later at Hiroshima. Some blame the Tunguska explosion on a comet that vaporized in the atmosphere – or on a black hole in space or the crash of an alien spaceship.

In ancient times, stones that fell from the sky were often worshiped. This one, in South Africa, is still an object of awe to scientists: at c.60 tons it is the heaviest meteorite yet found.

The Tunguska incident in 1908 flattened forests for miles around. This picture was taken in 1929, 4.3mi (7km) from the center.

❑ Some 100,000,000 meteors hurtle towards Earth every day (above), but disintegrate into dust before arriving. Most are only pinhead size to start with. Sometimes large fragments fall to Earth as meteorites, but even these are small cause for alarm. A 9lb (4kg) meteorite smashed through the roof of an Alabama housewife's home, and struck her. It only bruised her arm and hip – but gave her the distinction of being the only human on record hit by a meteorite.

❑ Centuries ago, the Inuit of Greenland developed iron tools despite not knowing how to smelt iron. Unlike most peoples, they had a stock of nearly pure iron at hand: three large meteorites that had conveniently fallen on their land in ancient times. Today one of them, weighing 34 tons, is on display in New York's Hayden Planetarium.

❑ Archeologists excavating a Mexican temple found a meteorite wrapped in mummy clothes.

The Bayeux Tapestry depiction of the Norman Conquest of England shows Halley's Comet bringing defeat to English King Harold in 1066.

About 20,000 years ago, a million-ton meteorite hit Arizona harder than a 30 megaton H-bomb. Meteor Crater, 1mi (1.6km) wide and 570ft (174m) deep, was blasted out by its impact.

Corpse-candles, goblins, and Merry Dancers

A rare photograph, taken in Austria in 1978, of the elusive and eccentric ball lightning – a luminous globe that does not act like lightning at all.

Modern science can explain most of Nature's firework displays. Our ancestors thought lights flickering over marshland were "corpse-candles" borne by lost souls, or goblins' lanterns – Will o' the Wisp, Jack o' Lantern, Kit Candlestick – luring travelers into bogs. Now we know the *ignis fatuus* (foolish fire) is just burning marsh gas from rotting plants. Electrical storms at sea can create "fire" that plays along ships' upperworks: St. Elmo's fire (from St. Erasmus, patron of seamen), or corposant (holy body). Most spectacular is the aurora: bands of colored light in the sky, usually seen in high latitudes – hence the name Northern Lights. (The Southern Hemisphere has its *Aurora Australis*, or Southern Lights.) In Norse folklore the aurora shone from the golden shields of Valkyries, warrior maidens who led souls to Valhalla. France calls the lights *les chèvres dansantes*, or dancing goats; Britain knows them as "the Merry Dancers"; in Celtic tales they are the *Fir Chlis* – fairy fighters whose blood stains the sky and falls as red pebbles, "blood stones." Scientists ascribe the Northern Lights to electrically charged solar particles striking Earth's magnetic field – but they cannot explain ball lightning. For years they denied its existence: now they say this rare type of lightning in the form of a luminous sphere denies all laws of physics. Lightning balls may enter houses by closed doors or windows and explore the interior with erratic movements: they spin, hover, or bounce, without burning what they touch. Soon they may slip out as mysteriously as they came – or explode. Such explosions melt metal, kill animals, or blow up fuel supplies – but rarely hurt people. A woman who brushed a lightning ball away got a sore hand – and a scorched skirt where the ball exploded. Witnesses say ball lightning acts as if it has a mind of its own.

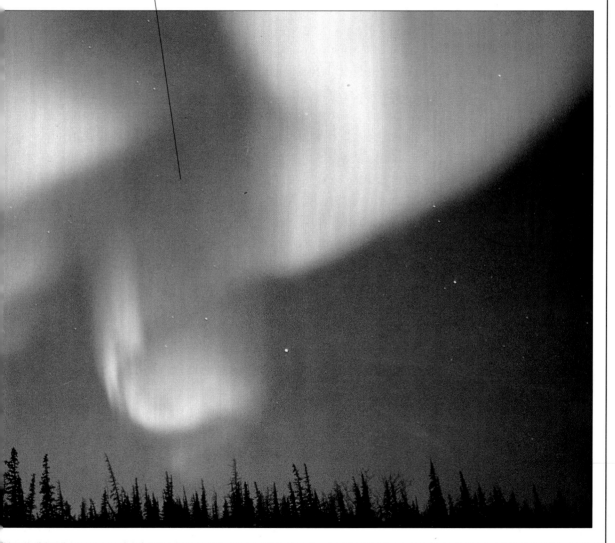

Folk traditions ascribe the shimmering lights and colors of the *Aurora Borealis*, or Northern Lights, to the activities of Otherworld beings – shield maidens or fairy warriors – in the sky.

A spectacle literally out of this world: an expanse of the *Aurora Australis* (Southern Lights) photographed by astronauts on the space shuttle *Atlantis* while orbiting Earth.

43

Fire from Heaven

Mary Reeser was reduced to ashes, yet the fire hardly touched her apartment. The local Police Chief commented: "this . . . just couldn't have happened, but it did."

Late at night on May 25, 1985, teenager Paul Hayes was walking down a quiet road in London when he burst into flames. Enveloped in fire from the waist up, he thought that he would die – but 30 seconds later the flames vanished as inexplicably as they began. With badly burned hands, arms, and head, Paul was one of the rare survivors of a phenomenon reported some 200 times since the 1600s: spontaneous human combustion. Most victims burn to death in an unnaturally intense fire of unknown source, eerily localized in a small area. As in Paul's case, it strikes suddenly – victims rarely have time to call for help – and without apparent external source: sufferers seem to self-ignite. The fire can reduce a body to ashes more quickly than a crematorium. Yet little else is touched: clothes over charred bones, or a bed under a cremated body, may remain unburnt. When Mary Reeser burned up in her Florida apartment in 1951, nothing was left of the 175lb (79kg) woman but 10lb (4.5kg) of ash, a shrunken skull, a charred liver – and an unburned foot still in a satin slipper. So fierce a fire should have destroyed the apartment, but it was limited to a small circle: the victim's habit of sitting with a leg outstretched had preserved her foot. Forensic scientist and fire death specialist Dr. Milton Krogman found it all unaccountable: "As I review it, the short hairs on my neck bristle with vague fear. Were I living in the Middle Ages, I'd mutter something about black magic." A rational explanation is hard to find. Victorian doctors blamed drinking. Victims, they said, were drunks who had imbibed so much alcohol they became flammable – a view the temperance movement welcomed. Modern theories include internal disorders, static electricity, high-frequency sound, and microwave radiation – but all fail to explain how these might work.

A movie stuntman dares the flames with fireproof gear and helpers nearby – but spontaneous combustion has no such escape clauses.

A 1966 victim of spontaneous combustion was retired Pennsylvania physician Dr. John Bentley. Intense heat reduced his body to fine ashes and burned through the floor beneath him – yet spared most of the room, his metal walker, and half his right leg.

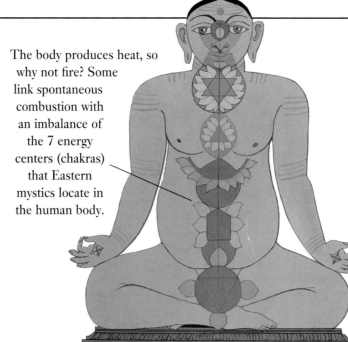

The body produces heat, so why not fire? Some link spontaneous combustion with an imbalance of the 7 energy centers (chakras) that Eastern mystics locate in the human body.

FACT FILE

❏ In 1725, French innkeeper Jean Millet was condemned to death for murdering his wife, found burned to ashes in her kitchen. Luckily for Millet, trainee surgeon Claude-Nicolas Le Cat, a guest at the inn, realized this was no normal fire. It had almost consumed the woman's body and burned the floor under her – but nothing else. Le Cat was so struck by this unnatural effect that he persuaded the court to change its verdict to "visitation of God."

❏ Spontaneous combustion usually limits itself to humans and objects: animals seem exempt. A possible exception was Hayes, a retriever pup that caught fire next to its home in England in 1978. Owner Jean Payne looked out of the window to see her dog "with flames leaping up from his belly." The police assumed a case of human sadism; but no one was seen nearby, and flesh does not normally catch fire so easily. (Hayes survived his ordeal to make a full recovery.)

❏ Fires sometimes break out for no apparent cause in houses afflicted with poltergeist activity, a phenomenon that may be connected with spontaneous human combustion. Researchers also note cases of "fire-prone" individuals, in whose presence fires repeatedly break out – but are not, apparently, deliberately caused by them.

Cereal stories

Farmers who find crops crushed by trespassers are justifiably annoyed. But – in England at least – if wheat is flattened in a symmetrical circle, neither careless picnickers nor hikers are likely to be blamed. Media reports over the past decade identify such effects as "crop circles" – although the irate farmer may not know whether to blame freak winds, hoaxers, or U.F.O.s. Crop circles have been in the news since the early 1980s, when most reports came from southern England, but still remain a mystery. Unlike typical cases of careless or deliberate damage, the crop is flattened in a precise design: usually a single ring, sometimes with a curved or straight tail, sometimes multiple rings, sometimes linear patterns. The stalks are not broken, only bent over at the base. Still most common in England, crop circles are known also in the United States, Australia, Canada, France, and Japan. They seem to be a 20th century phenomenon; although an English report of 1678 told of a field of oats mysteriously mown overnight in circles – "as if the Devil had a mind to shew his dexterity in the art of husbandry." Today we are more likely to blame strange occurrences on space aliens than on the Devil, and some Ufologists identify the circles as flying saucer landing sites, or "U.F.O. nests." Other theories include secret military devices, sportive animals, and hoaxers. Some circles are admitted fakes – at least one complex example was instigated by a tabloid newspaper – but it is difficult to believe in teams of hoaxers working worldwide over so many years. Most scientists say freak weather conditions are the cause: Dr. Terence Meaden of the British Tornado and Storm Research Organisation suggests an electrically charged atmospheric vortex, formed when air passes over certain landscape features.

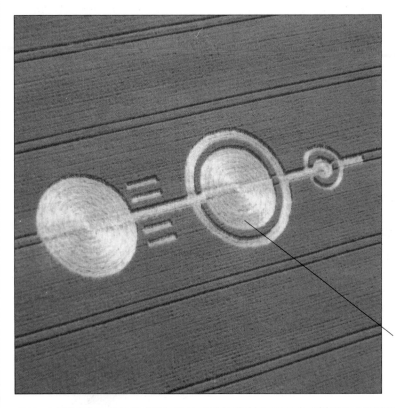

Crop circles are reported worldwide, but most appear in southern England. This impressive triplet group appeared on July 13, 1990, in the English county of Hampshire.

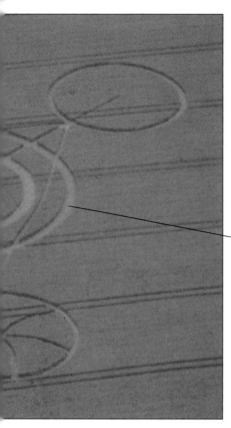

It is hard to believe that such elaborate and symmetrical geometric patterns as this July 1991 example from Wiltshire, England, are accidents of nature.

In August 1678 a crop of oats in Hertfordshire, England, was mysteriously mown in rings. Ascribed to a Mowing Devil, was this the first recorded crop circle?

Prehistoric cup and ring marks carved in rocks in northern Britain puzzle scholars – but some researchers link the patterns with crop circles.

Hoaxers and serious students of crop circles can produce pretty convincing crop circles such as these made in England in July 1991.

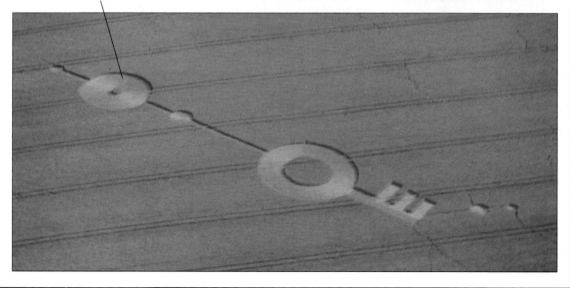

Strange rains

It never really "rains cats and dogs," as the saying goes; but apparently it does sometimes rain other animals – and vegetables and minerals. In ancient times folk saw edible rains – of grain or shellfish – as manna from heaven, while rains of "blood" literally put the fear of God into them. Today we explain such strange rains as the result of freak wind conditions, and know that showers of blood are only red sand, or bug droppings. Harder to explain away are accounts of animals falling from the sky – typically in large numbers of the same species, size, and age. Fish or frogs are the most common of these uncommon rains; lizards, snails, mice, and insects are also recorded. Some are dead, like the eels that fell on Hendon, England, in 1918 (providing plentiful fertilizer), or the stinking, headless fish that hit Jelalpur, India, in 1830. But many reach the ground alive and wriggling, apparently unharmed by the fall. Skeptics ascribe "frog rains" to the overactive imaginations of people who see frogs hopping around during rainstorms, and "fish rains" to hoaxers throwing buckets of river water. But faced with reliable eyewitness accounts, others seek explanations. Scientists in the 17th century thought that fish or frogs might be birthed in the sky by "spontaneous generation" and then fall to earth; today's theory is that freak whirlwinds or waterspouts draw up creatures from one spot to drop them elsewhere. Student of odd events Charles Fort (1874-1932) thought the only explanation to fit the facts was teleportation: a natural force transporting objects instantaneously through space. As he argued, no one can explain how a whirlwind could deposit its living load undamaged – or pick up a few thousand well-matched fish and nothing else.

Patrolman James Johnstone holds a steel chain that fell from the sky across a tractor driven by Wallace Baker at Rock Hill, Mo., on May 15, 1959.

A 1658 woodcut depicts a fall of fish, or rain of fish from the skies – a phenomenon first recorded in the early third century A.D. by Greek scholar Athenaeus.

Most animal showers comprise a matched set of beasts of identical size and age, like these fish that fell in London, England, in May 1984.

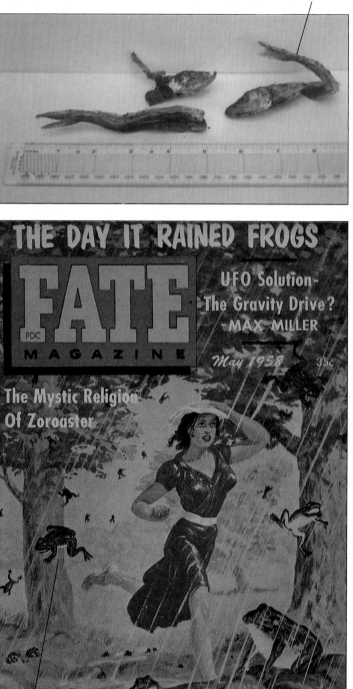

A frog rain depicted on the cover of *Fate* magazine, May 1958. It was once thought that little frogs hatched in the air from wind-borne frog spawn, to fall to earth in a shower.

Charles Fort saw teleportation as a force that once moved mountains or dispersed species around the world and now just toys with frogs and small fry.

Wild children

In 1920 missionary Joseph Singh went ghost hunting in the Indian jungle. He led a party to dig out the lair of half human, half beast "man ghosts" reported by the people of Midnapore. What he found was three wolves guarding a strange family – two wolf cubs and two human "ghosts": dirty, snarling little girls who seemed to think they were wolves. He took the children, whom he named Amala and Kamala, to an orphanage, where they acted like wild beasts. They ran on callused knees and elbows, could not stand upright, use their hands, or talk, and ate only raw meat. Amala, the younger, survived only a few months; Kamala lived eight years more, learning a few human skills and some 30 words. These wolf children of Midnapore were not unique. Legend says that Romulus and Remus, founders of Rome, were raised by a wolf; a "wolf boy" was captured in Germany in 1344; others in India in the 19th century; and a "monkey boy" in Sri Lanka in 1973. Like Amala, such children rarely live long after capture; although an Indian boy stolen by a wolf in 1843 and later restored to his family survived to return to the jungle in 1851. Skeptics say young children cannot survive in the wild: they believe "wolf children" are retarded youngsters abandoned by their parents and later found, by chance, in close proximity to animals – when their abnormal behavior is attributed to animal upbringing. They may be right. But many animals, including wolves, show innate compassion for youngsters of any species. In 1982 charity workers in the slums of Manila, Philippines, took an orphan child from a mongrel dog said to have adopted him more than a year earlier, suckling him like her own pup and driving off would-be rescuers. They reported that two-year-old Joel acted just like a dog.

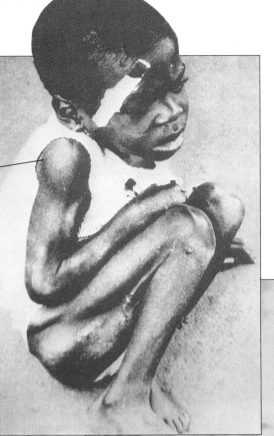

This boy, captured in Uganda in 1986, was said to have been living with a family of apes. He lacked speech and apparently feared humans.

"The wild boy of Aveyron" was captured in his late teens in 19th-century France, living like a wild animal. He was eventually taught to walk upright and speak a few words, but remained severely subnormal until he died, aged about 40.

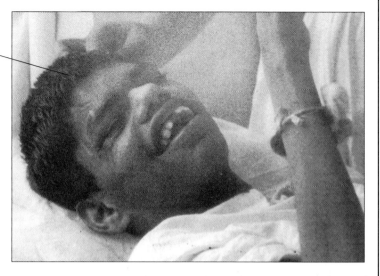

A modern "wolf boy," Ramu was found in the Indian jungle, playing with two wolf cubs, in 1960. His finders believed he had been raised by wolves: skeptics reject the idea.

"Wild children" show no sign of human socialization. But is their abnormal conduct learned from animals, or merely disturbed behavior caused by brain damage and increased by parental neglect?

FACT FILE

❏ While scientists argued about whether Amala and Kamala were really raised by wolves, theologians debated with equal heat whether they had souls. Many thought they had not, since they had lived as animals and failed to develop normal human minds.

❏ In 1963 French anthropologist Jean-Claude Armen reported a "gazelle boy" (above) – a 10-year-old child living with wild gazelles in the Sahara. He acted like one of the herd, communicating with sniffs and licks and sharing their diet of roots. He also ran like a gazelle: Armen estimated his speed at more than 30mph (48kmh), which would leave champion sprinter Carl Lewis, who covers 100m at c.23mph (37kmh), almost standing still.

Numerate nags and complaining cats

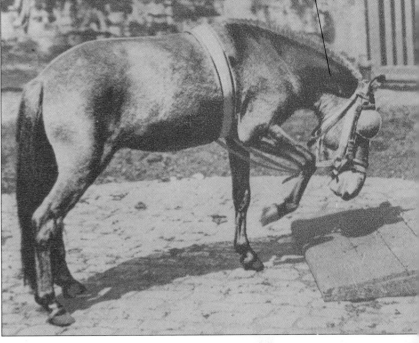

Clever Hans began by learning numbers and went on to demonstrate advanced math and reading. Here he spells out his name.

Christmas Eve once saw children hiding in stables to eavesdrop on talking animals – an annual miracle said to occur to honor the beasts at the manger in Bethlehem when Jesus was born. More sinister were the talking "familiars" (demons in animal form) attributed to witches; in the 16th century John Banks was charged with witchcraft when he claimed his performing horse Marocco could talk. Scholars said animals might acquire speech: in 1661, English diarist Samuel Pepys, impressed by a baboon that "understood much English," thought it capable of learning speech or sign language. Some 300 years later scientists took up the idea. Since the 1960s apes have been trained to "talk" with humans via symbols or sign language – but not speech, for which apes' voiceboxes are ill-suited. Outside the laboratory, such programs appeared earlier. In the early 1900s Wilhelm von Osten taught a horse, Clever Hans, sign language, math, reading, and musical appreciation. Early investigators compared Hans to "an intelligent 14-year-old boy."

In the 1500s, when performing horse Marocco told numbers on a pair of dice, people called it witchcraft: today most put it down to a skillful trainer.

Academics ridiculed these claims, but when von Osten died, Hans continued his schooling with a string of learned nags owned by Karl Krall of Elberfeld, Germany. The Elberfeld horses baffled researchers with complex feats – but whether such animals use reasoning power, have psychic gifts, or are just well-trained performers is still debated. A few animals are reported to use human speech: Batir, a Russian zoo elephant, is said to have some 20 phrases, from "Batir is good" to "Have you watered the elephant?" Cats and dogs are reported to have said things such as "I love you," or "I want a biscuit" – and Whitey, a Florida tomcat, sounds positively human. Sounding whining and self-pitying, he expressed dislike of other cats and moaned, "Why no one love me?"

An investigatory committee found that Hans performed just as well in his teacher's absence.

Some class educated animals with circus performers like these "liberty horses." Others are convinced they use their own brain power to think, calculate, and communicate.

We are always ready to humanize animals. In 1986 Morris the cat ran as a Democratic candidate for the U.S. presidency – and scored high in popularity polls.

❑ Many parrots (below) mimic human speech, but do not understand what they say. But in the 1980s one called Alex was reported to have gone beyond "parroting" speech. At Purdue University, Alex learned to link words with objects (mostly food and toys), and went on to express simple thoughts in speech. He asked for objects by name – and said molting depressed him.

❑ In the 1960s an English setter named Arli learned to operate the keys of a giant typewriter with his nose to produce messages such as "Arli go car," or "be good dog get ball and go bed." Some 50 years earlier, an Airedale terrier put on a more sophisticated performance. Using a paw-tap code, he solved math questions – and showed a certain wit. When a woman asked how to please him, he told her: "Wag your tail."

❑ When the gorilla Koko was taught sign language, she promptly used it to ask for a kitten of her own. In 1984, she was presented with a kitten and signed "Love that," to her trainers. She adored her pet, which she named All Ball, describing it as "soft good cat" and signed to it.

Nazca Lines: art for aeronauts

A page from the Nazca picture book: a giant spider, 148ft (c.45m) long. The shallow lines scraped in the soil have been preserved by the still, dry desert air.

The airplane had to be invented before we could appreciate the Nazca Indians' art. Between 400 B.C. and A.D. 600 this mysterious people turned Peru's Nazca desert into a giant picture book. They scraped in the soil huge birds and animals, each drawn in a continuous, fluid line, and c.13,000 straight lines, some more than 25mi (40km) long. But none is apparent from ground level: the Nazca Lines were spotted from the air in 1927. Their purpose is a puzzle. Perhaps they were astronomical pointers, but a 1968 study concluded: "Astronomically speaking, the system is random." Ufologists see them as runways for alien spacecraft, but the soft ground led researcher Maria Reiche to dismiss the idea: "The spacemen would have gotten stuck." Some, admiring their modern minimalist style, see the Nazca drawings as art for art's sake. A "birth control theory" claims they were made just to occupy a large labor force and thus keep down the population! But a religious function is most likely. Andean Indians still walk lines for spiritual reasons in rituals dating back to the Incas: perhaps the Nazca had such rites. Drawings of water animals (frog, cormorant, duck, killer whale) may have been rain-bringing magic. How the lines were made also intrigues scholars. Ufologists insist it took extraterrestrial intelligence. Research suggests the Nazca worked out their designs on dirt drawing boards some 6ft (2m) square, then plotted out full-scale versions with cords strung between wooden posts. Pondering the fact that Nazca artists could not have seen their work from the ground, American businessman Jim Woodman decided they must have flown over it in hot air balloons and built one from primitive materials to make his point. But his project showed only that the Nazca could have mastered flight; not that they did.

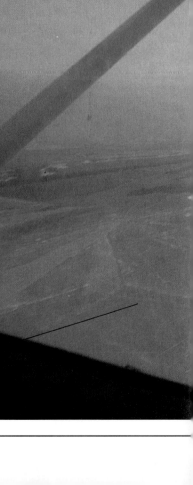

The Nazca Lines run perfectly straight for miles, regardless of terrain. Many cross each other to form complex networks of triangles, rectangles, and trapezoids.

Ufologists seeking evidence that the Nazca Lines relate to visitors from outer space claim this Peruvian rock drawing of a figure with a halo – probably a god – shows an ancient astronaut in a space helmet.

Ancient landscape art may be worked in rocks as well as soil. This Arizona medicine wheel was outlined in boulders for ritual purposes.

The first aerial study of the Nazca Lines was made in 1940 by American Paul Kosok.

❏ German-born Maria Reiche devoted her life to the study of the Nazca Lines. At first local people thought she was a witch because she bought so many brooms – which quickly wore out in the marathon task of sweeping the lines clear of debris. Later they came to honor her labors, naming after her a school and street in Nazca town.

❏ California's Mojave Desert also has landscape drawings. Since 1923 some 275 designs have been found, most since the 1970s. Archeologists estimate that they span a period from 3000 B.C. to the late 18th century A.D. Some are outlined with boulders, others scraped in soil, with added details: basalt eyes for a rattlesnake; a glittering spearpoint of hundreds of quartz pebbles. Some may be totems, some astronomical markers: the Black Point Dance Circle is thought to be a map of the Sun, Moon, and Milky Way.

❏ Jim Woodman's balloon, *Condor I*, used only materials available to the Nazca. The basket was made of woven reeds. The air bag, of cotton cloth similar to Nazca fabrics, was made airtight by curing it over a smoking fire in a burn pit suggestive of the piles of charred rocks within the lines. The shape was based on images from Nazca textiles and pottery – and on an account of a Brazilian hot air balloon flown in 1709.

Monuments of the Mound Builders

Moundville, Ala., boasts the tallest surviving U.S. temple mound – an earth version of the stone temple pyramids of Central and South America.

American pioneers moving west in the 1780s were puzzled to find thousands of imposing earthen mounds. Some – such as Monk's Mound, Ill., 100ft (30m) high and covering 16 acres (6.5ha) – were like the bases of Egyptian pyramids. Others were sculpted into the shapes of giant birds, bears, or reptiles. Clearly they were monuments of a major culture. But who were the Mound Builders? Local Native Americans were simple hunters, whom white settlers would not associate with such stupendous and wonderful works. They theorized that the Native Americans had destroyed a lost civilization: perhaps one founded by Egyptians, Greeks, Romans, Phoenicians, or Danes – even by a race of giants, the lost tribes of Israel, or colonists from Atlantis. No one believed Native Americans who said their ancestors built the mounds. In the 1840s a shaman, De-coo-dah, explained: "The face of the Earth is the red man's book, and those mounds and embankments are some of his letters." But it took a government survey 40 years later to persuade scholars he spoke truly. We now know the Mound Builders comprised not one but three Native American cultures: Adena (1000 B.C.-A.D.200), Hopewell (300 B.C.-A.D.700), and Mississippian (A.D.700-c.1550). Many Adena and Hopewell mounds were built as chiefs' tombs; Mississippian mounds were temple platforms. But the great animal sculptures remain a mystery. They are certainly of ritual significance, perhaps – as De-coo-dah claimed – astronomical. Most were built by Hopewell peoples, but the best known is Adena work: the Great Serpent Mound in Ohio, a 1,330ft (405m) snake whose gaping jaws reach for the "egg" of a smaller mound. The Mound Builders' civilization endured until Spanish conquerors came in 1539 to wipe out their culture. Only their earthen monuments remained to awe later generations.

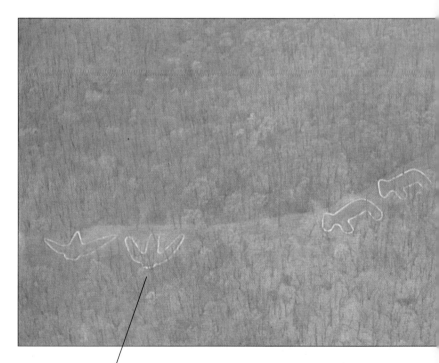

The 19th century shaman De-coo-dah described effigy mounds – earth sculptures in geometric, animal, or human shape – as symbols of heavenly bodies in which the gods were secretly entombed.

❏ The wealth of grave goods in Adena and Hopewell burial mounds bears witness to a rich culture with a vast trading network. Local craftsmen worked in raw materials imported from across the continent: gold, silver, copper, obsidian, sheets of mica, turtle shells, shark teeth, and freshwater pearls.

❏ Some Mississippian mounds were not only platforms for temples but apartment houses, with dwellings for priests and nobles built on the terraced sides. A house's position indicated the resident's social status. Higher ranks lived higher up the mound, and the chief sometimes built his house on top (see reconstruction above), beside the temple. Commoners made do with ground-level dwellings. This class-consciousness continued among the Mound Builders' descendants, such as the Natchez, who maintained a rigid caste system. The upper classes, in descending order, were Suns (royalty), Nobles, and Honored Men and Women (lesser nobles). Commoners were called Stinkards – though not in their presence.

Best-known of the many Adena earth sculptures, the Great Serpent Mound in Ohio may commemorate a lunar eclipse. The moon is shown as the "egg" that the snake is about to swallow.

A display model demonstrates the structure of the Great Serpent Mound – a colossal work requiring months or years of cooperative labor.

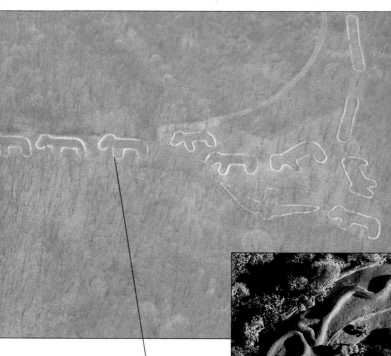

Earthwork bears marching along an Iowa ridge in single file are now a national monument.

Secrets of ancient stones

Through the late Stone and early Bronze Ages (c.3300-1500 B.C.) the peoples of Britain spent much time and effort building nearly 1,000 huge stone monuments, such as the stone circles of Stonehenge and Avebury. Historians, scientists, engineers – and cultists – have labored almost as hard trying to figure out why. Some medieval scholars believed that Merlin, magical mentor of King Arthur, built Stonehenge. Later, popular theory favored the Druids, the Celtic priests credited by 18th century romantics with mystic powers (but who flourished c.1,000 years after Stonehenge was built). Those who thought the technology beyond the Ancient Britons proposed Romans, Phoenicians, Danes, Egyptians, Greeks, Trojans, envoys from the lost world of Atlantis – even Martians. As for the function of stone circles, ideas ranged through cities, temples, cemeteries, schools, trade and social centers, and sports stadiums. The discovery that many stones align with the Sun, Moon or major stars gave rise to theories that the stone circles were prehistoric planetariums, observatories, or "computers" for calculating sunrises, sunsets, lunar cycles, and eclipses. Today most scholars agree that astronomical observation was one motive for the erection of circles – but probably not the only one. The scale seems excessive for the one purpose: Stonehenge alone was more than 500 years in building. Some recent discoveries have given new life to the medieval belief that stone circles were raised for (if not by) magical purposes. Dowsers report high magnetic fields and corkscrews of electromagnetic energy (now known to have healing effects) at many sites. Geiger counters detect natural radioactivity – triggering New Agers' claims that the circles focus beneficial "earth-energies" and are charged with ancient occult powers.

Begun by late Stone Age farmers, Stonehenge took its final form under wealthy Bronze Age warlords.

Despite this fanciful 19th century view of Druid rites at Stonehenge, its ceremonies remain unknown – but folktales of dancers turned to stone may hark back to ritual dances.

Few modern visitors would agree with scholar Dr. Johnson, who in 1773 dismissed stone circles as not worth visiting, "for there is neither art nor power in them, and seeing one is quite enough."

In 1990 dowser Ron Perry tried to cure "bad vibes" at this standing stone in Wales by driving stakes into the soil. Earth acupuncture, or archeological vandalism?

❑ The notion of Stonehenge as an astronomical computer has taken a few knocks. It relies mainly on the alignment of the Heel Stone with Midsummer Day's sunrise – but this alignment is not, and never was, quite accurate. So the temple theory resurfaces. Most recently, Dr. Terence Meaden sees Stonehenge as a vast image of the union of Father God and Mother Goddess. Just after Midsummer sunrise, he points out, the Heel Stone casts a long shadow into the heart of the stone circle – which he sees as an annual picture show of the Sky God's phallus fertilizing the Earth Mother's womb.

❑ A 1991 open air production of Shakespeare's *The Tempest* in a stone circle in Oxfordshire, England, had problems. Performing among the Rollright Stones (above) (noted among stone circle buffs for high magnetic fields and radiation levels), actors suffered brief memory losses and fainting spells; watches went haywire and power drained from batteries. "There's no doubt," the play's director concluded, "the Rollrights have a strange magnetism."

Riddle of the stone giants

In 1722, Dutch Admiral Jacob Roggeveen came upon remote Easter Island in the Pacific Ocean – and a mystery. Huge statues lined the coast: nearly 1,000 stylized figures, 12-30ft (3.6-9m) tall and weighing 12-80 tons, with glaring, inlaid eyes and red stone topknots. In contrast to the islanders' crude stone tools and unseaworthy canoes (described as "the worst in the Pacific"), they were clearly monuments of a skilled society. Researchers guessed at a range of ancient races or even visitors from space. But they were indeed, as the islanders themselves always claimed, the work of the Easter Islanders' ancestors. Possibly Polynesians from the western isles, or South Americans from the east, they settled Easter Island around A.D.380 to found a unique culture, with a complex picture script (still undeciphered), fine cave art, and the famous statues. They prospered for centuries, lining the shore with stone burial platforms (*ahus*) crowned by statues carved from the crater of the extinct volcano Rano Raraku. But from about 1600 famine and war – and, later, European slavers' raids – wore them down. Roggeveen, the first European to see the statues, was also the last to see worshipers attend them. By 1864 not one statue remained upright; many had lost their heads. Recent studies explain the islanders' decline and the statues' fate. Soil analysis shows that the bleak, treeless island was once densely wooded (so much for the idea that its sculptors chose stone for lack of wood). Cut for timber and to clear land for farms and roads, the trees were gone by about 1400. With them went farmland and fishing grounds: the fertile soil washed away without tree roots to retain it, and there was no timber to build boats. The good life was at an end. Losing faith, the islanders turned on their statues and felled them.

Today, reerected statues once again gaze impassively out to sea; but whether they represent gods or mortal chieftains remains a mystery.

Few credited Easter Islanders with the technology to create such colossal statues; but in 1956 explorer Thor Heyerdahl showed how they softened rock with gourds of water and carved with stone tools.

Easter Island's complex *Rapanui* picture script, still undeciphered, is inscribed on tablets known as *Kohau Rongo Rongo*.

Only the vestige of the inlaid eye remains.

Elongated earlobes suggest that the statues depict the ancient ruling caste of "long ears," whose earlobes were stretched with weighted earrings.

❑ Carvings and paintings (below) of a winged figure adorn rocks and caves – relics of a late (post-A.D.1500) Easter Island birdman cult. Each year, when the sooty terns returned from migration, cult followers raced by land and sea to their nesting site on a nearby island to gather eggs. The one who brought back the first egg won great honor for his clan chief.

❑ Easter Island's sculptural tradition began with dressing stone blocks to face burial platforms, where the dead were interred after the elements and birds cleaned their bones. Later, sculptors turned their skill to statues to crown the platforms. In 1956 explorer Thor Heyerdahl showed how Stone Age tools and techniques served to hew these monuments from solid rock, haul them to their final sites up to four miles away, and erect them.

❑ Easter Islanders tell of two groups of settlers: "long ears" (whose image may be reflected in the statues' long earlobes) and "short ears." They fell into dispute when famine came, the "short ears" triumphing shortly before Europeans discovered the island.

England's holy hills

Joseph of Arimathaea with the Holy Grail – in Christian legend Christ's cup at the Last Supper, but probably also the sacred caldron of pagan Celtic religion.

For centuries the English town of Glastonbury, in Somerset, has been for pagans and Christians alike, as a medieval scholar wrote, "the holyest erthe in England." A conical hill, Glastonbury Tor, dominates the landscape. Pagans said it was a gateway to the fairy world, and it was identified with the Isle of Apples or Glass Island of Celtic mythology – and with the Avalon where King Arthur awaits recall. Christian legend says St. Joseph of Arimathaea founded the Abbey below the Tor as Britain's first church. In its Chalice Well he hid the Holy Grail (Jesus's cup at the Last Supper), and there he planted his staff, which, as the Glastonbury Thorn, still blooms at Christmas. The Tor itself defied Christianization: an earthquake felled St. Michael's Church on its summit, and today only ruins of a later church survive. Ancient Britons' reverence for hills like Glastonbury led them, about 2750 B.C., to build an artificial one that, modern researchers calculate, cost them more time, labor, and wealth than we invest in a space project. Over many years they built up an estimated 35,000,000 basketloads of clay rubble into Silbury Hill in Wiltshire, 130ft (40m) high: Europe's largest artificial mound. Excavations reveal the technical skill of the builders, but not their motive. We know Silbury was neither a tomb, despite local tales of a royal burial, which inspired treasure hunts; nor a fortress, for it lacks defenses; and neither site nor design suggests an astronomical observatory. In 1968 a writer suggested it was a beacon in a prehistoric system of signaling – but there are three taller, natural hills nearby. It is almost certainly a sacred site of some kind: an extreme view, held by archeologist Michael Dames, is that Silbury is a vast earth sculpture of the Mother Goddess.

Legend said Silbury Hill, long thought to be a king's tomb, held a solid gold statue of a horse and rider, but treasure hunters were disappointed.

Christian tradition honors the Glastonbury Thorn, a winter-flowering hawthorn, as a relic of Joseph of Arimathaea.

The ruined church crowning Glastonbury Tor is an interloper, for this dramatic hill

was a sacred site long before it entered Christian legend.

Giants on the Earth

Britain's most famous giants, the 231ft (70m) high Long Man of Wilmington, in Sussex, and Dorset's 180ft (55m) Cerne Giant, are huge outline drawings cut into chalk hills. Most of Britain's c.50 chalk figures (from military badges to white horses) are modern – but the giants, although much restored, are not. They may depict Hercules, a demigod with a popular cult in Roman Britain. Tales of giants exist worldwide. Mythmakers saw monuments such as Stonehenge (the "Giants' Dance") as giants' work and Stone Age burial chambers as giants' tombs. Archeologists still term massive Bronze Age masonry "cyclopean" because ancient Greeks attributed it to the mythical giant Cyclops. Scientists hunted "real giants" into modern times. In the 1930s they found fossil bones of an extinct giant – but it was a giant ape, *Gigantopithecus*. In 1931 they hailed giant footprints found in Mexico as "definitely human"; later studies indicated they belonged to a mammoth – or a U.S. Army camel. In the 16th century explorers reported living giants in Patagonia, South America, the leader "so tall that our heads scarcely came up to his waist." In 1831 naturalist Charles Darwin cut down the Patagonian giants: "their height appears greater than it really is, from their large guanaco mantles, their long flowing hair, and general figure." But some say Darwin missed the real giants, who hid – and still exist in hiding. In 1966 explorers found another giant tribe in South America. But the Krem-Akaore, "a ferocious band of savages more than 7ft [2.1m] tall," shrank on closer examination to an average 6ft (1.8m) or less. Among ordinary mortals gigantism is usually due to medical disorders. This was the sad case of the world's tallest man, Robert Pershing Wadlow (1918-40) of Illinois. When his condition killed him, he was nearly 9ft (2.7m) tall – and still growing.

Antiquarians have at various times identified the "Long Man of Wilmington" as Woden, Thor, Hercules, and other gods – or even Mohammed or St. Paul!

Two 19th century "giants" from Kashmir (near neighbors of another giant, the legendary Yeti) pose with a "normal" Westerner, Professor Ricalton. Like many "giant" races, they boost their height with tall hats.

Some say the Cerne Giant is just a 1539 cartoon of a corrupt abbot. Its phallus signifies his lust, its club his violence, and its marching feet his welcome departure.

The so-called Giant's Grave in Penrith, England, is an assembly of crosses and stones from several graves.

❏ One of the best-loved giants of English folklore was Little John, Robin Hood's sidekick. In 1784, Captain James Shuttleworth revealed an element of fact in the fiction when he dug up ''Little John's grave.'' A huge femur proved that the grave's tenant had been well over normal height. Shuttleworth hung his trophy over his bed despite warnings that ''No good will come of it'' – but after a run of bad luck he was persuaded to rebury it.

❏ Cutting white horses was such a popular custom in 18th century Britain that designers coined a name for it: leucippotomy. The only example from ancient times is the Uffington Horse (above), which gave its name to Berkshire's Vale of the White Horse. Some think the dragon-like beast was an Iron Age Celtic totem; others say it was cut by Saxon invader Hengist (Horse) in c.450, or by King Alfred the Great in 871. It has even been identified as a sketch of an ichthyosaur – a beast extinct c.65,000,000 years ago!

The cursed seas

In 1492, Columbus had compass trouble and saw strange lights in the sky as he sailed the Atlantic off Bermuda. Today the so-called Bermuda Triangle, some 250,000sq mi (650,000sq km) of ocean between Florida, Bermuda, and Puerto Rico, is said to have swallowed hundreds of ships and aircraft, leaving no wreckage or survivors. Early losses include the U.S. Navy's *Cyclops* with about 300 persons aboard in March 1918. The modern saga dates from the loss of 6 aircraft and 27 men on December 5, 1945. Flight 19, five Grumman Avenger torpedo bombers, flew from Fort Lauderdale, Fla. – and vanished, after a radio message: "Everything is wrong . . . ocean doesn't look as it should." A seaplane sent to look for them vanished too. Many ships and aircraft have reported instruments going haywire and "lights in the sky." Triangle "experts" speak of "pockets of magnetic energy" that affect electronic gear – and attribute disappearances to "warps in space-time," "black holes," even alien kidnappers in giant U.F.O.s. But statistical analysis suggests that the number of disappearances is about the average to be expected in waters where sudden, violent storms occur and strong currents swiftly disperse wreckage. In 1992, U.S. geologist Dr. Richard McIver theorized that undersea landslides release huge clouds of methane gas. Rising, the methane makes the sea "boil," swamping ships, disrupting navigational instruments, and making planes wander off course and crash. Continuing undersea seismic activity buries the wrecks beyond all finding. One expert charts some 12 cursed seas worldwide. Among them are the Devil's Sea, centering on the Bonin and Mariana Islands in the Philippine Sea, south of Japan, and the Triangle of the Damned in the Tyrrhenian Sea, between Sardinia, Sicily, and mainland Italy.

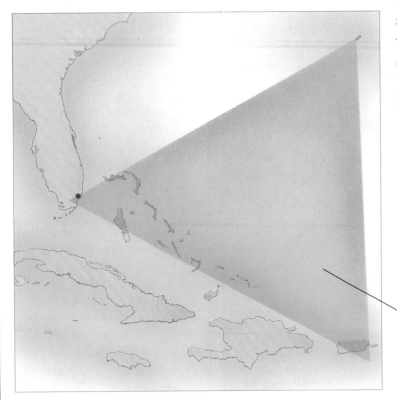

The U.S. Navy supply ship *Cyclops*, steaming from Barbados to the U.S. East Coast, had a radio – but sent no distress call before she disappeared in the Triangle in 1918.

The map shows the generally accepted area of the Bermuda Triangle. But some say the perilous zone runs from the Gulf of Mexico to mid-Atlantic – the Devil's Triangle – or even to the coast of Ireland.

Horseshoe Bay, Bermuda, looks like a vacation paradise. But does some strange power, capable of snatching away ships and aircraft, lurk under or above these waters?

Tales of the Atlantic curse date from the 1800s – and inspired a sci-fi writer's "non-gravitational vortex," sensationally illustrated in *Amazing Stories*, June 1930.

AMAZING STORIES

Scientifiction Stories by

A. Hyatt Verrill
John W. Campbell, Jr.
Edmond Hamilton

Lands beneath the oceans

The Greek philosopher Plato (427-347 B.C.) told how 9,000 years before his time a great people ruled the island continent of Atlantis until "in a single day and night . . . Atlantis disappeared into the sea." His account of an ideal state destroyed by the gods when it fell from grace – probably modeled on the Minoan culture of Crete, destroyed by a volcanic eruption c.1400 B.C. – was a moral fable, not history. But later scholars took it as fact that a drowned continent lay under the Atlantic Ocean. Advances in geographical and historical knowledge only added to the myth. With the discovery of the Americas, Atlantis became a "lost land bridge" between the New and Old Worlds. Later theorists located it all over the map, from Sweden to Africa, and peopled the ancient world with Atlantean refugees. In 1882, Ignatius Donnelly, ex-Governor of Minnesota, published his belief that Atlantis invented human civilization: *Atlantis, The Antediluvian World.* An instant bestseller, it inspired modern mythmakers' views of an Atlantean master race (perhaps colonists from space) with a supertechnology based on occult powers. The Atlantis craze also bred new "lost continents." Lemuria, in the Indian Ocean, began as a scientific hypothesis to explain animal distribution (notably of lemurs); Mu, in the Pacific, as a mistaken reading of Mayan script. Both quickly entered popular myth. Lemurians (Martians, Venusians, or telepathic, giant, hermaphrodite apes), and Muvians (the original, superior human race) joined Atlanteans as founders of human culture. In 1926 writer James Churchward popularized Mu as the Biblical Garden of Eden, sunk by exploding gases 12,000 years ago. Today, New Agers perpetuate the legend, but seabed surveys convince most scientists that these lands are imaginary.

Attempts to understand the restricted range of lemurs led to the idea of a lost continent: Lemuria.

Real lemurs are a far cry from the giant, preternaturally gifted Lemurians of fantasy.

Legendary priest-king Prester John was said to command a "lost land" in the East – a kingdom of perfect peace and justice, free of poverty, sin, and venomous plants or animals.

U.S. politician and author Ignatius Donnelly (1831-1901) believed Atlantis saw the first highly advanced civilization and the dawn of all our arts and sciences.

This rather uninformative 19th-century map of Atlantis is based on the diagram published by Donnelly in 1882 – which he in turn based on the sketchy information provided by Plato.

❏ Legend fills the seas of the world with lost lands. Factual coastal erosion inspired fictional drowned seaside kingdoms such as England's fabled Lyonesse. When maps were made by hearsay and guesswork, travelers' tales spawned many mystery islands. As recently as 1969 a U.S. Navy destroyer logged a new example: a Caribbean island about 45ft (14m) across, bearing large palm trees, and sailing west at about 3mph (5kmh).

❏ English geologist Philip Lutley Sclater (in 1855 one of the "inventors" of Lemuria) believed that tales of lemmings diving into the sea and swimming towards the horizon proved that lost continents had existed. Clearly, he said, the lemmings had a racial memory of Atlantis and were trying to migrate there.

❏ Lemuria fanciers claim some Lemurians survived the loss of their continent by migrating to Atlantis – or possibly to the United States. Some say they still inhabit caves near Mount Shasta, Cal. Dan Fry, who claims to have met Lemurians in 1950 in New Mexico, explains they have now moved to Mars but still visit Earth (by U.F.O.) as sightseers. Hollow Earthers, however, tell us Lemuria is not lost at all but remains inside the Earth, emitting harmful rays that cause our nightmares, wars, pestilences – and U.F.O. sightings.

Lure of the "Money Pit"

In 1795 a hunter on tiny, uninhabited Oak Island in Mahone Bay, Nova Scotia, found traces of excavation and remains of block and tackle gear. Rumors of pirate gold soon spread. By 1804 searchers had uncovered a 13ft (4m) wide shaft, sealed every 10ft (3m) by oak and clay platforms. At 90ft

Villainous Captain William Kidd supervises the burial of his (suitably personalized!) treasure – perhaps on Oak Island – in this magazine illustration of 1902 by American artist Howard Pyle, famous for his stirring pirate pictures.

(27m) lay a "cipher stone," said to mean "40ft [12m] below £2 million [then about $12 million] are buried." But at 110ft (33.5m) water flooded the shaft. At that depth, an 1849 expedition found, the Money Pit's designers had dug a c.150ft (46m) tunnel to the shore, so that the change in air pressure when the shaft was excavated siphoned in the sea. In 1894 treasure seekers dynamited the flood tunnel, drilled to 175ft (53m), and found three links of a gold (or copper) chain. Then the sea poured in again: the explorers went broke trying to sink parallel shafts. In 1938 a U.S. engineer found a second flood tunnel at 150ft (46m). Undeterred by tragedy in 1965, when four men in the pit were killed by a pump's exhaust gases, a Canadian syndicate launched a $600,000 effort in 1967. A TV camera lowered to 212ft (65m) in the flooded shaft produced blurred images interpreted as a pickax, three treasure chests, and a severed human hand. Today, after some 13 expeditions, the site is so torn up that even the original shaft's location is uncertain. If there is treasure in the Money Pit, who put it there? Popular belief says it is the hoard of pirate Captain William Kidd, hanged in 1701. A more likely theory is that about 1780, in the Revolutionary War, when British headquarters in New York were threatened with capture, engineers constructed the elaborate hiding place for the army's pay chests. There is no record of the British Army losing this treasure, suggesting that it was recovered when peace came in 1783 – and that the Money Pit has been empty ever since.

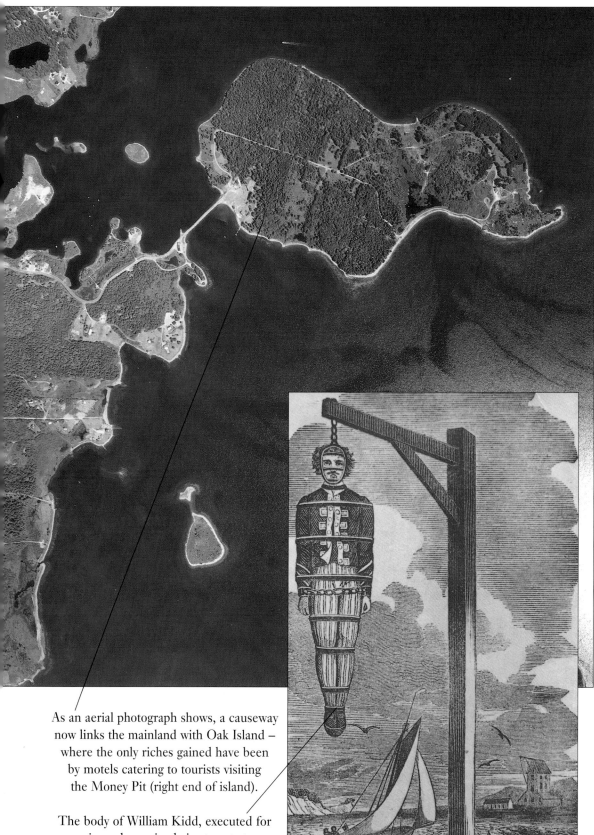

As an aerial photograph shows, a causeway now links the mainland with Oak Island – where the only riches gained have been by motels catering to tourists visiting the Money Pit (right end of island).

The body of William Kidd, executed for piracy, hangs in chains to rot at London's Execution Dock, 1701. Kidd's ghost is said to walk on Long Island, N.Y., one of his lifetime "haunts."

❑ Before his execution Kidd valued his hidden treasure at the then enormous sum of £100,000 (today equal to a multimillion dollar fortune). He vainly offered it to the British government in exchange for his life – then cursed all who went in search of it. Maps found in the 1920s among what were said to be Kidd's effects show an island much like Oak Island. Wilder theories link the Money Pit with fugitive Incas, Viking rovers, a crippled Spanish treasure ship – even with documents that may prove that Francis Bacon wrote Shakespeare's plays.

❑ In 1992 a U.S.-Australian syndicate invested some $160,000 in a hunt for a safe full of gold said to have been buried by outlaw Jesse James (above). According to his (self-styled) descendants Jesse James IV and his brother Woodson, the "Jesse" gunned down in St. Joseph, Mo., in 1882 was an impostor. The real Jesse lived on as railroad and mining tycoon J. Frank Dalton of Granbury, Tex., dying in 1951 at the age of 107. He married 26 times – but still found time to bury his loot somewhere near Waco, Tex.

Stately homes: stately ghosts

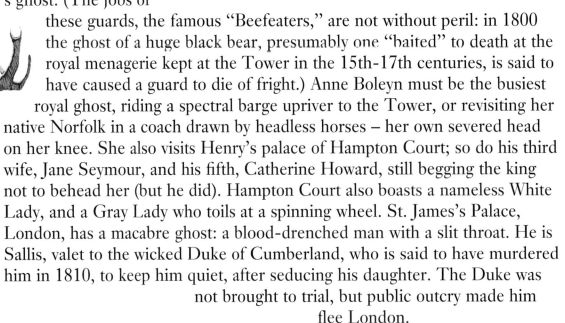

Holyrood Palace, where in 1556 Lord Darnley, husband of Mary, Queen of Scots, slew her reputed lover David Rizzio. Both are said to haunt the scene.

The stately homes of England house stately ghosts. A much haunted site is the Tower of London, "Death Row" for state prisoners for 800 years. The ghosts of the Princes in the Tower (King Edward V and his brother, murdered there in 1483) lingered until their belated royal burial in 1674. More persistent phantoms include Sir Walter Raleigh, recalling 13 years' imprisonment as he paces the walls by moonlight; shrieking Guy Fawkes, tortured for his attempt to blow up Parliament; the Countess of Salisbury, reenacting her grisly death in 1541 as the executioner chases her around the scaffold; and Anne Boleyn, second wife of much-married Henry VIII. In 1864 a Tower guard accused of sleeping on duty was cleared when witnesses backed his claim to have fainted when he met Anne's ghost. (The jobs of these guards, the famous "Beefeaters," are not without peril: in 1800 the ghost of a huge black bear, presumably one "baited" to death at the royal menagerie kept at the Tower in the 15th-17th centuries, is said to have caused a guard to die of fright.) Anne Boleyn must be the busiest royal ghost, riding a spectral barge upriver to the Tower, or revisiting her native Norfolk in a coach drawn by headless horses – her own severed head on her knee. She also visits Henry's palace of Hampton Court; so do his third wife, Jane Seymour, and his fifth, Catherine Howard, still begging the king not to behead her (but he did). Hampton Court also boasts a nameless White Lady, and a Gray Lady who toils at a spinning wheel. St. James's Palace, London, has a macabre ghost: a blood-drenched man with a slit throat. He is Sallis, valet to the wicked Duke of Cumberland, who is said to have murdered him in 1810, to keep him quiet, after seducing his daughter. The Duke was not brought to trial, but public outcry made him flee London.

At midnight, Windsor Park is haunted by the savage Herne the Hunter. Legend says he was a 14th century forester who hanged himself there, but the tale may have older roots in Celtic worship of a horned god.

A popular haunt, Hampton Court boasts a range of ghostly queens, ministers, royal servants, and royal victims – from Cardinal Wolsey to Edward VI's old nurse.

❏ Glamis Castle, Scotland (below), family home of Queen Elizabeth the Queen Mother, has several ghosts – including a party of gamblers condemned to play until Doomsday a card game begun in the 15th century. No ghost, but a sinister legend, is the Monster of Glamis, said to be a hideously deformed, unnaturally long-lived son of the house, kept in a secret room. In 1865 a workman found the hideaway, emerged in a state of terror – and was sent to Australia before he could tell his tale. Only the head of the family knows the true secret of "the curse of Glamis," and traditionally passes it on to his heir on his 21st birthday. But perhaps the Monster will now remain a mystery forever: the 14th Earl (grandfather of Queen Elizabeth II) is said to have been so appalled that he refused to share the secret with his son.

Ghostly queen Jane Seymour is said to flit nightly up the stairway to her private apartments at Hampton Court.

Curse, jinx, or hex?

Students of the occult make a distinction between a curse and a jinx. A curse is a weapon aimed at a particular person, as when an Aboriginal shaman "points the bone" at a malefactor or a Voodoo sorcerer makes, then mars, a doll in the image of an enemy. A curse may work because the intended victim knows of it, believes in the curser's power, thinks he or she cannot resist – and simply loses the will to live. A jinx is less personal: it is when bad luck seems to attach to a particular artifact, typically a structure or ship that has seen accidental death while being built, or to an object, usually associated with violence of some kind, that brings tragedy to a succession of owners. A useful word for all phenomena of this kind is hex (German: *hexe*; witch). The reader may decide whether the hexes examined here and on other pages are curses or jinxes. The Hope Diamond is certainly jinxed. The 44.5 carat stone sold to Henry Hope in London in 1830 was probably the remnant of King Louis XVI's Blue Diamond of the Crown, a 67.1 carat gem that disappeared when the monarch lost his head in the French Revolution. Legend says it was mined in India in the 15th century, set in the forehead of a god's image, and stolen by a priest, its first victim. Some 20 owners have since suffered great misfortune. In the early 1900s a Russian prince decked his actress mistress with it, then shot her, and then was assassinated himself. Sultan Abd-ul-Hamid II (Abdul the Damned) of Turkey bought it for one of his wives in 1908, then tried to kill her, then lost his throne. U.S. press tycoon Edward Beale McLean bought it in 1911: he was ruined and died insane; tragedy plagued his family for 40 years. But the jeweler who bought the gem from McLean's heirs played it safe: he gave it to Washington's Smithsonian Institution.

The Koh-i-Noor diamond now adorns the crown of England's Queen Elizabeth the Queen Mother. It is said to bring bad luck to male wearers.

Possession of the fabulous Hope Diamond brought no joy to Turkey's Abd-ul-Hamid II (Abdul the Damned, or the "Great Assassin") (1842-1918).

The executioner holds aloft the severed head of King Louis XVI of France; January 21, 1793. The Hope Diamond is said to have been cut from the unlucky monarch's huge Blue Diamond of the Crown.

❏ Another gem said to carry a jinx is the 106 carat Koh-i-Noor (Mountain of Light) diamond. It belonged in the 18th-19th centuries to the Mughal emperors of India, whose realm crumbled; to a Shah of Persia, who was assassinated; to an Afghan ruler who was deposed; and to Sikh princes whose domains, along with the great diamond itself, were taken over by the British. It is said to be unlucky only for men: Queen Victoria and other British queens have worn it without harm, but no male monarch has risked it.

The 44.5 carat Hope Diamond in its modern setting. It is said to have first adorned the forehead of an Eastern god – whose vengeance has struck down later owners.

Although it is said to have brought tragedy to her family, Evelyn Walsh McLean seems calm as she wears the Hope Diamond at a ball, in 1941.

❏ In the opera *Charles VI* by French composer Jacques Halévy (1799-1862) there is a "cursing aria." On the opera's opening night a stage hand dropped dead as the song was sung. In 1858, Emperor Napoleon III of France (above) ordered a command performance – and narrowly escaped assassination on the same day. It is believed the unlucky opera has not been performed since.

Curse of the boy king

On November 26, 1922, Egyptologist Howard Carter broke a peace of c.3,000 years by opening the tomb of Egypt's king Tutankhamun (died c.1340 B.C.). "Can you see anything?" asked his backer, Lord Carnarvon. "Wonderful things!" cried Carter, seeing treasures buried with the pharaoh's gold encased mummy. Some four months later Carnarvon (57) died in Cairo. As he raved of "a bird . . . scratching my face," a power failure plunged Cairo into darkness – and in England his pet dog howled and fell dead. So began tales of a curse. It was said that Carter found in the tomb the inscription: "Death comes on swift wings to whoever disturbs the pharaoh's peace" – a reference to the vulture goddess Nekhbet. Her images were found with the mummy – and a great bird hovered above the tomb on the day of its despoilment. Sir Arthur Conan Doyle attributed Carnarvon's death to "elementals [spirits] . . . created by Tutankhamun's priests to guard the mummy." Within 7 years, only 2 of 13 Europeans present at the tomb's opening still lived; by the 1940s some 25 people involved had died unnatural deaths. Some theorized that the pharaoh's priests had "poisoned" the treasures; that unknown, deadly bacteria had remained effective for millennia in the sealed environment; even that ancient Egyptian scientists had impregnated the tomb with radioactive material. Howard Carter, who died in 1939 aged 66, opined, "sane people should dismiss such inventions with contempt." In 1966, Cairo Museum's Director of Antiquities was reluctant to send Tutankhamun's treasures for exhibition in Paris. Leaving a meeting where his objections were overruled, he was killed in an auto accident. His successor, Dr. Gamal ed-Din Mehrez, who dismissed all the deaths as coincidence, fell dead at age 52 in 1972, just as the boy king's gold mask left Cairo to be displayed in London.

This golden figure of a falcon goddess was among Tutankhamun's magnificent grave goods. Also found were representations of the less pleasant vulture goddess, Nekhbet.

In 1924, nearly two years after breaking into the tomb, Howard Carter opened Tutankhamun's sarcophagus (stone outer coffin). Carter, chief "guilty party" in disturbing the pharaoh, lived another 15 years.

As well as the sarcophagus for his mummy, the pharaoh's tomb contained several gold coffins like this, intended to hold various organs removed before mummification.

A golden fan with carved wood handle bears an embossed picture of the boy king, mounted in a chariot, drawing a bow to shoot down an ostrich whose feathers would line the fan's edges.

FACT FILE

❏ Most tombs (about 60) in the Valley of the Kings were probably looted not long after their building – suggesting that the ancient Egyptians cared little for curses. Tutankhamun's tomb remained virtually undisturbed because it was hidden by debris tossed aside by robbers of the nearby tomb of Rameses VI.

❏ Carter denied that he found a curse in Tutankhamun's tomb. Its only protection, he said, was a small lamp bearing the words: "I prevent sand from choking the secret chamber." Some say Carter destroyed the curse inscription to avoid scaring away his diggers; others believe he invented the curse to keep away sightseers and potential robbers.

❏ In September 1979, Tutankhamun's golden mask (above) was displayed in San Francisco. One of its guards, George LaBrash, suffered a stroke while on duty. In January 1982 he sued city authorities for having exposed him to the curse. His claim for compensation failed.

Doomed giants of the oceans

Although Captain Harrison commanded the 22,500-ton *Great Eastern* – the largest and fastest liner of her time – he was not happy. As the giant began trials in 1859, he learned of the death of her designer, Isambard Kingdom Brunel; a burst steam pipe scalded to death six engine stokers; and his off-duty rest was "rudely disturbed by constant hammering." *Great Eastern*'s construction had bankrupted her builders and had seen several fatal accidents: one riveter simply disappeared while working on her double hull. Her troubled career – with every unhappy incident – supposedly heralded by mysterious hammering from amidships – was never profitable, and in 1887 she was dismantled and scrapped. Found in the hull was a skeleton clutching a hammer: the missing riveter, whose spirit had banged out warnings of disaster for nearly 30 years. Not long after, in 1898, U.S. novelist Morgan Robertson published *Futility*, a tale of a 75,000 ton, unsinkable liner, *Titan*, sunk on an April night in the Atlantic after hitting an iceberg on her maiden voyage – with great loss of life because she carried only 24 life boats. On April 14-15, 1912, the unsinkable *Titanic* (66,000 tons) went down in exactly the same way: of 2,224 people aboard, 1,513 died – partly because she carried only 20 lifeboats. An unhappy giant of a later time was the German battle cruiser *Scharnhorst* (32,000 tons), launched in 1936 after a construction accident had killed 61 workmen and injured 110. In her first action in World War II, gun turret accidents killed 21 men: many more unlucky incidents followed until, on December 26, 1943, she was sunk by British warships. Only 36 of 1,900 crew members survived: 2 reached shore, lit an oil stove for warmth – and died when it exploded.

By far the largest ship of her time (1859-87), the *Great Eastern* is seen here in one of her few successful roles: laying the first undersea telegraph cable between Europe and North America in 1866.

Did her builders' boasts tempt fate? The unsinkable *Titanic* steams out of Southampton, England, on her maiden voyage, April 10, 1912.

Among those lost aboard the *Titanic* was British journalist and Spiritualist William T. Stead (1849-1912). Like Morgan Robertson, Stead had published a story about a huge liner, with few life boats, sunk by an iceberg. Shortly before embarking on the fatal voyage, Stead revealed that he had received spirit warnings not to go.

It was alleged that the *Titanic* was lost because her captain, eager to establish a record time across the Atlantic, steamed too fast in sea lanes strewn with icebergs.

❏ Famed French sci-fi author Jules Verne duplicated Morgan Robertson's "foreknowledge" – but his story had a happy ending in both fiction and real life. His novel *From the Earth to the Moon* (1865) "predicted" *Apollo 11*'s Moon landing in 1969. Verne's 3-man space craft the *Columbiad* was lauched from Cape Town, Fla; *Apollo 11*, with a 3-man command module named *Columbia* (below), from nearby Kennedy Space Center (Cape Canaveral). Speed and duration of the Earth-Moon journey in both novel (about 25,000mph (40,000kmh); 4 days 1 hour) and fact (about 24,000mph (38,600kmh); 4 days 6 hours) were nearly identical.

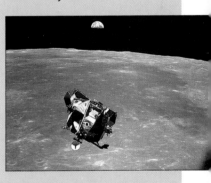

❏ One dark night seaman William Reeves was on lookout aboard a cargo boat in the North Atlantic. He had a premonition of danger and suddenly realized that the day, April 14, 1935 – his birthday – was the anniversary of the *Titanic*'s sinking in the same waters. Although he saw nothing, Reeves shouted a warning, and his ship changed course – just in time to avoid an iceberg. The name of Reeves's ship was *Titanian*.

Accursed autos and luckless locos

S ome believe ancient artifacts such as Egyptian mummies may carry a psychic charge, or be hexed. But surely not luxury automobiles – or diesel locomotives? On June 28, 1914, as Austrian Archduke Franz Ferdinand and his wife rode through Sarajevo, Bosnia, in a Graf und Stift touring car, Serbian terrorist Gavrilo Prinzip opened fire. The mortal wounding of the royal pair triggered off World War I. The car passed to Austrian General Potiorek, who went insane; then to another Austrian officer, who broke his neck when the auto killed two pedestrians. A Yugoslav diplomat sold it after four accidents (one cost him his arm) to a doctor, killed when it overturned. Suicide and fatal accidents claimed four more owners – the last with four passengers in a head-on crash. The accursed car survived, and was last reported in a Viennese museum. On September 23, 1955, when U.S. movie idol James Dean was introduced to famous British actor Alec Guinness, he proudly displayed his new Porsche sports car. Guinness, a "sensitive," warned: "If you get in that car you will be dead by this time next week." Days later the 24-year-old Dean lay dead in the wrecked auto. Towed away, it fell on a mechanic, breaking his legs. Its engine was fitted in a racing shell: its owner was killed in its first event. In the same race a driver using the Porsche's drive shaft in his rig also died. The original auto was reassembled and put on display – until it literally fell to pieces (11 of them) for no apparent reason. A jinxed locomotive was British Rail's 100-ton diesel *D326*, built in 1960. In 1962, hauling an express, it hit stationary passenger cars (18 dead; 33 injured). In August 1963, pulling a mail train, it was hijacked in the Great Train Robbery: the gang (later caught) snatched £2.6 million (c.$4.7 million). At last, renumbering (*40126*) seemed to lift the curse.

Britain's jinxed locomotive, diesel *D326*, on the day of the Great Train Robbery, August 8, 1963. It was involved in further incidents until renumbering seemed to lift the "curse."

The wreck of the Porsche sports car in which actor James Dean died; September 30, 1955. The "accursed" car survived to kill again.

Dean's role in *Rebel Without a Cause* (1955) seemed to foreshadow his death: he prepares to take part in a game of "chicken," a test of will that ends in death.

The assassination of Archduke Franz Ferdinand and his wife in a hexed automobile triggered a war in which many millions died.

❑ In 1991, British licensing officials announced that the number "666" (according to the *Book of Revelations*, "the number of the beast [Satan]'') would no longer be used on the license plates of British automobiles. "People complained of funny things happening whenever they encountered a vehicle with this number," said a spokesman for the government department, "and there was so much hassle about accidents that we decided to scrap it." Some religious leaders welcomed the decision, but the Evangelical Alliance spoke of "hysteria," pointing out that one of its own leaders was unworried by having "666" in his telephone number.

❑ In the late 1970s a British statistician made a detailed study of railroad accidents, comparing the number of passengers on a train involved in a crash with the number of passengers on the same scheduled service on uneventful runs. He found that there were always significantly fewer passengers on "unlucky" trains – giving rise to theories that many persons had been "warned" by premonitions of disaster.

❑ In July 1974, Neville Ebbin of Hamilton, Bermuda, aged 17, died after being knocked from his motorcycle by a cab. In July 1975 Neville's brother, 17, on the same cycle, died in a collision with the same cab and driver, on the same street.

Curse or coincidence?

Legend says that when Shawnee leader Tecumseh was killed by William Henry Harrison's troops in 1813, a shaman put a curse on American presidents.

Moments after this picture was taken on March 30, 1981, President Reagan, first elected in 1980, supposedly an accursed year, was badly wounded by a would-be assassin.

Many Americans were relieved when President Reagan's second term ended in 1989. Not because they disliked him – but because he broke a 120-year chain of deadly coincidence. From 1840 onward every president elected in a year divisible by 20 had died in office. Three – William Henry Harrison (1773-1841), elected 1840; Warren Harding (1865-1923), elected 1920; Franklin Roosevelt (1882-1945), elected for third term 1940 – perished from natural causes. Four – Abraham Lincoln (1809-65), elected for first term 1860; James Garfield (1831-81), elected 1880; William McKinley (1897-1901), elected for second term 1900; John Kennedy (1917-63), elected 1960 – fell to assassins' bullets. Reagan, elected for his first term in 1980, survived an assassination attempt in 1981. But legend says the deaths were more than coincidence. It ascribes them to a Native American shaman's curse called down when William Henry Harrison completed his crushing of the Shawnee nation, begun at Tippecanoe Creek in 1811, with victory over Shawnee leader Tecumseh at the Battle of the Thames in 1813. (Tecumseh himself is said to have been killed there by Richard Mentor Johnson, who ran for vice-president with Van Buren in 1836 on the regrettable slogan: "Rumpsey, Dumpsey – Colonel Johnson killed Tecumseh.") But coincidences, events that are remarkably similar but appear to have no common cause, may be just as mysterious as curses. Biologist Paul Kammerer (1880-1926) proposed "seriality," a theory that meaningful coincidences (which Carl Jung in 1952 termed "synchronicity") are far more common than we think and may represent an as yet unknown law of the universe. Nobel Prize physicist Wolfgang Pauli (1900-58) pointed out that meaningful coincidences are a recognized principle in subatomic physics – a principle, he suggested, that may extend into the everyday world.

Gunman John W. Hinckley, Jr., lurks in a crowd of press men, partly concealed by Police Officer Thomas K. Delahanty, one of the four people he wounded.

President Lincoln (first elected in 1860) falls to an assassin's bullet: shot in the head by actor John Wilkes Booth.

President Franklin Roosevelt was elected for the third time in 1940. He died in his fourth term; April 12, 1945.

President Kennedy slumps into his wife's arms as a bullet shatters his skull; Dallas, Tex., November 22, 1963. Kennedy was the last victim of the supposed curse on presidents elected in a year divisible by 20. Some say Reagan's narrow escape "broke" the curse.

❏ Early in April 1865, Lincoln told his friend Ward Hill Lamon of a dream in which he had gone to the White House's East Room and found a body lying in state. "Who is dead?" he asked a guard – who answered: "The president, killed by an assassin." Lincoln himself soon lay in state in the East Room.

❏ Lincoln and Kennedy (above) are strikingly linked by coincidence. Both were killed on a Friday, by shots to the head, with their wives present. Both assassins were killed before coming to trial, and the full names of both add up to 15 letters. Both presidents were succeeded by Southerners named Johnson, born in 1806 and 1906 respectively, both with forenames and surnames adding up to 13 letters. A Lincoln aide called John advised him not to visit Ford's Theater; Kennedy's secretary Evelyn Lincoln opposed the Dallas visit. Finally, a suggested running mate for Lincoln was a former Secretary of the Navy – named John Kennedy.

Hexes and hoaxes

Hexes may "work" not through supernatural power, but just because people believe they will. A case often quoted is that of a woman, apparently in perfect health, who died "in panic" at City Hospital, Baltimore, Md., in 1969. She told doctors that she was the only survivor of triplets born in 1946 (on a Friday 13th) in Georgia's Okefenokee Swamp. The midwife, for an unknown reason, told the mother that the babies were hexed: the first would die before the age of 16 (killed in an auto accident, age 15); the second before she was 21 (shot dead, age 20); the third before she was 23. The patient died on the eve of her 23rd birthday: an autopsy by specialists found no natural cause. But maybe hexes work because many people will believe anything – as editors of tabloid newspapers know. The British tabloid *The Sun* showed how easy it is to manufacture a hex. One of Britain's favorite pieces of "junk art" was a painting called *The Crying Boy.* In September 1985 *The Sun* announced that the picture was jinxed. Homes where it hung had been destroyed or damaged by inexplicable fires – which left the painting itself untouched. Hundreds of readers wrote in to tell of disasters caused by the picture; thousands packed up their paintings and sent them to *The Sun* – which on Halloween organized a giant bonfire of the accursed art. It reported that some fire companies had declined to assist because their personnel feared bad luck. In the United States in the 1970s-80s, reports of "unlucky stones" resulted in a deluge of mail for the staff at Volcanoes National Park, Hawaii, as tourists returned stones picked up on the slopes of the Mauna Loa volcano. Tabloids had reported a Hawaiian legend that said such theft angered the volcano goddess Pele – and had given a catalog of death and destruction.

A witch's doll made in the image of a person it is desired to hurt is hanged by the neck and skewered with a rusty nail. The pain should be transferred to the victim.

Is this the wrath of the goddess Pele? One of several active volcanic craters (among them two of the world's largest) on Mauna Loa, in Hawaii, erupts in smoke and flame, pouring out molten lava.

Stretching from Georgia into Florida, the Okefenokee Swamp is a wilderness about 700sq mi (1,800sq km) in area. Hexes are said to have struck down certain of its inhabitants.

An innocent seeming object – but this 18th century "witch bottle" holds nails meant to transfix dolls like that on the facing page.

❏ In 1978 the Chief Rabbi of Britain performed a solemn ceremony of purification at Clifford's Tower, York (below). The ancient fortification, it is said, had lain under a curse for nearly 800 years, since 150 Jews, falsely accused of ritual murder, committed suicide there to escape a Christian lynch mob on March 16, 1190.

❏ In the 1980s the council of an English town was asked to move an 18th century obelisk endangered by vandalism. The councillors refused, noting it bore the words: "Whoever moves this monument, let him die the last of his line." Town vandals then smashed it – but apparently still live on.

❏ British tabloid newspapers in the late 1980s created the Tamworth Triangle, an accursed area of Britain's railroad network, around Nottingham, where more than 100 fatal or serious accidents to people falling from trains had occurred within a few years. In 1991 an official investigation came up with a prosaic explanation: the doors on some of the passenger cars had faulty catches.

Lucky for some?

For vendors of lucky charms, superstitions mean good luck – and big business: Americans buy about 3,000,000 four-leaf clovers and 10,000,000 rabbits' feet a year; Europeans about 1,000,000 and 5,000,000 respectively. Centuries of disapproval by religious leaders have had little impact on our desire to believe in charms and omens. People worldwide touch wood, wish on a star, nail horseshoes over doors, throw salt over their left shoulders, dread breaking mirrors, and avoid walking under ladders. Few remember the meanings of these actions. A 1960 survey showed that 70 percent of pedestrians would venture into traffic rather than walk under a ladder – but probably few knew that they were showing respect for the symbol of the Holy Trinity, the triangle between ladder and wall – or avoiding a reminder of an old-fashioned gallows. Touching wood for luck, we do not recall prehistoric worship of tree gods; and only dedicated folklorists see an image of the Mother Goddess's womb or Moon Goddess's horns in the lucky horseshoe. Fear of the number 13 is so widespread it merits a name: triskaidekaphobia. It has been linked with the 13 at Christ's Last Supper; the 13 guests at the fatal feast of Norse mythology when the god Balder died; the 13 members of a witches' coven. But it was unlucky even before Christ's time – and not even those who fear it know why. Many people still carry lucky charms, although the gruesome amulets of the past – dried toads; bits of hangman's rope – have given way to St. Christopher medals or four-leaf clovers (said to be the one plant Eve brought out of Eden). Faith in a charm may really bring luck by inspiring positive thinking, and most such superstitions are harmless. Taken too far, they can dominate lives – and inspire evils such as witch-hunts.

Colorfully decorated sugar skulls are a traditional candy during Mexico's festival of All Souls' Day, when Death is feted in semi-Christian rites – to ward off his attentions.

Undertakers in ancient Egypt placed a carved scarab beetle, symbol of resurrection, over the heart of a mummified corpse as an amulet for the journey into the next life.

In England, "well dressing" – decorating wells with pictures made of flowers – survives as an annual Church festival; but it began as a pagan rite to honor "the gods below."

"Lucky" horseshoes: made of the sacred metal iron and with a significant shape – to pagans, a fertility image (honoring the Mother Goddess); to Christians, a "C" for Christ.

FOLLOW ME

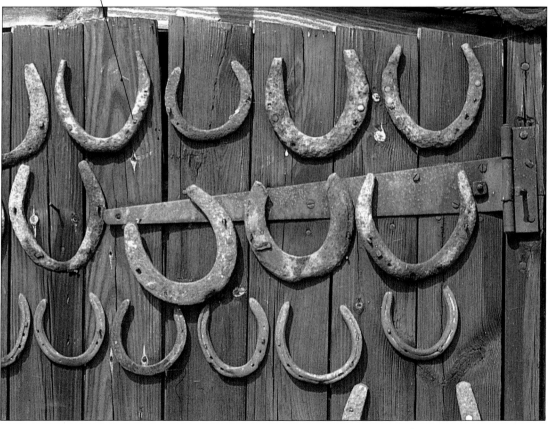

❏ Members of the National Society of Thirteen against Superstition, Prejudice and Fear in the United States and of Britain's Thirteen Club of London are devoted to breaking taboos. They meet on Friday the 13th to dine 13 to a table, spill salt, open umbrellas indoors, smash mirrors, and walk under ladders – and apparently have just as much good fortune as nonmembers.

❏ The idea that breaking a mirror brings seven years' bad luck derives from ancient belief that one's soul appears in one's reflection: to harm one harms both. Happily, it is possible to avert this fate. Europeans can "wash away" bad luck by throwing the mirror shards into a river; Americans counter it by making the sign of a cross and laying a five dollar bill on the broken glass. Such varying approaches between countries are common: black cats (below) are potent omens worldwide, but are thought to be lucky in Britain, unlucky almost everywhere else.

Doomsday!

Thousands of followers of U.S. prophet William Miller (d.1849) gathered on New England hills on April 3, 1843, to face Doomsday. When the day ended and the world did not, Miller made updates extending to October 22, 1844. Many Millerites sold their possessions, donned white robes (designed and profitably marketed by Miller himself), and headed for graveyards to meet the risen dead. One farmer bought robes for his cows, hoping to sell milk to thirsty travelers on the road to Heaven. Believing the dead would reach Heaven first, some tried to jump ahead by family murder and suicide. When the final Doomsday dawned without incident (except a "Last Trumpet" panic caused by a farmboy tootling a cow horn) most of the c.100,000 Millerites gave up. Today other prophets warn that Earth is at risk: from nuclear power, the greenhouse effect – or, say more way-out soothsayers, comet strikes, space aliens' attacks, or "polar shift" (the Earth tilting to spill sea over land). Their slogan, "The End is Nigh," is an ancient one. Many faiths have taught that God will end His creation in a cosmic battle between good and evil. This final conflict, Armageddon, will be preceded by war, earthquake, storm, famine, and flood and followed by Judgment Day for souls. In old times, natural disasters were believed to confirm such fears. Aztec, Buddhist, and Hindu teachers envisaged a cycle of creation and destruction, with each age worse than the one before, and the last (in which we now live) beyond redemption: the Hindu *kali yuga*, or black age. Although many modern cults say that the Last Day is near, we may take comfort from the many mistaken prophets of Doomsday – but not from the Anglo-Israelite sect. Calculating a 1953 Doomsday, they stuck to their guns when 1953 came and went: they said the world had ended – but unbelievers had failed to notice.

One of the Bible's most chilling images: the dawn of Armageddon, with the skeletal figure of Death, mounted on his pale horse, riding out to slay.

To some, Doomsday is part of a cycle – like the Flood of *Genesis*, which destroyed the world only to herald a new beginning in God's Covenant with Noah.

In Eastern religions the never-ending cycle of birth, death, and rebirth – repeated creations and destructions – is symbolized by the ever-turning Wheel of God.

Doomsday: angels pour "the vials of the wrath of God" on the guilty earth (*Revelations*. XVI).

❏ Armageddon (Hebrew: *har megiddo*, hill of Megiddo) takes its name from Megiddo in Palestine, where many major battles were fought in Biblical times because of its strategic position.

❏ Jehovah's Witnesses believe God set up His kingdom on Earth in 1914 to prepare for the end of the world. They teach that "many now living will not see death," for Armageddon is due any moment now – or overdue, for some in the movement expected it in October 1975.

❏ In 1964, Jim Jones, leader of the People's Temple Church, announced that the world would end in thermonuclear war on July 15, 1967. Despite his prediction's failure, his cult survived – until November 1973, when the world ended for Jones and 912 followers with mass suicide at Jonestown, Guyana.

❏ Christian faith in bodily resurrection of the dead at Doomsday was once very literal. People thought that bodies would rise in the same condition they were buried in – so amputees had severed limbs buried with them, for fear of facing the Lord short of an arm or leg. This was the reason people so dreaded "Resurrection men" who stole cadavers for surgeons to dissect – for how could bodily parts scattered among laboratories reunite on Doomsday?

The Devil's footprints

The Devil has left his mark on the map of Britain. Huge standing stones such as the Devil's Arrows in Yorkshire are known as rocks he hurled at churches; prehistoric tombs such as the Devil's Den in Wiltshire are his lairs. Legend says he dug the valley of the Devil's Dyke in a bid to drown Sussex churches and built the Devil's Bridge over a Welsh river to trap the souls of those who crossed. Another Satanic visit occurred in Devon in 1855, during an unusually bitter winter. People froze to death, and suffered bread riots or starvation when snow cut off supplies. It seemed only natural that the Devil should come to inspect his work – and on February 9 people all over Devon awoke to find his footprints in the snow. For that was the only explanation that seemed to fit the tracks that ran everywhere, crossing locked yards,

Local legend says these prehistoric monuments are the Devil's Arrows, with which the Archenemy sought (in vain) to smash a church in England.

inaccessible rooftops, and high windowsills; even passing through walls. They were apparently left by a being that walked on two legs, with cloven hoofs – and, some say, claws. Several witnesses said they resembled donkey tracks – if a donkey could walk upright, fly onto roofs, squeeze through tiny gaps, and cover hundreds of miles in a single night. Convinced that the Devil was abroad, people ran to consult the clergy or locked themselves indoors. Scientists tried to explain away the Devil's footprints, blaming animals from kangaroos to badgers, toads, birds with iced-up feet – and human pranksters; later, students of peculiar events added hopping mice, or attributed the tracks to marks caused by a rope trailed by a nocturnal balloonist! No one has explained why the tracks should dance across a single county for just one night. And if, as one clergyman held, his parishioners' rotten morals inspired Satan's Devon visit, was there no other district that similarly merited his attention?

The Devil's Bridge, in Wales. The tale goes that the Devil built it in exchange for a promise of the soul of the first creature to cross it – but locals outwitted him by sending a dog over first.

This contemporary sketch of the Devil's footprints shows the clear resemblance, noted at the time, to the tracks of a donkey's shoe.

Naturalists can read the story of animal tracks in snow; but some remain undeciphered, such as Yeti tracks in the Himalayas – and the Devil's footprints.

Cloven hoofs are the best-known distinguishing mark of the Devil, dating back to Rabbinical tradition of the goat as an emblem of uncleanness (unholiness).

❏ Similar mystery footprints are occasionally reported elsewhere. To records from Scotland and France, English explorer Sir James Clark Ross added one from the Antarctic. In 1840 he visited uninhabited, icebound Kerguelen Island – and was amazed to see prints in the snow. They resembled a donkey's (on an island where certainly no donkey existed) but were single-track, as if it walked on two legs: just like the prints in Devon.

❏ If the Devil's footprints were the work of a human agency, they may have been meant as more than a practical joke. At the time some clergymen were drawn to Puseyism, a neo-Catholic revival inspired by theologian Edward Pusey – to which traditionalists objected violently. This was the case in several of the parishes where the mystery tracks appeared – and led right up to church doors. At least one local newspaper saw the visitation as "a warning to the Puseyites."

❏ In the 1950s, Scottish explorer James Alan Rennie saw in Scotland "tracks every bit as mysterious as those seen in Devon." But they were no mystery to him. He had seen similar tracks in Canada in 1924, when they actually formed before his eyes – made, he said, by "some freakish current of warm air" condensing in the cold to deposit "water-blobs" that left weird prints in the snow.

Into thin air

People once blamed disappearances "into thin air" on lustful gods snatching up persons they fancied, or demons dragging off sinners to Hell. Now, some blame mysterious abductions on U.F.O.s, or theorize that locations such as the intersection of "ley lines," said to join ancient sites, may form "gateways" to another dimension. Ivan T. Sanderson mapped 10 "vile vortices" (one the Bermuda Triangle) where magnetic/climatic factors may create "gravitational whirlpools" that whisk away objects or people, who sometimes return; sometimes not.

Charles Fort called such removals "teleportation." A well-attested case is that of Spanish nun Mary of Agreda, who in 1620 claimed she had made flights to Mexico. Other nuns swore she had never left the convent. In 1622, Father Alonzo de Benavides, a missionary to the Mexican Jumano people, reported they had already heard of Christ from "a lady in blue." A chalice she had given them was later identified as one from Mary's convent. Among famous disappearances are those of British diplomat Benjamin Bathurst, from the yard of a German inn in 1809; Rudolf Diesel, inventor of the diesel engine, from a North Sea steamer in 1913; and British politician Victor Grayson, who stepped onto a train in 1920 and was never seen again. But Bathurst may have been abducted by Napoleonic agents; Diesel was in financial difficulties and was suspected by Germany of selling industrial secrets to Britain; and Grayson feared exposure of his bisexuality. More interesting is the case of U.S. author Ambrose Bierce. One of his stories (published 1878) created the legend (printed as fact as recently as the 1980s) of Tennessee farmer David Lang, who vanished in mid-stride in a pasture but whose calls for help were heard long afterwards. In 1913, Bierce announced that he was off to join Pancho Villa's rebels in Mexico – and vanished without trace.

American bandleader Glenn Miller, heading the American Band of the Allied Expeditionary Forces during World War II, was presumed killed in December 1944, when the plane in which he was flying from Britain to Paris disappeared. No wreckage or bodies were found. It was rumored that the plane had been mistakenly shot down by an Allied fighter and that Miller had survived the crash, but so dreadfully disfigured that he became a recluse.

Mexican bandit and revolutionary Pancho Villa (1878-1923) (left) with a henchman. Did U.S. writer Ambrose Bierce end his days among such tough customers?

Aviatrix Amelia Earhart and a copilot disappeared over the Pacific in 1937. Rumor says they had been asked to spy on Japanese-held islands.

Tales of mystery and horror made Ambrose Bierce (1842-?) famous. A noted cynic, nicknamed "Bitter Bierce," he disappeared after running off to Mexico at the age of 70.

❑ Church authorities recognized Sister Mary of Agreda's 500 flights to Mexico as genuine miracles. She was luckier than an unfortunate Portuguese merchant in Goa, India, who a few years after her flights, in 1655, was suddenly "teleported" back to his homeland. The Holy Inquisition got word of his experience – and had him burned at the stake as a sorcerer.

❑ Rumors that Adolf Hitler (above) survived World War II and "disappeared" to South America are certainly false – but stories that the body burned outside the *Führer*'s Berlin bunker after his suicide on April 30, 1945, was not his may be true. In September 1992, Moscow's K.G.B. archives released movie footage said to show Hitler's unburned corpse. One Russian historian claims that Hitler's body was secretly buried in the Soviet Union in 1945, dug up for reidentification in 1946, and finally destroyed in 1970.

From out of nowhere

Rarer than mysterious disappearances are people who appear "from out of nowhere." Some may be frauds, fleeing their pasts or seeking notoriety – such as Princess Caraboo, who appeared in 1817 near Bristol, England, claiming to be a Javanese princess kidnapped by pirates. She was hailed as "the Wonder of the West," until her mother turned up to identify her as Mary Willcocks. But what of the two "Green Children" found in England in the 1100s? They spoke an unknown tongue and had green skins. Lodged with local landowner Sir Richard de Calne, the boy soon died; the girl lived to learn English and tell of her home in "St. Martin's land." She served Sir Richard for years; but he reported she was "rather loose and wanton in her conduct." A teenage boy found in Nuremberg, Germany, in 1828 was also an enigma. He could write his name, Kaspar Hauser, but seemed ignorant of speech – or anything but sitting still, playing with toy horses, or eating bread and water. Within weeks he was able to tell of lifelong solitary confinement in a tiny, dark room. Was he the subject of a sinister experiment in sensory deprivation, or (as many thought) the secret heir of some great family, deprived of his birthright and brought up in secrecy? In 1829 he died as strangely as he lived, stabbed – he said on his deathbed – by a masked man. Another enduring mystery was a woman rescued from drowning in a Berlin canal in 1920. She claimed to be Grand Duchess Anastasia, daughter of Tsar Nicholas II of Russia, who had been reported killed with her family in 1918. The Tsar's surviving relatives could not agree whether she was or not, and for more than 50 years, under the name Anna Anderson, she was the center of a legal battle. Years after her death, scholars still debate her case.

Folktales tell of "alien" visitors such as the "Green Children" straying into this world from a parallel, yet totally separate, world – a theme taken up by modern "sci-fi" yarnspinners.

Kaspar Hauser appeared in 1828 in Nuremberg, unable to express himself but clutching a cryptic letter. The writer claimed to have kept him shut up for 16 years.

Tsar Nicholas II and his family in happier days. Today the skills of forensic scientists are turned to the task of identifying their presumed bones.

Did Grand Duchess Anastasia (seated far right with her family) die in 1918, as the official story has it, or did she escape, to reappear as Anna Anderson in Berlin?

Some mysterious appearances and disappearances may be cases of teleportation – an unlikely event that befell Victorian medium Mrs. Guppy.

FACT FILE

❏ Russian officials announced in 1991 that bones found near Ekaterinburg, in the Urals, were certainly those of Tsar Nicholas II, Empress Alexandra, and three of their children – but not of Anastasia or Tsarevich Alexis. In 1993 some of the remains that had been sent to Britain for D.N.A. ("genetic fingerprinting") tests confirmed the Russians. Prince Philip, husband of Britain's Queen Elizabeth II and near relation of Alexandra, had donated tissue for comparison testing.

❏ Victorian medium Mrs. Guppy vanished from her London home one evening and materialized soon after, with a heavy thud, at a séance a few miles away. The arrival of "the biggest woman in London" (230lb/104kg) made quite an impact, especially on one unfortunate who howled: "Good God – there is something on my head!" The random nature of teleportation led Charles Fort (below) to describe it as a cosmic practical joke: the case of Mrs. Guppy certainly suggests a paranormal sense of humor.

What happened at Philadelphia?

World War II's strangest secret weapon was tested, it is said, at the Philadelphia Navy Yard in October 1943. It was the U.S. Office of Naval Research's Project Rainbow, an attempt to make a ship invisible by electronic camouflage. Albert Einstein was personally involved in this practical application of his theories suggesting that space and time are not absolutes. An electromagnetic force field about 300ft (90m) across was created around the 1,240 ton destroyer escort *Eldridge*. A green mist enshrouded the ship; then, in a "space-time warp," it vanished – "teleported" to the harbor at Norfolk, Va., about 300mi (480km) away. Minutes later the *Eldridge* reappeared at Philadelphia, apparently unharmed. But the effects on her crew proved deadly. Some died; some went insane; some were mutilated by spontaneous combustion; some underwent periods of "transparency" during which they could walk through solid objects. The Navy confined survivors in top security hospitals. The story was not told until 1956, when Ufologist Morris Jessup made public information said to come from a merchant seaman who had been an eyewitness (although it seems unlikely that a top secret experiment would have been made in plain view). The U.S. Navy has always denied that the "Philadelphia Experiment" took place – but some allege a cover-up, seeing sinister implications in Jessup's suicide in 1959 and claiming surviving witnesses are still silenced by threats from government agencies. What really happened? The story may stem from garbled accounts of research into radar invisibility during World War II, when the German Navy once announced it had developed a magic paint that made U-boats immune to electronic detection. It had not, but certainly research in this field of "stealth technology" was made by both sides.

Surrendered U-boats, 1945. Late in World War II – as a cover-up for new snorkel gear that made submarines more elusive – the German Navy claimed to have developed a "magic anti-radar paint."

A nuclear submarine under repair at Norfolk, Va., long a major U.S. naval base – and the reported scene, in 1943, of the brief "materialization" of a "time-warped" warship.

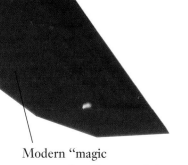

Modern "magic camouflage": state-of-the-art low observables technology and an ultra-streamlined body make the U.S. Air Force's F-117A "stealth fighter" nearly invisible to enemy radar.

The theories on time and space of Albert Einstein led some to consider the viability of invisibility or even time travel.

❏ The *Eldridge* was apparently none the worse for its experience. She was sold in 1951 to the Greek Navy, serving as the frigate *Panthir* into the 1980s.

❏ The U.S. Navy probably never practiced magic, but some top commanders of World War II were noted mystics. Air Chief Marshal Dowding, who led the Royal Air Force to victory in the Battle of Britain, was a Spiritualist. In 1943 he published a book, *Many Mansions*, containing "spirit messages" from dead fliers. U.S. General George S. Patton (above) was a believer in reincarnation, claiming to have been a "warrior woman" in one former life. Admiral Takijiro Onishi came close to dismissal from the Imperial Japanese Navy: first for suggesting that naval aviators should be selected by graphology (handwriting analysis); then for allocating billions of yen to fund a charlatan who claimed to be able to change water into gasoline. Onishi survived to help plan the Pearl Harbor attack and later founded the *kamikaze* suicide squadrons.

Invasion of the body snatchers

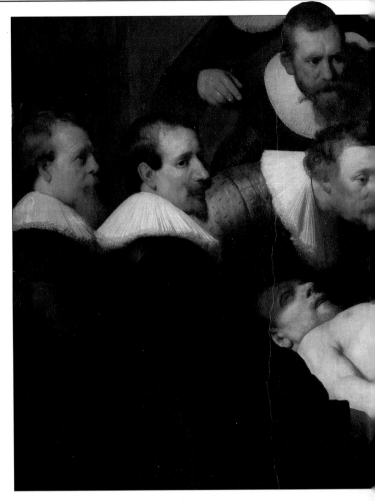

From early times cadavers were stolen from tombs for "medical magic." Physicians prescribed "mummy" (parts of corpses) for many ailments: leg bones ground up in wine for rheumatism, powdered skull for epilepsy. In 1300 the Church ruled that desecration of the mortal body harmed the immortal soul and forbade dissection of "images of God." For centuries this held back medicine: Andreas Vesalius (1514-64), pioneer anatomist, was condemned to death by the Inquisition for body snatching. By the late 18th century most civilized nations had relaxed anti-dissection laws (including most U.S. states, although New York Hospital was wrecked by an anti-dissection mob in 1788). But in Britain only the bodies of certain criminals (doomed to dissection after execution as "a peculiar Mark of Infamy") went to anatomists. Corpses (shipped as salt fish) were imported from Ireland and

Pioneer anatomist Vesalius was condemned to death for "body snatching." The sentence was commuted to a pilgrimage – on which he died.

France, but medical schools demanded fresh bodies. The years from around 1750 to about 1830 were the heyday of body snatchers, known as "Resurrectionists," "Grips," or "Sack-em-up men." The latter name came because bodies were taken naked from their graves: British law said stealing a body was only a misdemeanor, but stealing grave clothes or coffins a felony. One Grip caught with 30 corpses (including a tub of pickled babies) got a small fine for body snatching, but 7 years' jail for stealing a shroud. The trade was profitable – surgeons paid up to £12 (about $70) each for prime subjects – and it is estimated that more than 1,000 Britons a year were "resurrected" in c.1800-30. Two Edinburgh Grips spoiled it. Too lazy to dig, William Burke and William Hare murdered some 16 roomers at their squalid lodging house in 1826-28 and sold the still warm bodies to a local surgeon. The scandal of their trial was largely responsible for the Anatomy Act of 1832, which made about 600 corpses a year legally available for research.

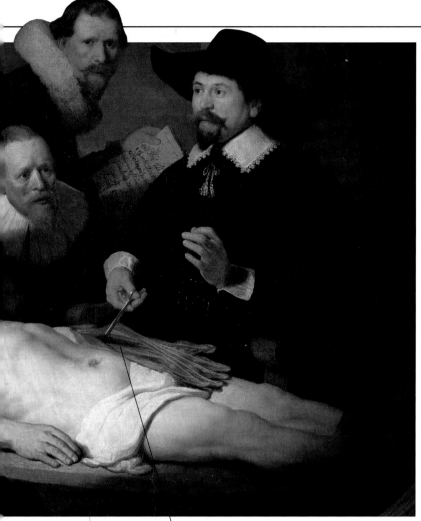

Body snatcher William Burke was hanged for murder (and then anatomized); January 1829.

Hare escaped the gallows by ratting on his partner – dying, it is said, a blind beggar.

❏ Resurrectionists invented a huge, iron "corkscrew" to split open the head ends of coffins, so that corpses could easily be winched out with block and tackle. Bereaved persons countered with heavy stone slabs (lowered into graves to cover the coffin for several weeks; then dug up to be used again); iron cages (mort safes) around graves; small forts to house armed watchmen (below); even graves boobytrapped with spring guns or explosive devices.

The corpse shown in Rembrandt's magnificent *Anatomy [Lesson] of Dr. Nicolaes Tulp* is said to be that of Adriaan Adriaansz, a 28-year-old criminal from Leiden, hanged in 1632.

"Mort safes" like these – heavy iron cages to be placed over a new grave – were developed in Scotland to keep out the "Grips" in the 18th-19th centuries. They were rented out by the week to cautious mourners.

❏ In 1819 Dr. James Jeffrey, Professor of Anatomy at Scotland's Glasgow University, gave a public demonstration of "galvanism," applying electrical current to the (legally acquired) corpse of an executed murderer. But when the current flowed, the corpse – in fact, only half hanged – revived. As the audience began to panic, Jeffrey calmly cut the subject's throat with a scalpel. Since the man was legally dead, Jeffrey was not charged with a crime.

Trial by fire

"Human salamanders" have been around since the *Old Testament* told how Daniel survived the Babylonian fiery furnace, and immunity from fire has long been seen as a mark of religious grace. In a medieval "trial by ordeal," an accused who could carry a red-hot plowshare three (or seven) paces without injury (or with burns that healed within three days) was judged innocent. It is said to be easy to walk swiftly across burning wood or ash, making only brief contact with a material of low thermal conductivity, but some firewalkers, notably Buddhist and Hindu holy persons, walk slowly over stones heated to about 800°F.(430°C.) – and skeptical witnesses have testified that their feet are not treated with protective substances. Most think firewalking is a matter of faith (a kind of self-hypnosis) or, in the case of Westerners who perform the feat, nerve: stride out briskly and all is well – he who hesitates gets burned. Scientific tests are said to show that some who withstand painful rituals are able to slow down their brain waves to the "theta frequencies" of sleep. At Kataragama, Sri Lanka, firewalking is part of annual Hindu religious ceremonies that include ritual mutilation. In religious ecstasy, devotees slash themselves with knives and thrust steel skewers through their tongues and cheeks. Some submit to having as many as 50 hooks embedded in their backs: with cords tied to these, some swing from frames, others pull loads of offerings to the temple. None shows pain; the wounds do not bleed. Young Westerners have now adapted a ritual of the Pentecost islanders of the South Pacific, who prove their manliness by jumping from 90ft (27m) bamboo towers with fiber ropes tied to their ankles to stop the fall. A bungee jumper plummets 200ft (60m) or more, then bounces like a yo-yo at the end of a latex rope.

A Hindu holy man stands on sharp sword blades during ceremonies at Kuala Lumpur, Malaysia. The devotees of many faiths practice mortification of the flesh as a sign of humility before their gods.

Although a fair number of Westerners have performed the feat, firewalking as a religious rite is mainly an Eastern practice. Here, a worshiper in Hong Kong crosses red hot embers during a Chinese Great Monkey God festival.

A needle pierces the cheek of a Javanese dancer. Laboratory experiments suggest that religious ecstasy helps such persons block out pain with "theta waves" from the brain.

Like their feet and bodies, the light silk or cotton clothing typically worn by firewalkers is unharmed.

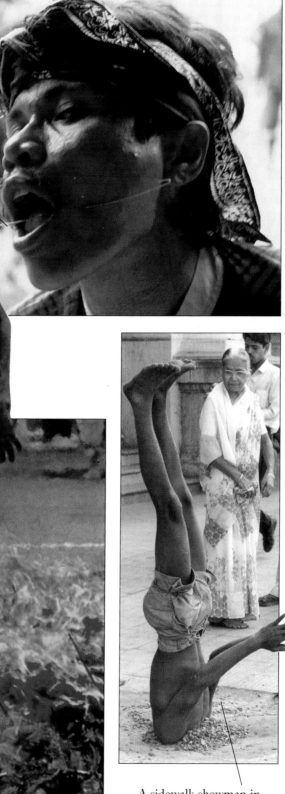

A sidewalk showman in Calcutta uses advanced yoga techniques, giving great control over breathing and other bodily functions, to perform a remarkable feat.

FACT FILE

❑ On May 21 every year, to mark the miraculous rescue of saints' images from a burning church about 1250, villagers in Lankadas, Greece, dance for up to 30 minutes in a fire pit about 12ft (3.6m) square. Scientists who studied the ceremony in 1980 measured the temperature of the coals at 932°F. (500°C.), while thermocouples fitted to the dancer's feet registered only 356°F. (180°C.). "Faith is needed," said a dancer in 1982 – after a witness who attempted to join in was rushed to the hospital with third-degree burns.

❑ One of the most famous U.S. "human salamanders" was, appropriately, a blacksmith: Nathan Coker of Easton, Md. In 1871 it was reported that he could stand with bare feet on a white-hot shovel until it cooled, juggle pieces of metal taken from his fiery furnace, and gargle with molten lead.

❑ Feats of tower divers, bungee jumpers, and base jumpers (who make parachute jumps from high structures) are overshadowed by the involuntary achievement of Nicholas Alkemade, a British Air Force sergeant of World War II. On March 24, 1944, Alkemade jumped from a flaming bomber over Berlin without a parachute and fell about 18,000ft (5,490m). Thick undergrowth and deep snow broke his fall, and he had only minor injuries.

Food for thought!

In the 1970s "anthropologist" Oscar Kiss Maerth claimed that early humans developed intelligence through a diet of brains. The cleverest "ape people" trapped and butchered less able contemporaries and ingested their abilities along with the contents of their skulls. (Maerth suggested that women, less physically capable of murder, were thus historically doomed to be less intelligent than men!) We may laugh at such theories, but if a rash of "cannibal killings" in the 1980s-90s – like the case of Jeffrey L. Dahmer, the Milwaukee Monster, convicted in 1992 of having slaughtered and eaten parts of several young men – is a guide, there are still people who hold the very ancient belief that human qualities can be "stolen" by eating the flesh and/or drinking the blood of their possessors. Cannibalism has been far more often practiced for magical purposes than out of a taste for human flesh. Most persons who have eaten fellow humans for nonmagical reasons have done so simply to survive. Even instances of ritual cannibalism may have been much exaggerated. Spanish conquerors claimed that the Aztecs and other South American peoples ate sacrificial humans. Those who unquestioningly accept this should remember that early opponents of Christianity made the same charge, pointing out that at their "love feasts" Christians ate the "body and blood" of Christ. Eating people is not only wrong – it may also endanger your health. Some tribal peoples of New Guinea consume the brains of a recently deceased (in former times, ritually slaughtered) relative at the name feast of an infant, who then takes that relative's name. It is now known that this practice spreads *kuru* (shivers), a fatal degenerative disease of the central nervous system caused by a virus like that responsible for Mad Cow Disease, a recent Western health scare.

Caged like a wild beast, Russian "cannibal killer" Andrei Chikatilo was convicted in 1992 of 52 murders.

Cannibals prepare to feast: an old engraving of a type once popular among people who liked to think themselves superior to "savage" races.

A tribeswoman in New Guinea displays a mutilated hand. She is said to have cut off her fingers and burned them as part of a religious ceremony.

❏ The most famous U.S. case of "necessary cannibalism" was probably that of the Donner Party. Trapped by snow in the Sierra Nevadas in winter 1846, some members of George Donner's California-bound wagon train ate each other in order to survive. One man from the party was later tried for murder (he admitted to eating five people), acquitted – and cashed in on his notoriety by opening a restaurant in San Francisco. He was luckier than a snow-bound trapper who is said to have been convicted of murder and cannibalism later in the century by a politically biased judge, who opined: "Maybe you had to do it to survive. But there were only five Democrats in this county – and you ate three of them!"

❏ Male chauvinists like to point out that women's brains are smaller than men's. They are – a male brain averages around 50.3oz (1,424g) in weight; a female brain around 44.7oz (1,265g) – but scientists say that brain size, within normal parameters, has little to do with intelligence. An autopsy on Nobel Prize winning novelist Anatole France (1844-1924) (above) revealed that his brain was only about half average weight.

Hit or myth?

Myth says that the sewers of American cities (some far from the Mississippi, where this specimen lives) are infested by alligators – perhaps originally dumped there as unwanted pets.

Most of us have heard an "urban legend;" typically, an amazing experience of "a friend of a friend of mine." Tales of venomous spiders that crawl from store-bought pot plants (usually yuccas) and alligators in the sewers are exaggerations of real incidents – poisonous insects are found in exotic plants and fruit; *The New York Times*, February 10, 1935, reported a 7ft (2.1m) alligator in a conduit on East 123rd Street, possibly dropped from a ship on the East River – but we must hope the microwaved cat (or baby!) is fictitious. Students of modern folklore say the new legends differ little from ancient ones. Medieval folk who said King Arthur "slept" to reemerge in time of need have much in common with moderns who like to believe Elvis Presley is alive (maybe as a short order cook in Minnesota). Many urban legends are international – but one recorded in 1991 is specific to southern France, where forest fires then raged. The body of a scuba diver, it is said, was found in a burned out area: he had been siphoned up by firefighting planes filling their water tanks from the ocean. A British classic is the myth of Springheeled Jack, a demonic figure who terrorized London in 1837-38 and made sporadic reappearances until as late as 1904. His mighty leaps were attributed to springs in his boot heels – but some said he was an insane circus acrobat, who vowed to frighten 30 persons to death, or even a trained (cleverly disguised!) kangaroo. A modern classic is the "vanishing hitch-hiker," perhaps dating from Chicago's Resurrection Mary of the 1940s. "Mary" hitches a ride with a young man, agrees to date him, and gives him her address. He later goes to her home and is told she died years ago – killed near the spot where he picked her up – and has been trying to get home, on the anniversary of her death, ever since.

Corporal Dawie van Jaarsveld gave a ride on his motorcycle to a female "phantom hitch-hiker" near Uniondale, South Africa, in April 1978.

One of Victorian England's favorite myths was that of Springheeled Jack. He was not always shown as a villain: here he scares away bodysnatchers from their prey.

Tabloid newspapers' frequent sightings of Elvis Presley (seen here in a 1973 photograph) are eagerly accepted by some fans unwilling to accept the fact of The King's death in 1977.

❏ The outrages (he specialized in sexual harassment of girls) of Springheeled Jack were probably the work of a succession of unpleasant practical jokers. The original in 1837-38 may have been Henry de la Poer Beresford, Marquis of Waterford (1810-59), a notorious and ruthless gagster. Beresford had protuberant eyes – Jack's victims often described him as bug-eyed – and, newpapers of the time alleged, he could often be located at or near the scenes of Jack's attacks.

❏ A grim tale that seems tailormade for today tells of a man or woman who has a one-night stand with a stranger. He or she wakes to find the partner gone, leaving a note: "Welcome to the A.I.D.S. club." But Dr. Paul Smith, Professor of Folklore, Memorial University, Newfoundland, traces this myth back to the Middle Ages – when the message read: "Welcome the Black Death!"

❏ A cautionary fable certainly for our time is that of a youngster who accepts a drink (or drugs) from a stranger. The victim wakes up hours later with a surgical scar on his or her back. Medical examination reveals a kidney is missing – "hijacked" by an unscrupulous surgeon for sale in the Middle East. Police in England claimed to have been told of some 50 such cases in 1992: all concerned "a friend of a friend"; none were genuine.

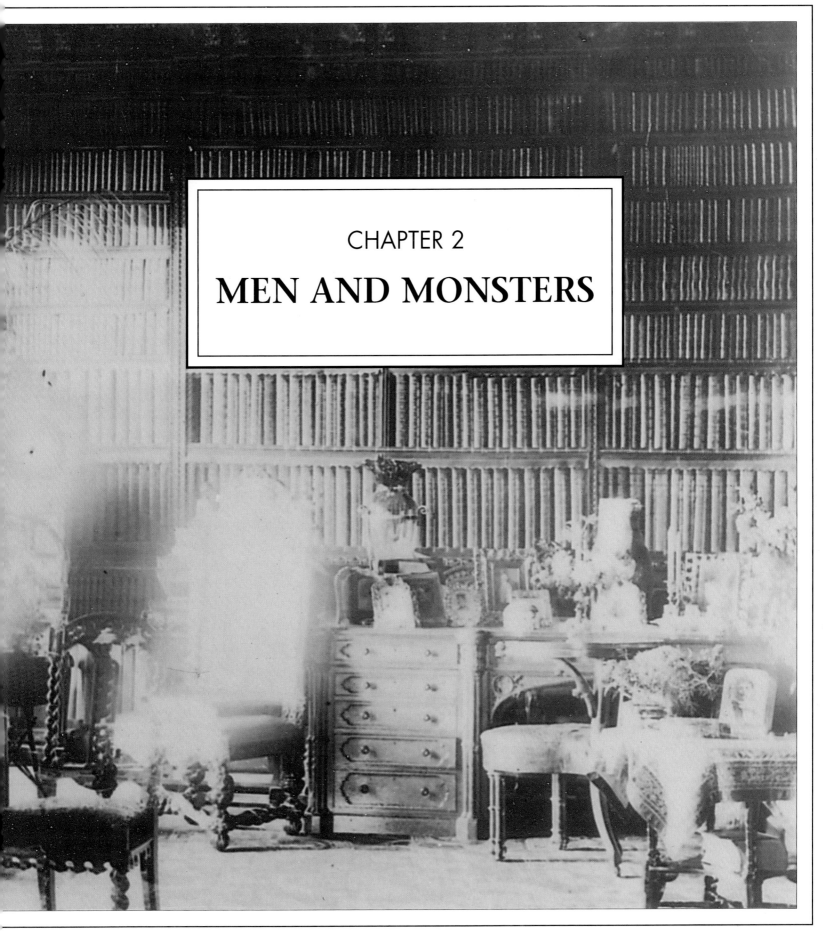

CHAPTER 2

MEN AND MONSTERS

Men of mystery and magic

Everyone loves a mystery, and this chapter, like its companions *Strange World* and *Gods and Demons*, examines many of the most intriguing mysteries of this world – and the next. The coverage of this chapter centers on living beings – men, women, and animals – who have become the stuff of legend. Its human characters range from seekers after eternal life to vaudeville performers; its animals from the monsters of antiquity to

Seen in 1914, master escaper Harry Houdini is about to be shut in a chest that will be secured with chains and then lowered into a river.

A 16th century print shows alchemists in their workshop. They seek the "Philosopher's Stone" that will change base metals to gold – and perhaps confer eternal life.

modern oddities, some the creations of movie special effects' workshops.

Each person has his or her own view on the paranormal, on those things that lie outside the boundaries of our everyday senses, and any writer – or reader – who approaches the subject needs to be aware of his or her own prejudices. People are frequently skeptical when they first encounter tales about men and women of "mystery," those who claimed to have (or were said by others to have) unearthly powers. Many people admire the magical feats of Harry Houdini, who himself never claimed to be a real magician, and of Uri Geller, in spite of the exaggerated claims of his less critical supporters. They respect ancient and modern alchemists, seekers after the Philosopher's Stone, for their intellectual dedication and for their many real contributions to scientific knowledge. Mesmerism, once considered a magical art, is now, as hypnotherapy, an accepted healing technique.

Where the author drew the line, as will many readers, was at outright magic. As the reader will see, the author held the view that the self-styled "Great Beast," Aleister Crowley, was no more than a sick prankster. But . . .

This book was written on a word processor: a piece of equipment the authors have used every day, for several years, without incident. As the author finished the piece on Crowley, a muffled "scream" was heard from the machine and then several hours of work dissolved from the screen, as if wiped away by an invisible hand – and even more disconcerting, it was impossible to enter any other files on the disk. It held all of the book then written; there was no backup copy.

It took a computer expert almost two days of electronic juggling to extract from the "corrupted" disk a jumbled printout from which the book could be reconstructed. When the author called the book's editor to explain the delay, the telephone conversation was interrupted by an angry scream and the line went dead. Finally, when it came time to print out the book's complete text, part of the "Crowley" piece had again disappeared, to be

Until as late as the 18th century many people believed witches flew to their evil revels (traditionally astride broomsticks, as seen in this print of 1612) with the aid of Satan.

Author Richard O'Neill at work on the final draft of this book – delayed by what may have been a manifestation of an offended Aleister Crowley!

Although he died in 1947, it may still not be wise to insult the "Great Beast," magician Aleister Crowley. Note the characteristic phallic "A" in his autograph.

replaced by a series of ***s and $$$s. Again the text was reconstructed, but if it is missing from your copy of this book, then perhaps the publisher is not to blame . . . !

New sciences and old oracles

The second part of this chapter begins by looking at scientific mysteries, those that may one day be explained, even controlled, by scientific techniques. These include extrasensory perception (E.S.P.); the photography of auras, which might revolutionize medical diagnosis; and the location of liquids, minerals, and objects by dowsing. Even such phenomena as time slips, which some have seen as partial proof of reincarnation, may be amenable to investigation by psychological, if not strictly scientific, methods.

The chapter then goes on to examine a more controversial subject: communication with the spirits of the dead. Spiritualism was sometimes denounced in the 19th century as un-Christian (the Roman Catholic Church still officially maintains this view) and an evil influence. It is now accepted by many people that, admitting fakery by early "materializing mediums," some mediums – such as Eileen Garrett – seem genuinely to be in touch with what we may call (whether or not we accept that the dead speak through the mouths of the living) "the other side." Garrett was typical of many modern mediums in insisting that there must be psychological and scientific explanations for her gifts.

But perhaps the day when science at last establishes the parameters of the paranormal will be a sad one for humanity. Most people probably would like to believe in miracles, for we all need to dream. But miracles can be dangerous. In the past, men and women were persecuted or killed because they claimed to have, or others accused them of having, paranormal powers. Levitation was thought to be a gift of God when holy saints rose aloft in religious ecstasy, but accused witches were said to fly through the air with the Devil's aid. The 16th century seer Nostradamus, the most famous name in the chapter of this book devoted to prophets and prophecy, deliberately made his forecasts obscure, fearing charges of wizardry.

Modern prophets such as Edgar Cayce and Jeane Dixon have spoken without fear of persecution, for people have grown more tolerant, more open-minded. For example, in the British elections of 1992, almost all of the 600-plus places in Parliament were contested by Natural Law Party candidates, followers of Maharishi Mahesh

Victorian Spiritualist medium William Marriott displays puppets used to fake "materializations," supposedly formed by a substance called ectoplasm from within the medium's body.

harmless, popular (with more than 3,000,000 adherents worldwide), and, its supporters maintain, beneficial movement.

It is possible, however, for people to be too open-minded. Few people now take seriously such methods of foretelling the future as palmistry and phrenology – but astrology, I Ching, rune-casting, and Tarot still flourish. They are even growing in popularity, as any glance at a tabloid newspaper or visit to a New Age shop will show. They are, for many observers, intriguing and amusing diversions. The fear is that all too many people are increasingly allowing them to direct their lives.

A dowser attempts to locate underground water with the aid of a wooden wand. Unlike some other paranormal powers, this ancient skill is of considerable practical use.

A table rises aloft: one of many levitational phenomena produced and recorded by the Missouri-based Society for Research into Rapport and Telekinesis (S.O.R.R.A.T.).

New Age enthusiasm has led many to investigate ancient methods of looking into the future. But should the Tarot deck and crystal ball be taken seriously?

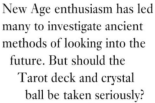

Yogi, an Indian *guru* (Hindu religious teacher) whose doctrines are based on the discipline of Transcendental Meditation (T.M.). The party's manifesto mentioned that all of its candidates were able to levitate. Apart from a few newspaper cartoons, no one seemed to think this particularly unusual (although none of the Natural Law candidates won many votes). T.M. is, of course, a

Monsters in fact and fiction

The final part of this chapter is devoted to animals – some mythical, some possible, some real – and monsters likewise. "Here be dragons," map makers used to record as confidently as they located rivers or cities. Today few still believe in the beasts that were real to our ancestors – dragons, unicorns, mermaids, and the like. We remember them in children's stories, place names, heraldic coats of arms, fantasy novels and movies, and sword and sorcery computer games. They show an occasional flicker of life. From time to time perfectly rational people claim to have seen such creatures ("What I saw was real," swore Scotsman Alexander Gunn in 1900. "I actually encountered a mermaid."), but usually we relegate the fabulous creatures of the ancient world to the land of myth and story book.

For other legendary beasts, the dividing line between myth and reality has grown blurred, as scientific discoveries make us aware how far we are from knowing everything about the natural world. Sea serpents, long dismissed as sailors' yarns, become credible in the light of deep-sea exploration that reveals previously unknown forms of marine life – like the coelacanth, a large fish thought extinct for 70 million years.

If sea serpents may exist, why not their cousins the lake monsters? Reported sightings of the Loch Ness Monster and some of its North American cousins, such as "Champ" of Lake Champlain, are no longer laughed at and scorned. On land, medieval tales of "wodwoses" (wild men of the woods) and modern

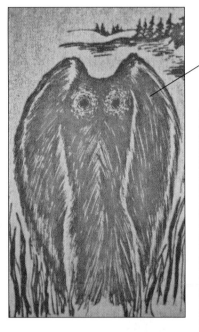

Mothman: artist's impression of a winged, headless being, with glowing red eyes in its shoulders, sighted in West Virginia in 1966-67.

Nessie, perhaps the world's best loved modern monster, posed for this photograph taken at Loch Ness, Scotland, in 1977.

Armored knights charge against monsters: the 14th century illustrator has rendered his scaly winged, flying dragons even more threatening by making them two-headed.

reports of "ape men" – the Yeti of the Himalayas and the Russian Alma; North America's Bigfoot – acquire new credence. Some even suggest they may be survivors from prehistory: Neanderthal men, or "missing links." Some weird and wonderful monsters reported in remote places have emerged as real species, previously unknown, so many zoologists now have open minds regarding the possible reality of Australia's Bunyip or Kenya's Nandi Bear – even of the "living dinosaurs" rumored to survive in African forest and swamp and other isolated regions of the Earth.

Since Gothic horror novels became best sellers in the 19th century, writers and then movie makers have breathed new life into old legends. Werewolves stalk the moonlit night; vampires and zombies rise again from their graves. Modern moviegoers seem to have an unlimited appetite for man-made monsters: from golems to Godzilla; from Frankenstein's undying humanoid to the mighty ape King Kong.

Monsters will always be with us, with or without the blessing of scientific evidence. They may be images from our subconscious, or inherited tribal memories of beasts our ancestors knew. New Age buffs favor the idea of alternative realities inhabited by beasts unknown to zoology, which we sometimes glimpse through "windows" between the worlds.

Some 43in (109cm) from nose to tail and with savage fangs, this wild, black cat was one of several shot in Scotland in 1983-85.

Bigfoot expert René Dahinden is dwarfed by a sculpted figure based on descriptions of the American wild man. It stands 8ft (2.4m) tall.

Perhaps we just need to believe in frightening things "out there" to underline our real safety (a view called the "bugbear hypothesis"). One thousand years ago, Viking heroes who feared no man shivered indoors at night, hearing trolls tearing at their roofs; many children today demand a night light as protection against the tiger under the bed; and modern adults, in a prosaic world, like to know that somewhere, still, there "be dragons."

The secret art of alchemy

Many scientists accept the "Baghdad battery," found in 1936, as a dry cell electric battery dating from the 1st century A.D., used by Middle Eastern metalworkers to electroplate (coat thinly with gold) silver objects. That process may have been the beginning of alchemy: the art of changing lesser metals into gold. The words "alchemy" and "chemistry" probably derive from Arabic *al-kimia* (art of the land of Khem [Egypt]), and from the 2nd century A.D. Arab alchemists made great contributions to early scientific knowledge. Their lore reached Europe at a time when most people saw no difference between science and magic. Early European alchemists, such as the philosopher St. Albertus Magnus (1206-80), were called wizards: an image that persisted. Popular belief was that alchemists aimed to change lead to gold by perfecting a chemical formula called the Philosopher's Stone and that they sought immortality by distilling the Elixir of Life. But some say true alchemists sought not wealth but spiritual development; that their writings, obscured by symbolism, refer not to laboratory experiments, but to journeys of the mind in search of perfection (symbolized by gold, a "perfect metal") both in this life and the life everlasting. Some alchemists were frauds, extorting the equivalent of modern research grants with false promises and conjuring tricks; others were genuine scientists. Some were both: Bombastus von Hohenheim (Paracelsus) (1493-1541) revolutionized medicine and hugely advanced chemistry, but ranted such nonsense about his magical powers that the word "bombast" (empty boasting) was coined from his name. Today's physicists have used nuclear fission to make gold from lead – but at a cost of millions of dollars per gram, so alchemists still seek the Philosopher's Stone. Some now seek it through Kundalini yoga, said to focus the body's sexual energy and enable the adept to exert "psychic force" on the material to be transformed.

Alchemists, like others who practiced magical arts, shrouded their secrets in symbolism. In this 17th century plate, the fire-breathing beast symbolizes base metal; its crown stands for the Philosopher's Stone that changes the metal to gold.

Taurus the Bull, symbolizing the Earth, and other Zodiacal signs reflect the alchemical doctrine that the principal metals were linked with the seven planets known to the ancient world.

The words and symbols on the outer rings are drawn from the Cabala (Qabbalah; Kabbalah), a mystical Jewish doctrine much studied by alchemists.

A stuffed alligator was a common feature in the workshop of a medieval wonder worker. Some early explorers of the Americas identified these reptiles with dragons.

FACT FILE

❏ The best attested "transmutation" of lead to gold was by the physician Johann Schweitzer (Helvetius) in 1666. He claimed to have received a tiny portion of Philosopher's Stone from a mysterious stranger. The philosopher Baruch Spinoza investigated the miracle and pronounced it genuine. Isaac Newton and Robert Boyle (whose *Sceptical Chymist* of 1661 discredited Aristotelian theories of matter held by alchemists) were firm believers in transmutation.

❏ German scientist Johann Rudolph Glauber (1604-70) is credited with the discovery of hydrochloric acid, the first production of nitric acid, and other advances in chemistry. He claimed one of his discoveries, sodium sulphate (Glauber's salt), was a breakthrough in the search for the Philosopher's Stone. It failed to produce gold – but is still used to cure constipation.

❏ The Anglo-American alchemist Israel Regardie (1907-85) claimed in the 1960s that he had made (or witnessed) a successful "transmutation" at the Paracelsus Research Institute, Salt Lake City, Utah.

❏ Chefs owe a debt to the alchemists who developed a double boiler – the "Bath of the Virgin Mary" – in which materials could be very gently heated. It survives in modern kitchens as the *bain marie*.

Paracelsus ("greater than Celsus," a famous doctor of ancient Rome), physician and alchemist, is shown with his magic sword and a volume of Cabalistic lore.

This reconstruction of the laboratory of an apothecary (a pharmacist) of the later Middle Ages gives us a good impression of how an alchemist's workshop of the time would have looked.

The immortal St. Germain

In January 1972, on a camp stove in front of French TV cameras, Richard Chanfray of Paris appeared to change lead to gold. Asked how he knew the art of alchemy, Chanfray claimed: "I am Count St. Germain." The supposedly immortal Count may have been born in 1710 (although the composer Jean Philippe Rameau claimed to have met him as a grown man in that year), son of a tax official. By the 1740s, "Count St. Germain" was charming the French court, displaying fine jewels – "from my friend the Shah of Persia" – and gifting ladies with magical anti-wrinkle cream.

Handsome, dressed always in black, he cleverly provoked gossip that marked him a miracle man. He neither confirmed nor denied that he was a master alchemist, that he could enlarge precious stones, and that he was many centuries old. Questioned, he said only: "Nothing is impossible." He had real talent as an industrial chemist – workshops set up to dye silk and cure leather by his patents made large profits – but preferred a riskier life. He was expelled from both England and France on suspicion of spying. As "Count Surmount" he prospered in business in Holland, but decamped with investors' funds to Russia, where he is said to have fought against the Turks as "General Welldone." In the 1770s he toured the courts of Germany as "Prince Rákóczy." His death was recorded at Hesse in 1784, but Franz Mesmer, the "magnetic man," claimed to have met him (then apparently aged about 40) in 1785 – and Queen Marie Antoinette recorded in her diaries that he warned her in 1788 of the coming French Revolution. Chanfray's claim to be St. Germain was the most recent: in the 1860s there were so many that Emperor Napoleon III ordered an inquiry.

A painting of the durable St. Germain thought to date from 1783 (when he may have been about 73 years old) shows him as a handsome man in the prime of life.

Artist Jacques Louis David made this sketch of Queen Marie Antoinette, her hair shorn, on the way to the guillotine in 1793. She wrote that St. Germain had warned her of her fate in 1788.

Occult symbols abound in the "Magic Mirror," an illustration in an 18th century alchemical book said to be the work of St. Germain.

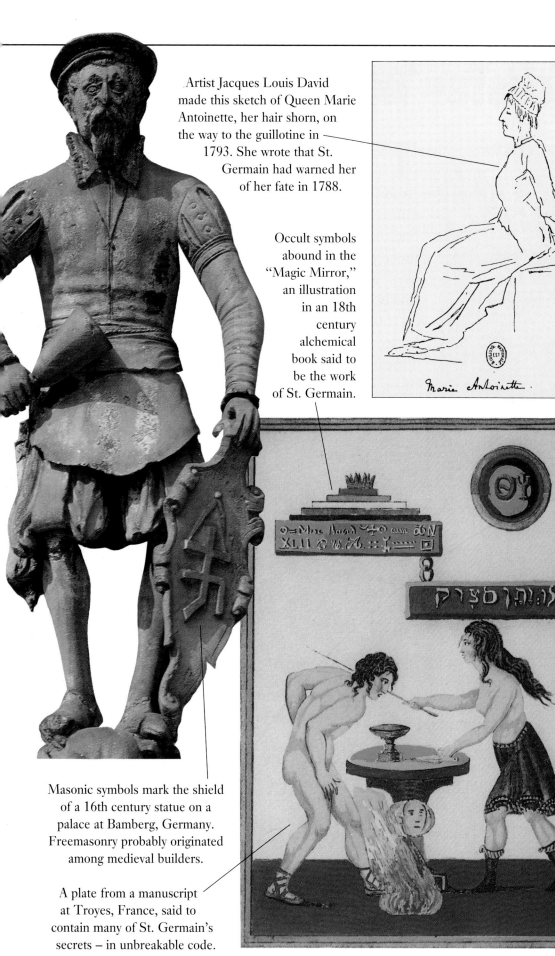

Masonic symbols mark the shield of a 16th century statue on a palace at Bamberg, Germany. Freemasonry probably originated among medieval builders.

A plate from a manuscript at Troyes, France, said to contain many of St. Germain's secrets – in unbreakable code.

❏ St. Germain fostered rumors that he possessed the Elixir of Life by never eating in public, talking non-stop through magnificent banquets (the great lover Casanova said he was "the best talker I ever met"). Some New Age thinkers today claim he was a vegan (strict vegetarian) and was disgusted by the gluttony and heavy drinking of his age.

❏ At the court of Prince Frederick Augustus of Brunswick in 1776, St. Germain claimed to be a Master Mason – a leader of the secret society (above) (today a social and charitable organization, although it still preserves an element of secrecy) that claimed to stem from the builders of Egypt's pyramids. The Prince then revealed that he himself was Grand Master of Prussia's Freemasons and gave a password St. Germain could not answer. The Count bluffed it out, implying that in the many centuries since he had helped found Freemasonry, he had forgotten its secret signs.

Houdini: trickster against trickery

As this flier from fairly early in his career shows, Houdini's magic act included card tricks. The sleight of hand they called for was invaluable also in his feats of escapology.

The best known illusionist of modern times was born Erich Weiss, son of a Hungarian-American rabbi, in Appleton, Wisc., in 1874. He entered show business as a trapeze artist, but decided his superb fitness and agility could be more profitably exploited in death-defying escapes. With a stage name taken from the French illusionist Robert Houdin, "Harry Houdini" was an international star by 1900. A master publicist, he would challenge police forces wherever he appeared to lock him, chained and naked, in their most secure cell. "The man who walks through walls" always escaped. He broke out of locked iron chests dropped into icy water, wriggled free of straitjackets suspended from cranes. He may have concealed picklocks in his bushy hair and beneath calluses on his feet, but he was also a master of advanced yoga. He showed near supernatural control of his metabolism in his greatest feat: remaining submerged for 91 minutes in an airtight tank, where a normal man might survive 5-6 minutes. The enormous strain of performing this trick at the age of 52 was mainly responsible for his death on October 31, 1926 (although it is also said he died from a stomach punch he had invited to show off his muscular control). Houdini's death on Halloween was seen as a judgment by some mystics, for he had savagely exposed mediums who purported to contact his beloved mother after her death in 1913, duplicating their "miracles" and revealing them as conjuring tricks. Spiritualists claim that Houdini used sleight of hand to frame the mediums he investigated, notably the respected Mina (Margery) Crandon. Houdini's superb collection of books on magic is now in the Library of Congress, Washington, D.C.

Houdini chats with Abraham Lincoln! One of the many photographs he released in his campaign to show how "spirit materializations" might easily be faked.

The master escaper jokes with helpers as they strap him into a straitjacket in 1915.

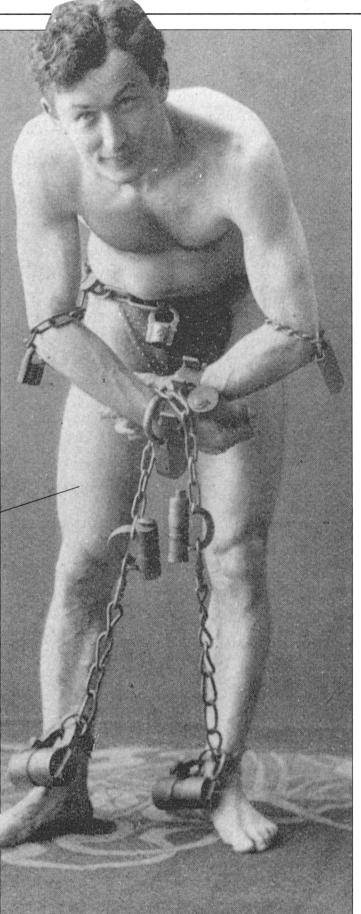

Photographed during a stage performance in 1905, Houdini obviously has nothing up his sleeve – but will soon be free.

FACT FILE

❏ Robert Houdin (1805-71), Houdini's inspiration, served his country by magic. In 1856 he was sent by the French government to Algiers, where *marabouts* (Muslim holy men) were using "miracles" to turn people against colonial rule. Houdin discredited the *marabouts* by showing how their tricks were done.

❏ Many people believed Houdini had supernatural powers, among them Sir Arthur Conan Doyle, creator of Sherlock Holmes and a dedicated Spiritualist. The two were close friends (above), but split when Doyle's favorite medium "received" a letter supposedly written by Houdini's late mother. Houdini objected that it was in English, a language his mother had never learned to write, and was infuriated by Doyle's insistence that she had "learned English in the spirit world."

❏ The most famous U.S. stage magician before Houdini was probably Alexander Herrmann, who once produced lighted cigars from the beard of President Ulysses S. Grant.

The holy terror

A monster appetite for drink and women won Grigori Yefimovich (b.1871), son of a Siberian peasant farmer, the nickname "Rasputin" (literally, "lowlife"). Around 1893 he joined a religious cult, the *Khlysty* (Whippers: their rites included ritual flogging), which preached "the greater the sin, the greater God's forgiveness." He may have learned from Siberian shamans (witch doctors) to develop occult powers, using herbal drugs and undergoing physical ordeals that included prolonged dancing. About 1903 he came to St. Petersburg, claiming to be a clairvoyant, prophet, and healer – but some said it was only sexual magnetism (and perhaps hypnotism) that lured many society ladies into his bed. He was often drunk and rarely washed, but the reputation of the *staretz* (holy man) in a greasy robe and peasant's high boots grew so great that in 1907 he was presented at the Russian court. Empress Alexandra became his disciple when his prayers proved able to stop the bleeding of the hemophiliac Crown Prince Alexis. Rasputin may have been a psychic healer, or he may have bribed servants to administer drugs to the young prince: either way, his power became immense. With Emperor Nicholas at the front in World War I, Rasputin governed at home through the German-born Empress: the pair were rumored to be both lovers and German agents. Late in 1916 aristocrats led by Prince Felix Yusupov invited Rasputin to an orgy. They fed him cakes and wine laced with cyanide: Rasputin simply demanded louder music on the phonograph, and girls. He was shot several times, castrated, beaten with iron bars, and at last tied up and shoved beneath the ice of the frozen Neva River – where, examination of his body later showed, he made a determined effort to escape.

Seen at the height of his fame, Grigori Yefimovich Rasputin narrows his notoriously hypnotic eyes and gives a sly smile. He seems to have washed, as he rarely did, before facing the camera.

The "holy man" in a simple peasant's smock is surrounded by well dressed "disciples." Many of St. Petersburg's finest ladies, it was rumored, shared Rasputin's bed as well as his discourses.

The hemophiliac Crown Prince Alexis (b.1904) is seen here before World War I. In 1918 Alexis died with his parents and sisters, murdered by the Bolsheviks.

❏ Rasputin's sexual career is said to have begun in his early teens, when he was "raped" by a local noblewoman and her maidservants. His wife (he married young and had several children) reportedly condoned his unfaithfulness, saying "He has enough for all." As late as 1968 an elderly woman in Paris (claiming to have been a maid in the Yusupov palace) gained publicity with tales of Rasputin's sexual prowess.

❏ Rasputin predicted that if he was killed by Russian aristocrats the Imperial family would die within two years (they did, murdered by the Bolsheviks); that the aristocrats would be swept away (they were, by the 1917 Revolution); and that Russia would face deadly peril in 25 years' time (1941, when a German invasion almost succeeded).

❏ In 1932, Metro-Goldwyn-Mayer released the movie *Rasputin and the Empress.* Prince Yusupov brought a successful law suit against M.G.M.: not because the movie showed him as Rasputin's assassin (he took pride in that), but because it implied that his wife (Emperor Nicholas's niece) had been seduced by the mad monk. One of Rasputin's daughters claimed that Yusupov hated her father for repulsing his homosexual advances.

The future Emperor Nicholas II and his wife-to-be, Alexandra, are seen in 1894, the year in which they married and Nicholas succeeded to the throne – long before both fell under Rasputin's evil spell.

Wickedest man in the world?

Contesting a libel case in 1934, Crowley adopts a "magical" stance that he claims may silence a lawyer for the opposition.

As a youth, Aleister Crowley (1875-1947), son of a British brewer and raised as a fundamentalist Christian, was denounced by his mother as "the Beast, 666" (the Biblical Antichrist). At 20, he was a student of magic, a drug addict, and, oddly, a respected mountaineer, leading Himalayan expeditions. His membership in a "white" magic sect, the Hermetic Order of the Golden Dawn, ended when his "black" practices alienated its leader, S.L. McGregor Mathers (1854-1918); the two men fought a magical duel, sending "elemental spirits" against each other. In 1903 he married Rose Kelly (like some others of his many women, she later went mad) who in drug induced trances put him in touch with Aiwaz, his devil god and the true author, according to Crowley, of his *Book of the Law* (1904). As "Frater Perdurabo" or "Baphomet" he traveled the world with a series of Scarlet Women on whom he tried in vain to beget "moon children" (with unearthly powers) by combining the sex act with magical rituals. He became a leader of the *Ordo Templi Orientis* (Order of the Temple of the East; O.T.O.): a Crowleyan O.T.O. sect, Children of Baphomet, now thrives in California. His peak came in 1920-23 as master of a "magical colony," the Abbey of Thelema in Cefalù, Sicily. Tales of bisexual, sadistic orgies (true) and child-abuse and murder (untrue, although Crowley sometimes pretended otherwise) in the world's tabloids, which named Crowley the "wickedest man in the world," brought down the Abbey. Having spent his inherited fortune and failing to restore it by exhibiting magic rituals in a London theater, Crowley spent his later years in an English seashore boarding house. Although possibly more of a sick jokester than the Great Beast he proclaimed himself, he became a cult figure to hippies of the 1960s-70s and is still of interest to many New Agers.

Grotesque faces ornament a sword and wand consecrated for use in witchcraft rituals. Both these objects are said to have once belonged to Crowley.

The Irish poet W.B. Yeats (1865-1939) was, like Crowley, a member of the Order of the Golden Dawn in c.1898. Yeats later denounced Crowley as "an unspeakable mad person."

A decoration for a temple of the *Argentium Astrum* (Silver Star) cult, founded by Crowley in c.1908, symbolizes the "male" physical world thrusting up towards the "female" circle of the Zodiac.

"I am a hell of a holy *guru*," boasted Crowley, who often posed in weird and wonderful magical regalia of his own design.

The book bears a pentagram, a powerful magic symbol; on its spine is one of Crowley's aliases: "Perdurabo Magister."

❑ Crowley defined magic as: "the science and art of causing change to occur in conformity with the will." He always spelled "magic" as "magick," a practice followed by many modern occultists. He claimed that "magick" signified "science of the Magi" (the three wise men of the *New Testament*), but also said that the "k" stood for the Greek word *kteis* (the female sex organs: vital to his rituals).

❑ Some of Crowley's admirers today claim he was a "white" (benevolent) rather than a "black" (malevolent) magician – and some even say that he was a "Hidden Chief" of the Great White Brotherhood, a powerful secret society that uses magic to guard humanity.

❑ Among those who do not admire Crowley are Scientologists, whose movement was founded in the 1950s by L. Ron Hubbard (1911-86; some say the announcement of his death was a ruse to mislead his enemies). When Hubbard tried to copy Crowley's "moon child" experiments in the 1940s, the Great Beast denounced him.

❑ A lifelong drug addict, Crowley daily took huge amounts of heroin and cocaine, seemingly without ill effect. His novels *The Diary of a Drug Fiend* (1923) and *Moonchild* (1929) and his pornographic poems are now prized collectors' items.

Jack the Ripper: black magician?

In England in September 1888, London newspapers received a macabre letter. "I am down on whores," said the writer, "and I shan't stop ripping them . . . ." He signed off with a name now immortal in infamy: "Jack the Ripper." In August-November 1888, in London's Whitechapel slums, six prostitutes were murdered, all apparently by the same "Ripper," who was never caught. Parts of their bodies were removed with, it was said, surgical skill, so many doctors were among the suspects at the time or suggested later. Even Sir William Gull (1816-90), Queen Victoria's physician, has been named. The most sensational theory came from Aleister Crowley, who boasted that he had befriended the Ripper

in later life. He named "a surgeon, Dr. Roslyn D'Onston," known as "Tautriadelta," a black magician so powerful he could make himself invisible, and said he killed to obtain various organs that, when buried at sites forming a mystic pattern, increased his magical powers. In fact, "Roslyn D'Onston" was Robert Donston Stephenson (1841-?1925) an alcoholic, ex-medical student, occultist, and hack journalist who "investigated" the murders. In December 1888, Stephenson accused Dr. Morgan Davies (1854-1920), a surgeon, of being the Ripper. The police did not even question Davies, but investigated Stephenson, who had recently been convicted of assaulting a woman. Stephenson had some surgical knowledge, was in Whitechapel at the time of the murders, and was, although shabby, a "gentleman" likely to attract slumland prostitutes. It is said he ceased to kill on becoming a "born again" Christian. Later he lived in the United States: in the late 1920s a former New York policeman, George Dougherty, claimed that Stephenson had confessed to the Ripper murders on his deathbed in a New York hospital.

The setting of the Ripper murders is recreated for *Hands of the Ripper*, one of the many movies inspired by the case: a "toff" encounters a woman of the streets in a sleazy alley in Victorian London.

Some connect Sir William Gull, physician to Queen Victoria, with the "eminent doctor" supposedly identified as the Ripper by a Spiritualist medium.

Newspaper illustrators all over Europe worked overtime to record and sensationalize the Ripper's killings. This is a French newspaper's version of the discovery of a victim.

Between five and ten murders are attributed to the Ripper: most Ripperologists now agree on six by the same hand. All of the victims were prostitutes.

PUBLIC HOUSE

❑ "Roslyn D'Onston" was not the only suspect fingered by Crowley. He once suggested, probably as one of his sick jokes, that Helen Petrovna Blavatsky (1831-91) (below), the Russian-American co-founder of the Theosophical Society, teaching Eastern mysticism and the doctrine of reincarnation, was involved with the murders.

❑ Experts doubt the authenticity of all of the supposed letters from the Ripper. They include one addressed "From Hell" and containing a piece of a human kidney ("the other I fried and ate"), and some in red ink ("I wanted to use blood").

❑ Strong cases have been made for the guilt of various suspects, ranging from Queen Victoria's supposedly degenerate grandson Albert Victor, Duke of Clarence (1864-92), to a mad midwife (Jill the Ripper), a Jewish ritual slaughterman, and Russian anarchists. The most favored candidate is Montague John Druitt (1857-88), a schoolteacher described in police records as "sexually insane." Druitt drowned himself in November 1888, just after the last Ripper killing.

Mind over matter

In 1854, Count Agenor de Gasparin concluded that "table turning" at séances (Spiritualist meetings) was achieved not by disembodied spirits but by the human will. Soon scientists began to investigate psychic force, and initial findings seemed to support the idea that the human mind can directly affect physical objects, without bodily contact. Research into what is now termed "psychokinesis" or "telekinesis" continues. Mediums have been studied while moving or bending objects by mind power alone under laboratory conditions; in other studies, scientists have devised minilabs in which objects are securely sealed – yet are found to move by some unknown power. But despite some intriguing findings, psychokinesis remained a fringe interest until, in the 1970s, Israeli "wonder worker" Uri Geller (b.1946) hit headlines worldwide by demonstrating a remarkable ability to affect metal objects by mind power alone. He was seen to bend or twist metal silverware or keys by gently stroking them, or even simply by looking at them; he made clocks and wristwatches stop or go by raising his hands over them. When he appeared on television, hundreds of viewers reported that metal objects in their own homes were affected during the broadcast – and some claimed that their children had taken to apparently paranormal spoonbending. Laboratory investigations of Geller's powers produced startling results. A Geiger counter held by him reacted as if to dangerously radioactive material; a gaussmeter (gauge to measure magnetic fields) over which he passed his hands indicated that his magnetic field was nearly half as strong as that of the Earth! Skeptics insist Geller is only a brilliant conjurer: others are convinced of his supernormal powers.

Researchers could detect no fraud when they studied Uri Geller bending metal apparently by mindpower alone, under controlled laboratory conditions.

Any movement of the objects in this 1979 sealed minilab activates lights and cameras and provides the S.O.R.R.A.T. team with film of psychokinesis in action.

Paperclips scrunched together, untouched by human hand, in an experiment at Professor John Hasted's University of London laboratory.

In the 1970s the image of a bent fork became familiar across Europe and the United States, as psychic metalbending became a craze.

❏ Hundreds of children in England, Japan, and elsewhere took to home spoonbending after seeing Geller on T.V. Under test conditions, some proved to be bending metal "by palpably normal means" (i.e. cheating). But some children, such as 15-year-old Monica Nieto Tejada (below), are reported to have performed feats beyond normal powers.

❏ Some experiments suggest that successful gamblers may rely less on luck than on psychokinetic ability to influence the fall of playing cards or dice.

❏ For 10 years Russian scientists studied Soviet psychic Madam Kulagina under laboratory conditions as she moved objects ranging from compasses to eggs by psychokinesis. They failed to establish how this "new and unknown form of energy" works, but noted that her feats put her under tremendous strain. During psychokinetic activity her pulse rate rose to 240 per minute, and she lost up to 4lb (1.8kg) of body weight within 30 minutes.

Mesmer the magnetic man

Ancient Greek physicians sometimes achieved cures through *mekhenesis* (removal of responsibility). An "entranced" patient was made to subject his will to that of the doctor and told that on waking he would be better. We do not know how ancient doctors induced a trance state, but some 2,000 years later their supposed technique was sensationally revived by Austrian physician Franz Anton Mesmer (1734-1815). He said magnetic force was an invisible fluid bathing the entire universe and that the astrological influence of the planets was caused by the interaction of their magnetic fields with that of Earth – and with the animal magnetism of each individual. Illnesses were caused by an "improper balance" of magnetic fluid and could be cured by putting patients into a trance by stroking them with magnets. Aided by showmanship – supervised by Mesmer in magician's robes – handsome young magnetizers gave stroking treatment to neurotic aristocrats (especially aging women).

He made a fortune in Paris before a royal commission declared Mesmerism a fraud. But some doctors were impressed by Mesmer's suggestive cures. Scottish surgeon James Braid (c.1795-1860) cut through Mesmer's gobbledegook and established that the voice alone could put patients into a hypnotic trance (Greek *hypnos*: sleep) in which they could withstand the pain of surgical operations. The development of chemical anesthetics set back medical use of hypnotism, as did its popularity as a vaudeville entertainment, but psychoanalysts and psychologists found it a valuable tool, giving access to buried memories of early life (and even, some say, releasing knowledge of former lives). Hypnotherapy is now a recognized treatment for addictions, allergies, and insomnia.

Franz Anton Mesmer made a fortune from cures by animal magnetism, but was denounced as a fraud. Now he is sometimes seen as a pioneer of modern methods of healing through hypnosis.

In the 1780s members of Parisian high society flocked to Mesmer's studio to absorb health-giving "magnetic fluid" through iron bars or cords fixed to a "magic tub."

A modern hypnotherapist has no need of Mesmer's showmanship. The technique is now an established treatment for a number of physical and psychosomatic ailments.

A contemporary caricature satirizes animal magnetism by showing Mesmer as a donkey and suggesting that his entranced patient also has no more sense than an animal.

❏ The composer Mozart satirized Mesmer, his contemporary, in his opera *Così fan tutte* (1790). Two lovers feign suicide, and are revived with magnetic treatment by a girl disguised as a quack doctor.

❏ Mary Baker Eddy (1821-1910), founder of the Christian Science church, was a firm believer in animal magnetism. Becoming eccentric in her old age, she maintained that her first husband had been poisoned by "evil magneticists," and always refused to travel by train unless another locomotive was hired to run ahead to dispel "adverse magnetism" that might be in the tracks.

❏ French pathologist Jean Martin Charcot (1825-93) helped pioneer medical hypnosis. He theorized that persons in a hypnotic trance could not be made to perform actions they would normally regard as morally wrong. He cited the case of an assistant who confessed that having hypnotized an attractive girl, he had made "improper suggestions" – whereupon she immediately awoke and slapped his face. A German contemporary, surgeon Rudolf Heidenhaim, disagreed. He hypnotized a man who took great pride in his huge mustache and ordered him to shave it off. He did – but his shock on waking is said to have caused him to become a lifelong drunkard.

Psychic detectives: hit and miss?

Police forces know that when a crime gets big news coverage they are likely to be deluged with offers of help from psychics. But serious students of the paranormal (and some seers themselves) agree that the success rate of the psychic detectives is low and that their work is hyped out of all proportion by popular media. The best-known psychic detectives are Gerard Croiset (1909-80) and Peter Hurkos (b.1911), both Dutch. They were clairvoyants, using psychometry (deducing facts from handling an object; typically something belonging to a missing person). In 1961, Croiset, in Holland, pinpointed the location of a child missing in New York and described her killer, after handling her clothing. He is said to have demonstrated knowledge of future events in the "chair test." In a hall where there was to be a large public gathering, he would be asked about one week before to take a chair at random and write down information about the person who would later sit on it. Many times he proved right. Peter Hurkos, a house painter, came out of a coma after fracturing his skull in 1943 to find he had become clairvoyant. After moving to the United States in the 1950s he won fame as a psychic consultant to movie stars and police departments. He worked on the "Boston Strangler" case in 1964 (he always maintained that Albert DeSalvo was not the killer) and claimed to have directed police investigating the killing of movie star Sharon Tate to "a bearded guy named Charlie" (Charles Manson's hippie "family" committed the crime). The contributions of Croiset and Hurkos to law enforcement may have been exaggerated, but both are said to have triumphed in less-publicized work, such as locating the bodies of people who drowned in Dutch and Belgian canals.

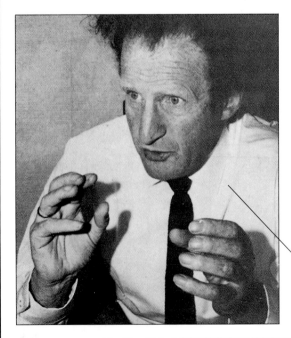

Gerard Croiset was credited with amazing telepathic powers, but some say his feats were exaggerated by his patron, parapsychologist Wilhelm Tenhaeff of Utrecht University.

Croiset and Hurkos are best
known for criminal cases.
They were more consistently
successful in locating
bodies in canals in Amsterdam
(above) and elsewhere.

Albert DeSalvo (left) admitted to
to the Boston Strangler
murders. Because of his
mental state he was not tried
for them. Hurkos believed
DeSalvo was not the killer.

Charles Manson (b.1934) led
a gang of killer hippies
in California in 1969. Peter
Hurkos claimed that he had
told police to look for "a
bearded guy named Charlie."

❏ The word "psychometry"
was coined by 19th century
American physician Joseph
Rhodes Buchanan. He was
inspired to investigate the
phenomenon after witnessing
the ability to detect various
metals, unseen, demonstrated
to him by Leonidas L. Polk
(1806-64), an Episcopal
Church bishop and a general in
the Confederate Army.

❏ Peter Hurkos claimed that
his first mental feat almost cost
him his life. While still in a
hospital in 1943 (when Holland
was occupied by German
forces) he "sensed" that
another patient was a British
secret agent and warned him
that he would soon be killed by
the *Gestapo* (German secret
police). When the prophecy
came true, the Dutch
Resistance briefly suspected
that Hurkos himself had
betrayed the agent and put
him on a hit list.

❏ A noted American psychic
detective is Dorothy Allison of
New Jersey. In 1967 she
correctly predicted that a
missing child would be found
dead in a storm drain (she
accurately described the
location), wearing a green
snowsuit, with sneakers on the
wrong feet. But she had less
success in the Patty Hearst
kidnaping case in 1975 and
herself estimates that of some
4,000 cases on which she has
worked, either by police
invitation or independently, she
has had a decisive effect on
fewer than 100.

131

Mental radio: extrasensory perception

Under controlled conditions, a psychic concentrates on the images on the E.S.P. cards and attempts to transmit them telepathically to a partner.

Until as late as the 18th century, people who seemed able to read others' minds or see into the future risked persecution as witches. Today, a growing number of scientists accept the existence of senses beyond the familiar five and of extra-sensory perception (E.S.P.). Convincing evidence of telepathy (direct transmission of thoughts from mind to mind), clairvoyance (awareness of events taking place far away), and precognition ("seeing" events in the future), has stimulated serious research. This was pioneered from 1927 at Duke University, N.C., where Dr. Joseph Banks Rhine (1895-1980) used "Zener cards" bearing simple symbols to test for telepathy. An agent in one laboratory tried to send the image of a random card to a receiver in another. By the law of probability, receivers should guess 5 out of 25 cards correctly. Some subjects got far better results (by telepathy) – some even predicted the order of cards before the agent shuffled them (precognition). Rhine's results are not accepted by all. But more recent, more sophisticated experiments seem to prove the existence of telepathy – though they cannot show how it works. Scientists can now detect physical effects in telepaths (persons transmitting and receiving thoughts), and are investigating methods of controlled telepathic communication. Russia leads the field. When a telepath in Siberia "sent" intermittent signals of set lengths to a contact, Moscow scientists read dots (15-second transmissions) and dashes (45 seconds) via the contact's brain waves – receiving the word *mig* (instant) in Morse code from a distance of 2,000mi (3,200km). An Anglo-U.S. study using measurements of blood volume (intense concentration on a particular subject has been found significantly to increase this) has also succeeded in transmitting Morse code. Telepathy has progressed from witchcraft to mental radio.

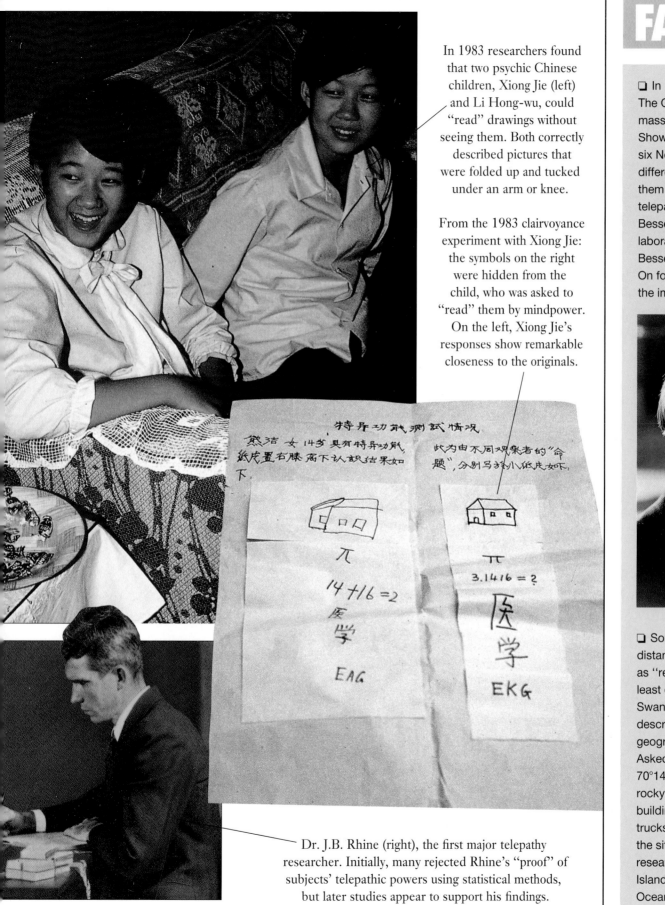

In 1983 researchers found that two psychic Chinese children, Xiong Jie (left) and Li Hong-wu, could "read" drawings without seeing them. Both correctly described pictures that were folded up and tucked under an arm or knee.

From the 1983 clairvoyance experiment with Xiong Jie: the symbols on the right were hidden from the child, who was asked to "read" them by mindpower. On the left, Xiong Jie's responses show remarkable closeness to the originals.

Dr. J.B. Rhine (right), the first major telepathy researcher. Initially, many rejected Rhine's "proof" of subjects' telepathic powers using statistical methods, but later studies appear to support his findings.

❑ In 1971, the cult rock group The Grateful Dead headed a mass E.S.P. experiment. Showing audiences at each of six New York concerts a different picture, they asked them to try to transmit it by telepathy to psychic Malcolm Bessent. Meanwhile, in a laboratory 50mi (80km) away, Bessent recorded his visions. On four nights, these related to the image being "sent."

❑ Some psychics can "see" distant places — a skill known as "remote viewing" — and at least one, Californian Ingo Swann (above), can apparently describe what lies at any geographical coordinates. Asked what lay at 49°20'S, 70°14'E, he said it was a cold, rocky island, with a few buildings (one orange) and trucks — a fair description of the site, a French-Soviet research base on Kerguelen Island in the southern Indian Ocean.

Kirlian photography: pictures of the unseen

Mystics have long believed that every living thing has an astral body, a spiritual twin of its earthly form. Now, some say "Kirlian photography" has proved the astral body's existence. In 1939 the Soviet engineer Semyon Kirlian watched a hospital patient undergoing electrotherapy and saw that as the electrodes touched the skin there was a flash of bright light. This inspired Kirlian and his wife Valentina to begin some 20 years' experimentation in "electrography." A Kirlian photograph is obtained by placing an object – such as a human finger – between two electrodes (metal plates), on one of which is light-sensitive film, and pulsing high frequency electric current between them. The image obtained reveals that all objects are surrounded by radiant patterns of colors, invisible to the normal eye, popularly called auras. The colors and forms of inanimate objects' auras do not vary – but the auras of living things change according to their condition. The human aura varies according to the mental and physical state of the subject; the aura of a fresh vegetable is much brighter than that of the same vegetable after cooking. Further, a Kirlian image of, say, a leaf from which a piece has been cut will show the missing piece still in place. This, some say, proves the existence of the astral body (and, incidentally, accounts for the well-known phenomenon of an amputee feeling pain in a missing limb). It is suggested that changes in the aura may be used to predict health problems well before they could be found by conventional diagnosis. Although some scientists reject Kirlian theory, serious research at Kirov State University, Kazakhstan, and at The University of California, Los Angeles (U.C.L.A.) is believed to have at least partly proved its validity.

This Kirlian photograph of human hands has been subjected to color translation by computer, thus bringing the radiant auras into sharper contrast.

Kirlian photographs of a patient's fingertips are taken for diagnostic purposes in the laboratory of a German naturopath (holistic, or natural healer).

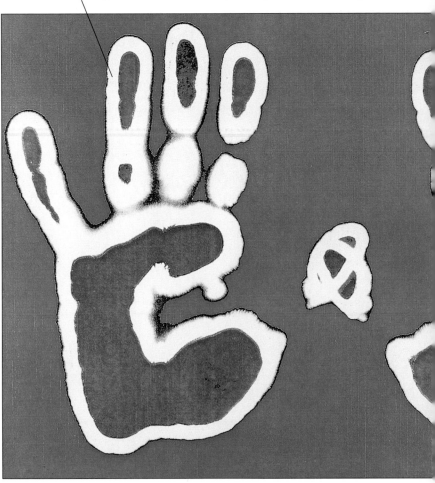

Auras around the fingertips record electrobiological energy, common to all living things. Some seek to identify it with the astral body.

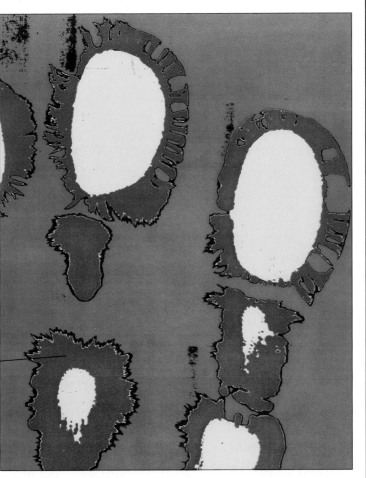

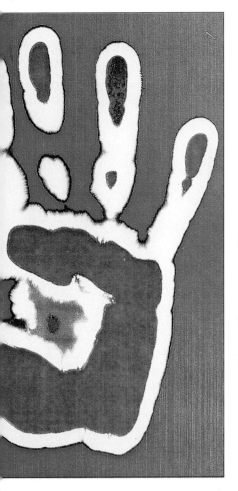

As with the fingertip auras, Kirlian enthusiasts claim that from the aura around a leaf a healer may deduce the state of health, even the mood, of the plant.

❏ Kirlian photography may prove invaluable in the investigation of such mind over matter phenomena as psychokinesis – energy discharges from the fingers of Uri Geller as he performs his feats have been photographed – extrasensory perception, and psychic healing. It may show that healers emit a special "healing energy." Kirlian pictures of the Georgian healer Alexei Krivorotov are said to show that during his "laying on of hands," beams of light radiate from them to the subject. Experiments with U.S. healers at U.C.L.A. showed that after the healing session the healer's aura was dimmer and the patient's brighter, suggesting "energy interchange."

❏ During Kirlian experiments at U.C.L.A., where the process is called "radiation photography," it was found that the aura of a male subject dramatically increased in brightness when a male researcher was suddenly replaced by a female. If subject and researcher were friends (regardless of sex), the subject's aura was brighter than when the researcher was a stranger.

❏ Some Kirlian researchers say that "flares" of energy emitted by humans subjected to various stimuli can be shown to come from the same areas of the body as those identified as vital spots by acupuncturists.

The twitching twig

Dowsing, a technique of sensing the presence of buried objects, has been widely practiced since at least the Middle Ages. Today many major mining companies are convinced that it beats modern technology at detecting underground water or minerals. Typically, the dowser walks over the site holding out a divining rod: a traditional Y-shaped wooden stick (often of hazel or willow), or a pair of L-shaped metal rods. At the spot where the buried object lies, the rod twists in the dowser's hand. The actual detecting agent is the human body, which reacts to signals from the buried object with involuntary movements of the hand muscles: the rod simply amplifies these. Research suggests that dowsers work by sensing tiny variations in Earth's magnetic field – an ability apparently present in everyone, though some are more sensitive than others. Experienced dowsers can tell the exact position and nature of a find from the rod's reaction. While dowsing seems to have a scientific basis, nobody can explain how some dowsers achieve results by dangling a pendulum over a map of the site, without needing to go there. Such "map dowsers" have successfully located underground water and, in "psychic archeology," ancient sites such as burial chambers. Noted British dowser Tom Lethbridge (1901-71) developed a system of pendulum dowsing not only for objects but also for colors, emotions, and even dates – his pendulum dating of a stone circle gave the same result as was later achieved by carbon dating. Pendulum readings have a long folklore history, as in the method of sexing an unborn child by dangling a wedding ring as a pendulum over the mother's abdomen. Japanese agriculturists claim a 99 percent success rate in sexing day-old chicks with pendulums.

The dowser walks steadily over the ground, holding out her divining rod (a Y-shaped hazel twig) until she feels it swing sharply downward.

Dowser Hamish Miller investigates a crop circle in England in 1990. No one has yet resolved the mystery of crop circles, but many dowsers report detecting particularly strong magnetic forces within them.

Dowser Erich Schuck and psychic Umberto di Grazia went to hunt buried treasure. Here Schuck demonstrates he can locate gold coins hidden by experimental researchers.

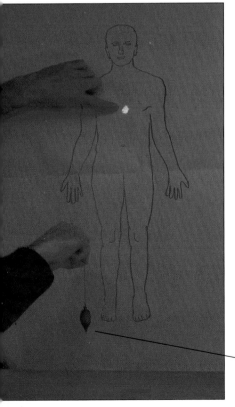

In radiesthesia, an alternative medicine technique, a pendulum is used to diagnose illness even in the patient's absence. Here we see a session of color healing, with the pendulum operator using a chart to represent the patient.

Defying the law of gravity

Scots-American psychic Daniel Dunglas Home (1833-86) scorned such trivial feats as table rapping. At séances he would levitate (rise into the air), once floating out of a window 80ft (24m) above the ground and in at another. Many reputable witnesses – among them Mark Twain and Napoleon III of France – saw him "fly," or make objects and people rise without touching them. Even those who thought him a fake (including poet Robert Browning, who satirized him as "Mr. Sludge the Medium"), failed to catch him in any fraud. People who defy the law of gravity have been found worldwide. Eastern mystics claim to become airborne by mental discipline. Some may be con men, but others seem genuine: in 1936 *The Illustrated London News* photographed Indian fakir Subbayah Pullavar as he lay prone in midair for 4 minutes before 150 witnesses. Modern *gurus* of transcendental meditation teach students to levitate in a seated, cross-legged posture. In the early medieval West, levitation was sometimes said to be a sign of God's blessing (several saints are reported to have risen into the air in holy ecstasy) – and sometimes Satan's work, his gift to witches. St. Augustine (354-430) refused to believe that witches could fly, but the Catholic Church later ruled that they did, and medieval witch trials produced many confessions (often under torture) of levitation. Some witches may have believed they flew, for their "magic potions" often included hallucinatory drugs. Perhaps some really did: it is recorded that a French witch trial in 1591 was disrupted when the accused woman rose aloft. So perhaps the human mind, as well as human science (in the space program), may be able to defy the law of gravity.

In the Indian rope trick, perhaps the most famous feat of Eastern wonder workers, a boy climbs an unsupported rope and disappears on reaching its top.

Few people have seen the rope trick performed, and this photograph of Indian magician Karachi and his son Kyder, taken in 1935, is perhaps somewhat suspect.

Anthony "Doc" Shiels, well known in Britain as an explorer of paranormal phenomena, performs a tongue-in-cheek levitation act with his daughter.

Medium Colin Evans rises aloft at a London Spiritualist gathering in 1938. Several photographs taken then convincingly show Evans levitating.

❏ Levitating saints include Francis of Assisi (c.1182-1226), Dominic (c.1170-1221), Catherine of Siena (1347-80), Edmund of Canterbury (c.1170-1240), Teresa of Ávila (1515-82), and Joseph of Copertino (1603-63) (below). St. Teresa described levitation as a feeling of great sweetness, or, if she resisted, of "a great force under my feet." Returned to earth, her body seemed to her "as if all weight had departed from it, so much that now and then I scarcely knew that my feet touched the ground."

This levitation of scissors was faked, using a wire support. It duplicates a c.1910 photograph showing the supposedly genuine feat.

❏ Levitation is popular with stage magicians. A girl lies on a board balanced on two pedestals, which the magician removes to leave her apparently floating in midair (actually supported by a hidden bar). The magician passes a hoop around the girl to "prove" the absence of support. It is another illusion: the hoop passes halfway down the girl's body, then enters a hidden gooseneck metal bar from which it can be rotated around her feet.

Talking with the dead

Spiritualism is based on belief in the survival of the individual human spirit after death. This, Spiritualists say, is proved by communication with the dead through a medium, a person who can contact "the other side," usually when in a self-induced trance state. Spiritualists may be devout Christians, and many Christians (but not Roman Catholics) believe that there is nothing contrary to Biblical teaching in Spiritualism. Modern Spiritualism had its origin in Hydesville, N.Y., where for months the home of the Fox family was troubled by strange "rappings." On March 31, 1848, using a tapping code, the Fox sisters Margaret (15) and Kate (12) began to "talk" with Mr. Splitfoot, said to be the spirit of a man murdered in the house (a skeleton was found in the foundations about 1900). News of the wonder spread and, managed by their sister Leah (34), the girls demonstrated their powers widely – and profitably. "Table rapping" and "turning" – when a table levitates under spirit influence – became first a craze, then a new religious manifestation, and soon spread to Europe.

Catherine (Kate) Fox: the modern Spiritualist movement had its origins in strange noises 12-year-old Kate and her sister heard in 1848.

Sitters at a séance hold hands to concentrate their power and call spirits to the medium. Flowers are believed to attract well intentioned spirits.

Although orthodox churchmen and militant unbelievers alike opposed Spiritualism, many rejoiced that life after death was at last "proved." In the United States, noted journalist Horace Greeley and philosopher William James spoke in support of Spiritualism. By c.1870 some groups were calling themselves "churches," and using Christian hymns and prayers as a way to create a favorable atmosphere for spiritual communication. Physical mediums – claiming to produce materializations of spirits and objects and quite often exposed as frauds – gave way to mental mediums, who give only spoken or written messages, and Spiritualism slowly achieved the respectable religious status most accord it today.

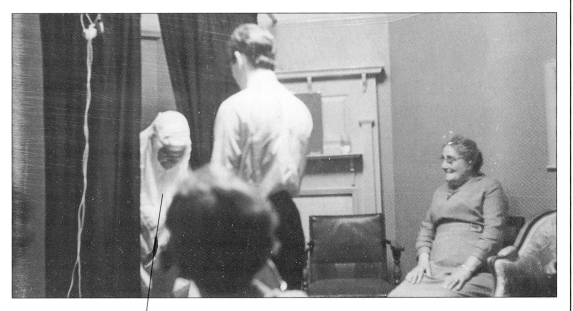

A spirit "materializes" from the medium's cabinet at a séance in 1967. It is obvious how easily such photographs might be faked.

From interpreting spirit rappings, the Fox sisters quickly progressed to other paranormal feats – such as amazing people in Rochester, N.Y., by levitating a heavy table.

R101: the medium and the messages

On the evening of October 4, 1930, the 777ft (237m) long dirigible *R101*, then the world's largest airship, left Britain on her maiden flight, non-stop to India. Aboard was British Air Minister Lord Thomson, who believed, as many then did, that the future of civil aviation lay in airships. Squalls over the English Channel buffeted the huge craft, the weather grew worse, and at 2:05 a.m. on October 5, in driving rain, *R101* crashed on a hillside near Beauvais, France. Within seconds her gasbags, with more than 5,000,000cu ft (140,000cu m) of hydrogen, ignited: of 54 passengers and crew, 48 died, including Thomson. Two days after the tragedy, in a séance at the National Laboratory of Psychical Research in London, medium Eileen Garrett (1893-1970) was trying to contact the spirit of recently-deceased Spiritualist Sir Arthur Conan Doyle. Suddenly she began to speak rapidly in an anguished, male voice: "Engines too heavy. Useful lift too small. Oil pipe plugged." With technical detail far beyond Garrett's conscious knowledge, the speaker described more than 40 design and management faults that had contributed to the loss of *R101*. He identified himself as "Irwin": Flight Lieutenant H. Carmichael Irwin, *R101*'s commander, who had died in the wreck. At later séances Irwin, speaking through Garrett, was questioned by aeronautical experts. Not all believed they were speaking to the dead aviator – but they admitted it was far more likely that Garrett had "supernatural knowledge" of the crash than that she could have studied the complex technology in so short a time. An official inquiry into the loss of *R101* in 1931 (describing records of Garrett's first séance as an "astounding document") confirmed that the bulk of Irwin's account was correct.

The success of modern blimps (nonrigid airships) such as *America*, seen here, has reawakened interest in such craft. Their development was curtailed after *R101* and other airships crashed in the 1930s.

Graceful, fragile *R101* swings at her mooring mast in 1930. Her construction was rushed, fatally as it turned out, by politicians anxious to increase the prestige of British aviation.

October 5, 1930: on a hillside near Beauvais, France, a twisted skeleton is all that remains of the flying giant: 48 men died when her huge bags of hydrogen ignited.

❏ Many connected with *R101* had premonitions of disaster. Irwin's wife, when told of his death, said "We both knew he wasn't coming back." The young son of Walter Radcliffe, a rigger who died in the crash, began to cry shortly before *R101*'s take-off: "I haven't got a daddy." Among the dead was Britain's Director of Civil Aviation, Sir Sefton Brancker. He had told friends of an occasion in 1924 when he had consulted a palmist — and had learned that only six more years could be traced in the lifeline on his hand.

❏ Although the foremost medium of her time, Eileen Garrett (above) was skeptical of supernatural powers, which she maintained must have a scientific explanation. She believed her "spirit guides" might be secondary personalities produced by her subconscious mind. In 1931 she settled in the United States, where she worked with E.S.P. researcher J.B. Rhine and, in 1951, founded the Parapsychology Foundation in New York.

Voices from beyond the grave

The dead have no voices; but Spiritualists believe that they desire to speak with the living. Some mediums "hear" the dead in trance; others invite communication by physical means. Table rapping evolved into the Ouija board (French *oui* and German *ja*, both meaning "Yes"), printed with Yes, No, and the alphabet. The inquirer rests a hand on a pointer or an upturned glass, which moves to the letters of the answer, apparently of its own accord. Believers say the spirits of the dead – and sometimes darker forces – communicate thus; others say the pointer is controlled by the inquirer's subconscious mind, or by a telepathic group consciousness formed by séance members. Some striking results have been gained, along with the merely silly – and the sinister. Another technique is automatic writing, holding a pen loosely and inviting spirits to steer it. Some prefer to use a *planchette* (French: little board), a wooden, wheeled, pencil carriage. Results range from meaningless squiggles to coherent messages, sometimes in handwriting not the medium's own. They range from simple, sometimes obscure, statements to long descriptions of the afterlife – or even "new" works dictated by dead authors and apparently beyond the medium's own capacity. Brazilian medium Chico Xavier spent 50 years transcribing more than 100 books "dictated" by dead masters. With limited schooling, Xavier says he cannot understand all he writes. Automatic writers often work not only above their own literary level but at amazing speed. Some set down more than one work at a time: the Rev. Stainton Moses (1839-92) used both hands at once for two pieces on different topics – in different languages.

Oh! is that his own writing?
It is, with our help.
He is with you now:
and also another

L. v Beethoven

Beethoven! And were they there?
Yes: they were present,
and are with you now.
They both aid in the
education of the boy,
and feel pleasure
and delight in their
work.

The Reverend Stainton Moses filled 24 notebooks with automatic writing. This extract features the "spirit autograph" of the composer Ludwig van Beethoven.

The *planchette*, a small board holding a pencil and mounted on wheels or castors, was invented in 19th century France as an aid to would-be psychics dabbling in the field of automatic writing.

This medium, Anita (from Italy) is normally right-handed. For automatic writing she holds the pen in her open left hand. The messages she records hold information apparently unknown to the medium herself.

The message in automatic writing, written by Anita's left hand and signed by her spirit guide, is in a script unlike the medium's own.

The same message, copied out by Anita in her normal (right-handed) handwriting for comparison.

A reluctant medium, Stainton Moses experienced table rapping, levitation, and psychokinesis, as well as automatic writing, but distrusted information from such sources.

❏ In the 1960s-80s, Ouija boards were a craze, moving out of the hands of earnest spiritualists to become a party game. But many fun-seekers were disturbed by supernormal manifestations. Some makers took Ouija boards off world markets because of their "disturbing and dangerous psychological effect."

❏ The Roman Catholic Church in Brazil condemns Chico Xavier's work as the product of demonic possession. Others see him as a a saint – and even say he is the reincarnation of St. Francis of Assisi.

❏ In 1972 the Toronto Society for Psychical Research experimented by inventing a fictitious 17th century English aristocrat, "Philip," and seeking to contact his imaginary ghost. Their results – table rapping, object levitation, flickering lights – resembled those of mediums seeking to contact "real" spirits and supported the theory that supernormal phenomena owe more to telepathy than to the spirits of the dead.

❏ One of the most startling forms of automatic writing is "cross-correspondence": when two separate mediums receive different parts of the same work. When Chico Xavier wrote down *Evolution in Two Worlds*, he produced only alternate chapters. He was "told" to contact Dr. Waldo Vieira, who proved to have received the other chapters.

In touch with genius?

When London housewife Rosemary Brown says she knows the great composers, she does not only mean she is familiar with their works – she claims to communicate with their spirits. More, she believes Beethoven, Liszt, and others dictate to her music composed after their deaths – first by using her hands "like a pair of gloves" to play the piano, then through automatic writing. Normally unable to compose music, while in trances she has transcribed many pieces – all in the style of their alleged composers, though not, critics say, up to their lifetime best. Rosemary Brown is not unique. Other mediums claim to have received "new" works by dead authors and artists. Automatic art, like automatic writing, occurs when the medium (often, but not always, in a trance) allows his or her hand to act independently of the owner's will. In the 1970s, British teenager Matthew Manning (born in 1955, just after his mother received a massive electric shock) found himself producing automatic art, at great speed and with no preliminary sketches, by concentrating on a particular artist – ranging from Leonardo da Vinci to Beatrix Potter. "It's not me," he said, "I simply switch on the energy." Brazilian trance artist Luiz Antonio Gasparetto does "spirit paintings" at an even faster rate, often two at once, using both hands or even his toes. He was filmed for television painting 21 new "Renoirs," "Cézannes," and "Picassos" in 75 minutes – viewers accused the T.V. company of speeding up the film. The source of such "spirit creations" remains a mystery. The mediums sincerely believe they receive messages from the "other side," but those who refuse to believe that the dead communicate with the living suggest that mediums tap the unconscious mind or draw on ancestral memories.

In October 1980 a U.S. television company filmed Rosemary Brown "receiving" and transcribing music from dead composers. While writing, she chats with the spirits, occasionally asking them to slow down for her.

146

Does automatic art derive from spirits, or the artist's own subconscious? In this automatic drawing by mediumistic artist Narciso Bressanello, the "spines" represent the protection of prayers.

Painting in the style of Cézanne by Brazilian trance artist Luiz Gasparetto. Unable to paint at all in a normal state, by psychic means he has produced works in 30 different styles.

This is the manuscript that Rosemary Brown transcribed during her television interview, a *Mazurka in D flat* that she believes was dictated to her by the spirit of Chopin.

FACT FILE

❏ Rosemary Brown's ghostly friends include not only composers but philosopher Bertrand Russell, scientist Albert Einstein, and artist Vincent van Gogh. She has produced, by automatic art, "new" works by van Gogh – and by the composer Debussy, who, she says, has taken up painting in the afterlife.

❏ Brown reports that the composer Chopin sometimes slips into his native Polish when communicating with her. She writes down his words as best she can, and a Polish friend translates.

❏ Trance artists find Picasso's spirit troublesome. Luiz Antonio Gasparetto, who painted "new" works by many dead artists, reported: "Picasso sometimes used to be violent. If anyone whispered, he would throw the paper away."

❏ In 1905, U.S. goldsmith Frederick L. Thompson began to feel driven to paint landscapes that he saw in his head. A year later he attended an exhibition of paintings by the late Robert Swain Gifford – and recognized the style in which he had been working. Then he heard a voice in his head saying: "You see what I have done. Can you not take up and finish my work?" Later, it emerged that the scenes he painted were real places unknown to him – but known to, though never painted by, Robert Swain Gifford.

Travelers through time

Several great scientist-philosophers have suggested that time is not simply chronology, or clock time, a linear progression from one unique moment to the next, as most of us experience it. "The distinction between past, present, and future is an illusion," said Albert Einstein. J.W. Dunne (1875-1949) defined time as "one moving point on the plane of possibilities," and declared: "In real time . . . everything which has established its existence remains in existence." Support for such theories comes from many persons who have experienced "time slips," in which they have found themselves witnessing events that took place in the past – or things still to come. The best documented time slip was that experienced in 1901 by two prominent British educators, Charlotte Moberly and Eleanor Jourdain. Visiting the Petit Trianon at Versailles, France, playground of ill-fated Queen Marie Antoinette before the French Revolution of 1789, they saw and spoke to persons in 18th century dress and noticed that the site did not conform to their modern guidebook's description. Detailed questioning by historians revealed that they had seen Versailles as it had been in the 1770s-80s. Although both ladies, whose truthfulness was beyond doubt, returned several times to Versailles, they could not repeat the experience. Some parapsychologists ascribe precognition (knowledge of events before they occur) to time slips, rather than to supernatural ability on the part of the prophet. In October 1966, when an accident in a coal-mining town in Wales killed 144 persons, a British scientist asked anyone who had "seen" the disaster in advance to contact him. No fewer than 76 people did so – and 24 were able to produce convincing witnesses to their foreknowledge of the event.

The magnificent palace and gardens at Versailles were constructed for King Louis XIV of France in 1676-1708. In the grounds stood a smaller palace, the Petit Trianon, where luxury-loving Queen Marie Antoinette liked to masquerade as a simple shepherdess.

There have been few more reliable witnesses to a paranormal experience than Eleanor Frances Jourdain, head teacher at an exclusive prep school near London at the time of her adventure.

Mathematical physicist Albert Einstein (1879-1955) suggested in his theories of relativity that Space and Time were not absolute, fixed dimensions.

In 1901, when she was "time slipped" to old time Versailles, Charlotte Moberly was head of a women's college at Oxford University.

❑ Historian Arnold Joseph Toynbee (1889-1975) spoke freely of his experiences of "falling into a time pocket." In Greece, he "saw" the riots caused by St. Paul at Ephesus; was horrified to find himself in the midst of the battle of Pharsalus (197 B.C.); and witnessed a massacre at Mistra (A.D. 1820) in the Greek War of Independence. These experiences, he said, inspired him to write his 10-volume *History of the World*.

❑ Royal Air Force Wing Commander Victor Goddard experienced a time slip to the future in 1934. Flying over Scotland in heavy rain and fog, he descended to check his bearings at a disued airfield. Moments later he found himself above the field in bright sunlight; below, buildings he knew to be derelict were now intact, and ground crews in blue uniforms (not then used) worked on unfamiliar aircraft. In 1939, Goddard was sent to the now reopened field. He flew in – to find the scene he had witnessed in 1934.

❑ Some parapsychologists equate Life Review Experiences (L.R.E.) with time slips. L.R.E. are the occasions, usually in times of extreme danger, when the whole of one's life is replayed in detail in a few moments. Some individuals have reported seeing their future lives, as well as their pasts, during L.R.E.s.

More lives than one?

When the Dalai Lama, Tibet's spiritual ruler, dies, his followers do not elect a successor. They know that their new leader will be the old one – in a new body. The child in whom he is reborn will bear identifying signs and will recognize the Dalai Lama's possessions. The belief that death is followed by rebirth into a new physical body – reincarnation – is shared by many peoples, including Hindus, Buddhists, and Australian Aborigines. Western Judaeo-Christian religions have resisted the idea, but today many Westerners find it persuasive. Many report memories of previous lives, often supported by accurate historical detail that they cannot have gained in a normal way. Some have tried to uncover past-life memory under hypnosis, by regression – a technique used by hypnotherapists to bring out buried memories of infancy, and now used in search of memories dating back before birth. Results have been both dramatic and confusing. Subjects tell of past lives in the language of the time, showing a mastery of linguistics and history far beyond that of either the hypnotist or, in a waking state, the subject. Yet, there is much

inconsistency: often the subject shows great knowledge of trivial details of everyday life, but ignorance of major historical events. A classic case was that of Virginia Tighe of Wisconsin, who, in 1952-53, underwent hypnotic regression to "Bridey Murphy," a 19th century Irishwoman. Under hypnosis Tighe (who had no knowledge of Ireland) spoke with an Irish accent, danced Irish jigs, accurately described customs such as the use of uillean pipes (an ancient musical instrument) at funerals, even named shops in 19th century Belfast. Research confirmed some details, but others, like the existence of a historical Bridey Murphy, remain unproven.

"Bridey Murphy" described how people kissed the Blarney Stone, an old custom believed to give one the "gift of the gab." Today, an easier method to kiss the stone has been devised. How did Tighe know of the earlier method?

Social reformer Annie Besant (1847-1933), a president of the mystical Theosophical Society, believed she had known a previous life as 16th century philosopher-monk Giordano Bruno.

Elaborate mummy cases attest to ancient Egypt's devout belief in preserving corpses to ensure life after death. Joan Grant, a medium who claimed a previous life in Egypt, said priests were taught to recall past incarnations.

Tibet's 14th Dalai Lama was born in China. At 2 years old he claimed objects owned by his late predecessor. This, plus marks on his body, told monks that they had found their spiritual leader's latest incarnation.

FACT FILE

❏ In 1929, three-year-old Shanta Devi of Delhi, India, shocked her parents by insisting that she was Ludgi, a married woman of the town of Muttra. She described her "real" family and home in great detail – and also her death in childbirth in 1925. When Ludgi's widower visited her, she knew him at once. Taken to Muttra, she went straight to Ludgi's home, identified her family, all but the youngest child – born when Ludgi died – and located jewelry hidden by Ludgi before her death.

❏ In the 1960s, English psychiatrist Arthur Guirdham found a group of people who shared recurrent dreams. In these they lived the lives of 13th century Cathars (a French religious sect condemned by the Catholic Church as heretical). Their massive knowledge of obscure historical detail convinced Guirdham of the group reincarnation of a band of Cathars who had been burned alive together in 1244.

❏ People blind from birth are known to dream nonvisually – but under hypnotic regression they are sometimes able to describe past lives as if they were sighted.

❏ Many religions that teach the never-ending cycle of life and rebirth regard reincarnation as a return to the sufferings of life, a punishment for faults, and try to break the cycle by leading a virtuous life.

Written in the stars

Astrology is the study of the effects of heavenly bodies on life on Earth, from which astrologers claim to predict the future. "Star reading" began in the Middle East about 3,000 years ago, as a science (astronomy) and a method of prophecy (astrology). Astronomers predicted such events as eclipses: astrologers used the same observations to read the fates of people, even nations. By c.600 B.C. the Chaldaeans (modern Iraq), believing that an individual's character and fate are influenced by the position of heavenly bodies at the time of birth, developed personal horoscopes. Until at least the 17th century A.D., astrology was an honored science, closely linked with medicine and alchemy. As astronomical knowledge grew, it was dismissed as fantasy. Yet, today it thrives again. Few take seriously newspapers' horoscope columns, simply based on birth dates (Sun signs). But professional astrologers maintain that detailed horoscopes, based on the positions of Sun, Moon, and planets in the Zodiac at the exact time and place of a person's birth, tell the truth. Scientists say that Zodiacal lore stems from ancient Greek legends with no modern relevance – but admit that heavenly bodies do influence life on Earth. In recent years they have found links between the Moon's cycle and the functioning of life forms from oysters to rats; between women's fertility cycles and the positions of Sun and Moon at their birth; and between radio disturbances and planetary positions that astrologers call "malign." French psychologist Michel Gauquelin made extensive computer analysis of birth times and found a correlation between planetary position and success in certain careers. Scientists were typically born under Saturn; soldiers under Mars or Jupiter; writers under Venus or the Moon.

Chinese astrological signs are all animals, such as this snake, ascribed not to months but to individual years within the 60-year cycle of the Chinese lunar calendar.

A 16th century woodcut combines Zodiac signs with a farming almanac, showing the appropriate labor for each month as well as its star sign.

The sign of Libra is a pair of scales: Librans are supposed to be well balanced and to need to form half of a pair.

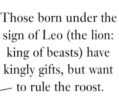

Those born under the sign of Leo (the lion: king of beasts) have kingly gifts, but want to rule the roost.

Sagittarians might wear this earring set with their birthstone, rubies, as a magic amulet as well as an adornment.

A Mayan Zodiac figure: Venus. The Maya, learned astrologers, revered Tlauixcalpantecuhtli (Venus) as the chief and most sacred of all planets.

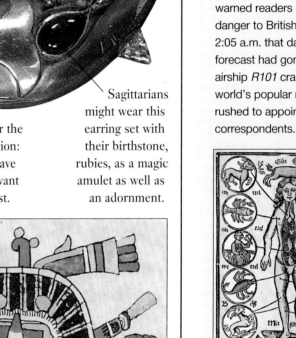

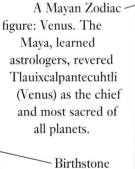

Birthstone jewelry (a gem associated with the owner's star sign) is worn to bring good fortune.

FACT FILE

❏ The first major newspaper to carry regular astrological predictions, now common worldwide, was the London *Sunday Express*, which featured astrologer R.H. Naylor (1889-1952) from August 24, 1930. His pieces provoked little interest until October 5, when he warned readers of "serious danger to British aircraft." At 2:05 a.m. that day, just after his forecast had gone to press, the airship *R101* crashed. The world's popular newspapers rushed to appoint astrological correspondents.

❏ Until the 17th century, medicine was inseparable from astrology, and doctors began diagnosis and treatment by drawing up the patient's astrological chart. Each star sign was believed to rule part of the body (above; a 16th century print), so the patient's birth sign indicated his physical weaknesses. Aries ruled the head, so it was to be expected that Arians should be prone to headaches. Aquarius ruled the circulation, so Aquarians were condemned to varicose veins and hardening of the arteries.

Hands of fate

Every human hand is different. Shape, skin color and texture, finger length, musculature, and nails all vary, and the pattern of lines on fingertips and palms is unique to each individual. The art of palmistry (in ancient times called chiromancy; Greek *cheir*, hand) is based on the belief that this variation is not random, but reflects a person's character, state of health – even destiny. Palmistry evolved in the East more than 4,000 years ago. In Europe it appeared in the Middle Ages as a magical art linked with astrology. It was regarded as a science by many 18th century thinkers and even taught in some universities. Today its status lies somewhere between that of outright superstition and alternative medicine. Fortune tellers retain links with medieval astrology, ascribing hand shapes to the four elements (Earth, Air, Fire, and Water), and each finger and mount (the fleshy pad below a finger) to a particular planet. Each palm line (the most important are the head, heart, and life lines) is associated with an aspect of the subject's life pattern. Significance is read in the line's position, clarity, and any breaks. The left hand is said to show a person's potential at birth; the right, actual traits (reversed for left-handers). Most people now take palmistry light-heartedly, as a "fun" way of fortune telling, ascribing accurate predictions less to hand reading than to the palmist's genuine if mysterious intuition. Serious practitioners read the hand to diagnose bodily and psychological states. This may have some scientific basis, for more than 30 congenital disorders, including Down Syndrome, are now known to produce typical palm lines. Japanese scientists have used palm prints to detect organic diseases such as thyroid deficiency and even to predict vulnerability to certain illnesses, including tuberculosis.

Despite the name, palmists study the whole hand, not just the palm. Hand shape, skin texture, flexibility, fingers, and nails, as well as mounts, lines, and lesser markings, all contribute to the serious palmist's interpretation.

The Duke of Beaufort consults a palmist. To the British, the Gypsy fortuneteller (authentic Romany or local minister in costume) is part of any seashore vacation or charity fete.

Fig 222. Hand of an Avaricious and Thoughtless Man

Eastern palmistry is a discipline of its own, but the poster suggests that this street palmist in Bangkok, Thailand, may be cashing in on Western tourists' exaggerated respect for "the mystic East."

Palmists take into account fingers' lengths and shapes, span, set on the hand, and whether joints are smooth or knotty, as well as relating each finger to the mount below it.

The Life Line is held to represent "life energy" (vitality).

❏ Some think the Hebrews practiced palmistry. The *Bible* holds two possible references: "He [God] seals up the hand of every man, that all men may know His work"; and "Long life is given in her right hand. In her left are riches and honor" (*Proverbs*, Ch.3, v.16).

❏ Early in the 20th century palmist Count Louis Hamon (also called Cheiro) read the hand of King Edward VII of England, and told him: "You will not die, sir, until you are in your 69th year . . . but a namesake will give up his crown for love." His prediction was exactly fulfilled. In 1910 Edward died as foretold; in 1936 Edward VIII abdicated in order to marry Mrs. Simpson.

❏ Some Hindu palmists base their entire reading on the thumb alone – and many Western palmists agree that the thumb is the key element in disclosing character.

❏ Traditionally, the length of the life line was said to show its owner's lifespan. People with short life lines may be pleased to know that few palmists today hold this view.

❏ When French palmist M.A. Le Normand read the hand of Napoleon Bonaparte, he was impressed by her detection of his secret plan to divorce his wife Josephine. Her memoirs note that his hand was "brutal and unattractive" at first glance, but aroused "keen emotion" on closer inspection.

155

Oracles of east and west

The history of the I Ching, the Chinese system of divination now internationally popular, began under the Shang Dynasty (1766-1122 B.C.). Shang emperors consulted oracle bones for everything from military strategy to toothache cures. These were tortoiseshells or ox bones, heated until they cracked into lines, which were "read" by diviners. Later, oracular lines were formed by tossing yarrow stalks to form hexagrams (groups of six lines): interpretations were set down in book form as the I Ching, or Book of Changes. It was revised in c.1150 B.C. by the nobleman Wen and expanded by generations of Chinese scholars, notably Confucius (551-479 B.C.), to become the basis of the manual now used. Traditionalists still make hexagrams with yarrow stalks, but some use dice, coins – even computer programs. Like most oracles, the I Ching rarely gives simple answers, but many feel it responds directly to the inquirer, not at random. In the 1980s some Western diviners turned instead to runestones. Pieces bearing the letters of the old runic alphabet are cast like I Ching tokens or laid out like Tarot cards. Historically, rune casters are on shakier ground than I Ching buffs. The runic alphabet was developed in northern Europe in the 1st century A.D., primarily as a writing system. Mass illiteracy linked it with sorcery, especially in Norse lands, but the popular view of runes as an occult tool comes largely from romantic 17th century scholars. Norse legends tell of magicians using runic books; victory runes were cut on weapons to evoke divine aid; and charms and curses might be written in runes. But modern diviners might bear in mind that runes were primarily the medium of epitaphs, name tags, graffiti, bills, receipts, letters – and tax notices.

A modern Chinese girl turns to an ancient Chinese oracle, using the traditional yarrow sticks (yarrow was once a sacred plant) to consult the I Ching.

Eastern students of the *Book of Changes* expect to learn its text by heart before ever using it. Few Western I Ching readers would have such patience!

A late 19th century Chinese depiction of the 8 trigrams that make up the 64 hexagrams of the I Ching, with their Chinese characters. A meaning is assigned to each line as well as each complete hexagram.

Lao Tzu's I Ching scroll features a Yin-Yang symbol. Yang (positive or masculine force) is represented in the I Ching by unbroken lines, Yin (negative or feminine) by broken.

Runes: magic tools for divination, or just handwriting? This Danish-inscribed stone is a Viking ruler's cenotaph and probably has no more mystic significance than as a memorial.

Chinese sages such as Lao Tzu ("the Old Philosopher") saw the I Ching as a tool for the intelligence.

❏ In 1936 archeologists working on the Shang Dynasty site of Hsiao-t'-un uncovered a pit holding 17,096 pieces of oracle bone. With them was a skeleton – perhaps the diviner, buried with his "tools" after an oracle failure.

❏ Nazi enthusiasts of the occult associated runes, the ancient Germanic alphabet, with German racial superiority. They adopted the sig, or "S" rune (above), as the emblem of Heinrich Himmler's infamous *Schutzstaffel*, the S.S.

❏ Icelandic legend says all magic lore was recorded in two great runic books. *Grey Skin*, by white wizard Eirikur Magnusson (c.1637-1716), was a primer for sorcery, black or white. But *Red Skin* was devoted to black magic and gave unlimited power for evil. It was said to be the work of Bishop Gottskalk "the Cruel" (1497-1520), an unpopular cleric whom folklore magnified into a high black magician. Fortunately it was buried with him: attempts to wrest it from his ghost failed horribly.

Cards of destiny

The cartomancer Dale Brown consulting the Tarot – the Thoth deck devised by occultist and magician Aleister Crowley – using a pattern of double eight.

Tarot is the oldest and best known of the many methods of cartomancy (predicting the future with playing cards). It originated in the *tarots* (French: trumps) of the earliest European card decks, after c.1300. The belief that it embodies the wisdom of the ancient Egyptian *Book of Thoth* may stem from the fact that Gypsies, early fortune tellers with Tarot, were often called Egyptians or Pharaohs in medieval times, but most agree its symbols echo very ancient occult beliefs. The deck is of 78 cards: four suits, Cups, Coins (Pentacles), Swords, and Wands (Rods), of 10 numbered cards and 4 coat (court, face) cards: King, Queen, Knight, Page (Knave, Jack), and 22 tarots. The tarots are the Major Arcana (greater secrets), representing human characteristics and earthly and unearthly powers; the rest form the Minor Arcana. The cards (sometimes a full deck; sometimes tarots alone) are laid out in various patterns, such as the Tree of Life and Celtic Cross, and interpreted in relation to each other. The cards themselves are not magic, but they liberate the occult powers of those who sincerely strive to interpret them. The great psychiatrist Carl Gustav Jung (1875-1961) said that concentration on the cards helped tap the powers of the subconscious mind, and Tarot is used as an aid to meditation as well as for prediction. Although some still condemn ordinary playing cards as "the Devil's picture book," Tarot is among the few modern occult practices that is seldom criticized. It remains very popular: the standard Rider Waite deck (codified by British occultist A.E. Waite in 1910) has been supplemented more recently by a Witches Tarot, a Native American deck, even a Feminist deck.

The Death card. The Tarot's images are powerful archetypes aimed directly at the unconscious mind.

Many of the Tarot's images recall ancient tradition. The Hanged Man may derive from Norse hanged god Odin.

Body language

In Shakespeare's *Macbeth*, Duncan laments: "there's no art to find the mind's construction in the face." But folk tradition says character may be read from such physical features as a cleft chin or long index finger. The first "scientific" study of physiognomy ("knowledge from the body") was made by Swiss mystic Johann Lavater (1741-1801). Italian physician Cesare Lombroso (1836-1909), after long study of the inmates of prisons and insane asylums, claimed to have identified a "criminal" head shape. Modern science rejects physiognomy – as it does phrenology, developed by Austrian physician Franz Gall (1758-1828). He claimed that intelligence and character traits could be deduced from reading the bumps on a person's skull, which he said were caused by development of the underlying areas of the brain, thus showing which parts of the brain the individual used most. In linking mind and brain and theorizing that different parts of the brain have different functions, Gall was ahead of his time – Catholic authorities had his teachings suppressed as heresy – but most of his allocation of functions to brain areas was guesswork: he located memory in the frontal lobes, behind the eyes, just because two of his friends with good memories had bulging eyes. Scientists now know brain use does not affect brain shape, but Gall was widely accepted in the 19th century. England's Queen Victoria hired a phrenologist to assess her children, and U.S. carnivals and medicine shows added "bump reading" to their attractions. As late as the 1940s, Nazi German theorists believed phrenology could reveal "racial purity," and S.S. murder squads in Russia were ordered to collect the skulls of Jews and Communist officials for analysis by the Third Reich's pseudoscientists.

Phrenologists divided the skull into various sections, each of which they related to an area of brain held to control some particular character aspect, such as generosity, greed, or secretiveness.

Veneration

Spirituality

Hope

LANGUAGE 35

Phrenologists went to some trouble to find significances in head shapes – as appears from this 1863 diagram, based on Johann Lavater's work, depicting "asinine" and "simian" (monkey-like) heads.

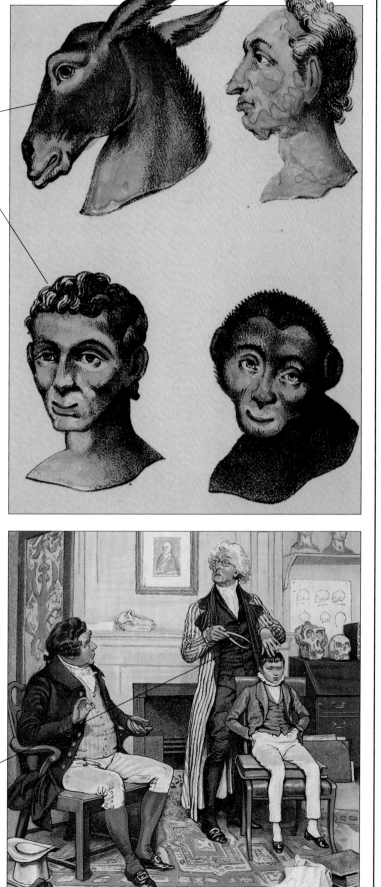

Parental love

Conjugality

Love

Combativeness

Destructiveness

Fashionable Victorian parents hired phrenologists to reveal children's characters and talents – though this small boy having his bumps read seems quite unimpressed.

❏ People whose eyebrows meet in the middle are harshly judged by popular physiognomy. A 16th century author said that this feature indicated "a wicked person, and an enticer of servants, and given to unlawful and naughty arts." A saying still heard is: "Trust not the man whose eyebrows meet, for in his heart you'll find deceit."

❏ As well as showing character, certain parts of the body, even bodily functions, may be used to predict the future. Methods include palmistry; moleosophy: from moles or warts; and onychomancy: from fingernails. Odder methods include geoloscopy – prediction from an individual's way of laughing.

❏ French policeman Alphonse Bertillon (1853-1914) used physical measurements for his criminal identification system. "Bertillonage" (above) called for detailed records of such features as height, length and breadth of head, length of fingers, forearms, and feet, shape of nose and ears, color of eyes. Effective but complex, it was soon replaced in most countries by fingerprinting.

Nostradamus: prophet of doom?

No one has made more far-reaching predictions than the French seer Michel de Notredame (Nostradamus) (1503-66). Born a Jew but raised a Catholic, he was a noted physician who, in c.1555-66, published some 1,000 predictions in rhymed quatrains (four line verses). They were hugely successful then – he was made court doctor to Kings Henry II (whose death he correctly predicted) and Charles IX – and remain so today, when new editions and interpretations appear regularly. He gained visions of the future by "scrying," staring into a bowl of water while in a semitrance. His quatrains are in a mixture of Greek, Latin, Italian, and French dialect, with anagrams, and are in random order, rarely indicating the date of predicted events. The obscurity was deliberate – in Nostradamus's time, straightforward prophecy might lead to accusations of heresy and witchcraft – but ever since it has led to some doubt about what he really meant. It is generally accepted that he foretold such events as the rise and fall of Emperor Napoleon ("Napoloron . . . born near Italy"), and the Spanish Civil War of 1936-39. He made predictions concerning "Hister" (Adolf Hitler, some say), and during World War II both sides employed Nostradamus (both genuine quatrains and forgeries) in propaganda. We must hope that at least one of his predictions (precisely dated) is wrong: "In the year 1999 and 7 months, from the sky will come the great king of terror . . . war reigns happily." Some commentators now think this refers to war between a U.S.-former Soviet states alliance and China; others say Nostradamus means World War III, begun by a Middle Eastern "Antichrist," that will last 27 years. Better news is that the end of the world, according to Nostradamus, is not due until A.D. 3797.

Long dead physician and seer Nostradamus is still a best-selling author. New editions of his prophetic verses appear almost every year.

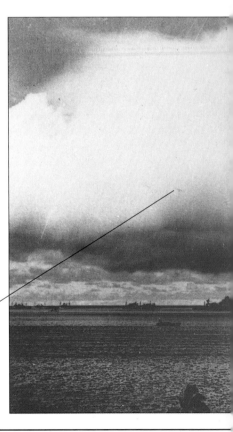

A mushroom cloud marks the experimental detonation of an atomic bomb. Nostradamus seems to have accurately predicted the atomic bombing of two Japanese cities in 1945.

Many of Nostradamus's quatrains are open to a variety of interpretations. But one actually names French bacteriologist Louis Pasteur (1822-95), who advanced medicine by showing diseases are caused by living organisms.

Nostradamus is said to have foretold such dictators as Emperor Napoleon I of France ("Napoloron" in a quatrain) and Adolf Hitler ("Hister") of Germany.

❑ Some of Nostradamus's prophecies were fulfilled in his own lifetime – as when he fell to his knees before a young Franciscan, hailing him as "Your Holiness." Many years later the monk became Pope Sixtus V (1521-90).

❑ Nostradamus foretold the time and place of his own death. He was buried standing upright in a church wall. In 1791, it is said, grave robbers disturbed his rest, hoping to gain prophetic powers by drinking from his skull. Around the neck of his skeleton hung a metal plate bearing the numerals "1791." One man drank from the skull and very soon died. The seer's remains were swiftly reburied.

❑ Walter Schellenberg (1910-52), a Nazi intelligence officer in World War II, claimed in his *Memoirs* that Nostradamus had aided the German conquest of France in 1940. Schellenberg ordered air drops of leaflets with faked quatrains suggesting that southeast France was a place of safety. Hordes of civilians fled in that direction, impeding the Allies but clearing roads for a speedy German armored advance farther north.

❑ One quatrain says that "Near the harbor and in two cities will be two scourges the like of which have never been seen." Many have interpreted this to be a forecast of the atomic bombing of Hiroshima and Nagasaki in 1945.

From crystal ball to computer

Edgar Cayce performed acts of of healing and made accurate prophecies while in a trance state, and was often called the "Sleeping Prophet."

The predictions made by carnival Gypsy fortune tellers with the aid of a crystal ball are usually taken lightly, but the forecasts of some modern prophets must be considered more seriously (although they may still use the much derided crystal ball as an aid to concentration and to achieving a prophetic state of trance). Those who use computers to build models of the future are called scientists, not prophets; but the visions of things to come obtained in trances or dreams may be as accurate as those gotten by modern technology. A famous modern dreamer was Edgar Cayce (1877-1945). After undergoing hypnotic treatment for a throat ailment, this Kentucky farmboy fell into trances in which he was both a healer and "sleeping seer." By clairvoyance, he diagnosed and cured patients he had never met. As a seer, he correctly forecast (among many other things) the Wall Street Crash of 1929, the invention of lasers, and the discovery of the Dead Sea Scrolls. His successor in popularity was Jeane Dixon of Washington, D.C., famous for publishing in a national magazine in 1956 her prediction that the 1960 Presidential election would be won by a Democrat who would die in office. She correctly foretold the Watergate scandal and (like Cayce) the fall of Communism in the U.S.S.R. (C.I.S.) in the early 1990s. Both Cayce and Dixon forecast global calamity in the late 1990s. Dixon warned of the rise of an Antichrist; Cayce's warning was of catastrophe caused by a polar shift (displacement of Earth's axis). His visions of huge earthquakes on the U.S. West Coast and of New York City, Japan, and parts of Western Europe submerged by floods are uncomfortably close to some of the consequences of global warming foreseen by ecologists with the aid of computer models.

Acting as aids to concentration, so that the user may focus his or her psychic powers, the crystal ball and Tarot deck are traditional tools of soothsayers. Today, some prophetic techniques, notably astrology, have been computerized.

❏ Some think Cayce's prediction in 1940 that part of the lost continent of Atlantis (where he believed he had lived in a former life) would rise again in 1968 has been fulfilled. In that year underwater explorers discovered the Bimini Road, a 2,000ft (610m) long avenue of huge stone pillars, some weighing more than 80 tons, in the sea northwest of Bimini Island, Bahamas. Many believe the stones formed part of a great Atlantean temple.

❏ Like Cayce, Native American legends predict catastrophe caused by a polar shift. An ancient Hopi belief is that this disaster will strike when "man puts a house in the sky." The launch of the first Soviet and U.S. space stations, Salyut and Skylab (above left), in 1971-73 was thought by some Hopi to fulfill the prophecy, and many took up survivalist lifestyles. Astrologers predicted polar shift disaster from the Jupiter Effect, an unusual planetary conjunction in 1982 and, when it did not occur, warned that a similar planetary lineup threatens Earth with upheaval on May 5, 2000.

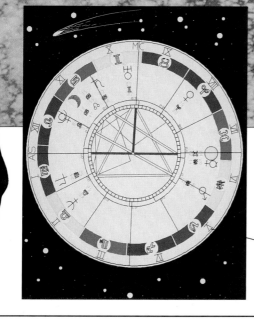

Skylab space station in orbit, 1974. Beyond, clouds shroud Earth: is the planet hiding its face from disaster stemming from the "house in the sky"?

A horoscope designed and printed by a modern computer is very different from the colorful charts made by traditional astrologers.

Monsters of olden times

From classical to medieval times the checklist of world fauna included many mythical beasts. Some clearly derived from travelers' tales, taken as fact by early scholars and accepted for centuries: the terrible nine-headed Hydra fought by the hero Herakles (Hercules) in Greek and Roman legend probably originated in an account of a real octopus. The common fear of snakes inspired fabulous reptiles such as the poisonous Salamander, dweller in fire, and the Basilisk or Cockatrice, King of Serpents, hatched from a rooster's egg brooded by a toad. Its glance was fatal (except, for some reason, to weasels): the only defense was to trick it into looking in a mirror, so it destroyed itself. That unique bird the Phoenix probably began as a religious allegory. There was only one Phoenix: it lived for millennia, then, grown old and weary, built its own funeral pyre and rose reborn from the ashes. Some fabulous beasts were composites, made from parts of different animals. Among the most fearsome were the Chimera, with lion's head, goat's body, and dragon's tail (we still use its name to mean a botched plan); the maneating Manticore, with man's face, lion's body, and scorpion's poisonous tail; and the Griffin, half lion and half eagle (dismissed by 17th century writer Sir Thomas Browne as "a mixt and dubious animal," but surviving into modern times in *Alice in Wonderland*). The Centaur, half human and half horse, was probably born when people who had not domesticated the horse first saw horsemen. Pure imagination supplied the winged bulls and horses of ancient art; the human-headed, lion-bodied Sphinx of Assyria and Ancient Egypt, and the Satyrs, human above and goat below, the lustful, drunken companions of the Greek wine god Dionysos.

China's *ky-lin*, a benevolent guardian despite its fierce appearance, is a composite with horse's hoofs, lion's body, dragon's head, and goat's horns.

Egypt's Sphinx symbolizes royal power, with a pharaoh's head and lion's body. The sinister Greek Sphinx was different: it had a woman's head and breasts, lion's body and paws, snake's tail, and wings.

This collection of medieval monsters (from a German woodcut of 1499) includes a dragon, a two-tailed Mermaid, and a wyvern (two-legged dragon), as well as some decorative composites likely to be the artist's own inventions.

❏ Roman Emperor Elagabalus (A.D. 204-22) hoped to gain immortality by dining on the deathless Phoenix. Since the Phoenix proved elusive, he ate the next best thing, a bird of paradise. An assassin soon proved the Emperor's dinner had not made him immortal.

❏ In the Middle Ages even scholars still credited many fabulous beasts such as the Salamander (below). Rich collectors bought such trophies as Griffins' claws (fossil mammoth tusks and antelope horns); fireproof Salamander wool (asbestos fiber); and preserved Hydras (at least one of which proved to comprise a snake's skin and weasels' heads and paws).

❏ The last recorded Basilisk hunt took place in 1587 in Warsaw, when a doctor identified the cause of death of two children as a basilisk's glare. A condemned prisoner was sent to seek out the monster. Encased in leather and armed with a mirror to reflect the beast's deadly glance back on itself, he captured what appeared to be an ordinary snake – which the doctor said was a Basilisk.

Lucky dragons and loathsome worms

Dragons occur in the myths of so many peoples that scholars have sought their roots in reality. One theory makes them a folk memory of dinosaurs – but these died out long before humans appeared. A more likely source is a basic human inclination to people the unknown with monsters. Different times and cultures created many kinds of dragons, and East and West developed quite different beasts. The Oriental dragon is a kindly demigod, "lord of the waters" and an imperial emblem; Chinese New Year festivities feature splendid dragons to bring good luck. The Western dragon is a darker force. Its ancestry includes Mesopotamia's creator-destroyer ocean dragon Tiamat; Babylon's dog-like Mushrushu, pet of chief god Marduk; and the poison-breathing, snake-like dragons of ancient Greece and Rome. The name comes from the Greek *drakon* (serpent): the word also implies sharp sight, and classical dragons, such as Ladon, who guarded the Golden Apples of the Hesperides, often served as the gods' watchdogs. Their miserly successors guarded treasures for themselves, like Fafnir of the Germanic Nibelung legend. In Norse myth the dragon Nidhoggr (corpse-eater) gnaws at the world from below. The medieval Church adopted the dragon as a symbol of evil, for the *Book of Revelations* calls Satan "the great dragon." Around this time dragons shifted shape from serpents ("worms") to heraldic winged quadrupeds; typically, fire-breathing monsters to be challenged by a hero. Belief in their reality was fostered by the discovery of huge fossil bones of extinct beasts (a woolly rhinoceros skull found in 16th century Austria passed for many years as a dragon's); and by medieval showmen, who made baby dragons by sewing bat wings onto lizard bodies.

The decorative Chinese dragon is a compound of nine everyday animals: camel, deer, hare, bull, iguana, frog, carp, tiger, and eagle.

The Western alchemist's symbol of unity, Ouroboros, the tail-biting dragon, dates back to ancient Egypt.

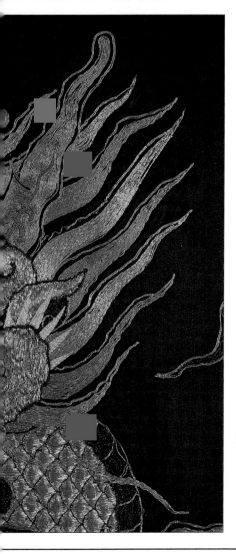

In Western tradition the fierce dragon must be slain by a hero. Popular tales often set a local farmer against a deadly "Worm"; while in religious art Christ or St. Michael is the dragonslayer who defeats "that old serpent" Satan.

❏ A dragon was reportedly sighted on the Kan River, in the Chinese province of Kiangsi, as recently as May 1931. Locals believed that river floods were due to the dragon's displeasure and wished to appease it by offering sacrifices.

❏ In 1912, zoologists investigated fishermen's reports of dragons on the Indonesian island of Komodo – and found they were true! The Komodo Dragon (above), a previously unknown giant monitor lizard, lacks the prototype's wings, fiery breath, and vast size: the record is a mere 10ft 2in (3.10m) long. But it does look like the dragon of popular tradition.

❏ In Old English dragons were *wyrms* – which meant snakes or dragons, interchangeably. British folklore preserves this usage, with dragons such as the Laidley ("loathsome") Worm of Lambton, the Linton Worm, and the Grisely ("grisly") Worme of Lofthouse.

Virgins' prey: the unicorn

Unicorns meant big money to early druggists. As late as the 18th century they were still prescribing alicorn (unicorn horn) for wealthy patients as the ultimate cure, charging its weight in gold.

The unicorn, loveliest of fabled beasts, was first seen about 2500 B.C., in carvings of the Indus Civilization (modern Pakistan). It was not then the dainty, horned pony loved by modern fantasists, but a one-horned ox. Ancient unicorn images range from the Indus ox to the Assyrian one-horned (sometimes winged) antelope. The first written description, by Greek physician Ctesias about 400 B.C., is of a large wild ass, with white body, dark red head, blue eyes, and a horn with magic powers as an antidote to poison. Despite the color scheme, he probably meant to describe the Indian rhinoceros (whose horn is still believed to be a magical sex stimulant). The Greek philosopher Aristotle (384-322 B.C.) listed two types of unicorn: Ctesias's "Indian ass" and a one-horned oryx (in profile, the two horns of the Arabian oryx are aligned and look like one). By the Middle Ages unicorns abounded in art and heraldry and in both love poems and religious texts. The unicorn was variously used to symbolize Christ, death, chastity, nobility, solitariness, and even violence. It had shed its origin in ox, rhino, and antelope to become a heraldic beast with a horse's head and body, goat's beard, lion's tail, cloven hoofs, and a long, straight, central horn. Two legends were firmly established: that the unicorn could be captured only by a virgin girl and that its horn guarded against poison. A unicorn horn (most were the long, straight tusks of the narwhal, a small whale) was a status symbol for the very rich. Until about 1600 most naturalists believed the unicorn existed. The zoologist Baron Cuvier finally laid to rest the legend in 1827, when he demonstrated that the skull of a cloven-hoofed animal always has a divided frontal bone, which cannot support a central horn.

Was this the inspiration for the unicorn legend? In profile, the long straight horns of the Arabian oryx appear as a single horn.

The fierce unicorn can be tamed only by a virgin. In this 16th century French tapestry, the unicorn appears as the lady's attendant as a testimony to her purity.

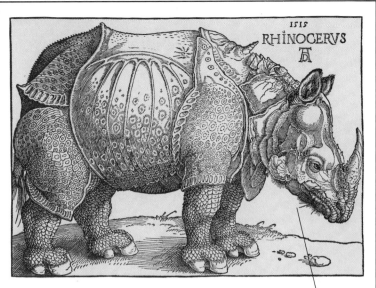

RHINOCERVS
1515

It may lack beauty to modern eyes, but the Indian rhinoceros was probably what classical Greece meant by a unicorn.

The unicorn of heraldry: horse's head and body, goat's beard, lion's tail, and cloven hoofs.

❏ The unicorn of the *Bible* is, alas, a translator's creation: in passages like "God . . . hath as it were the strength of a unicorn," the original texts almost certainly refer to the aurochs, a now extinct wild ox.

❏ In 1933, Dr. Dove, an American biologist, created a unicorn by surgery on a bull calf. He grafted its hornbuds together and transplanted them to the center of its forehead, where they grew to form a single straight horn. It is reported that the unicorn-bull grew up to be herd leader.

❏ Nature has its own "unicorns," single-horned beasts, from beetles to whales. As well as the rhinoceros (above) (whose horn is really a fibrous growth like a tight-packed mass of hair), there is a rhinoceros beetle, with an impressive horny outgrowth on its head. The tusk of the narwhal, once often taken as unicorn horn, occurs only in the male whale: it is the left upper canine tooth, which grows forward through the upper lip and may be up to 7ft (2.1m) long.

Terrors of the deep

Dead sea monsters found washed up on beaches generally turn out to be known animals whose remains are distorted past recognition by decomposition, such as this basking shark carcass.

Since humans first went to sea, they have reported meetings with monsters. In ancient mythology these are of world shaking proportions: the Mesopotamian ocean dragon Tiamat; Leviathan, the *Bible*'s terrible fish that "maketh the deep to boil like a pot;" and, later, the Vikings' Jormungandr, the World Serpent coiled under the sea, encircling the globe. For more than 2,000 years most scholars held as fact the existence of sea serpents and of the Kraken, a many-armed colossus that dragged down large ships with its tentacles. In 1555, Swedish Archbishop Olaus Magnus reported the appearance of a black sea serpent 220ft (67m) long, with a mane, glowing eyes, and a head raised "on high like a pillar." It is said to have plucked men from boats to devour them. By the 18th century disbelief set in: scientists rationalized sightings as floating trash seen in freak sea or weather conditions, or (a more modern explanation for "monsters" found dead ashore) the oddly shaped, decomposing remains of whales or sharks. But many 20th century experts are less dismissive, for new deep-sea exploration technology has revealed previously unknown species. These include the coelacanth, a large fish thought until 1938 to have been extinct for 70 million years, and in 1976 the megamouth shark. The mythical Kraken has emerged from legend as the giant squid – still never seen alive, but known from enormous remains found in sperm whales' stomachs or washed ashore. Reports of sea serpents continue, and remarkable similarities between many ancient and modern accounts contribute to a theory that the Plesiosaur, an aquatic dinosaur, may survive in the oceans to this day.

In 1848 a sea serpent "of extraordinary dimensions" was seen in the South Atlantic by the captain and officers of the British Navy's *Daedalus*.

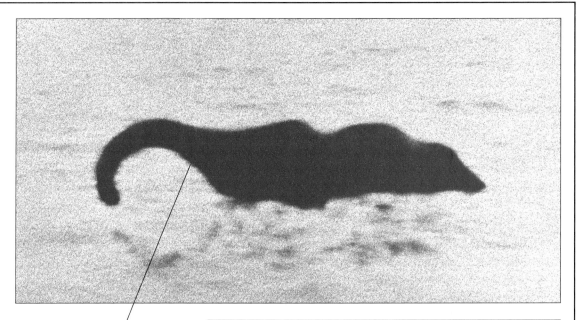

Nicknamed Morgawr (Cornish: sea giant), this monster has haunted Britain's Cornish coast since 1975. A woman calling herself Mary F took this picture in 1976.

In 1964, Frenchman Robert Le Serrec photographed this tadpole-shaped sea monster resting on the bottom in clear, shallow water off Hook Island, Australia.

❏ A sailors' legend says sea monsters are most often seen on a Thursday – the day of their creation according to the *Book of Genesis*.

❏ In 1845 a sea serpent skeleton, 114 ft (35m) long, was exhibited in New York and subsequently in Europe. It was a fake, made from bones of extinct whales – and was later bought by a German museum and disassembled to provide a less spectacular but authentic fossil exhibit.

❏ Although sea serpents are usually regarded as horrible monsters, one spotted off the coast of Vancouver Island several times since 1933 fails to arouse fear in locals. Nicknamed Caddy, it is described as "lovable and homely," with "kindly eyes."

❏ Some think sea serpents are not animals at all, but alien submarines. Certainly the "monster fish" encountered by the crew of the *Marion* in 1893, on the northwest American coast, sounds more mechanical than animal. It was more than 150ft (46m) long, brightly illuminated, driven by a propeller tail, and ringed with copper bands that gave off powerful electric currents.

❏ In 1876, a British newspaper reported that Cornish fishermen had caught a live sea serpent. But they killed it and dumped it back in the sea – missing a chance to make zoological history.

Lure of the mermaid

Sailors' stories, ships' logs, and eyewitness accounts by solid citizens attest to long belief in a race of sea people. Best known is the mermaid, woman above and fish below. Sometimes she was a wrecker, using her lovely voice to lure sailors to death, sometimes a friend who aided fishermen with their catch, warned them of storms, or fell tragically in love with a mortal. Mermaids probably originate in the fish-tailed sea gods of pagan cultures. Christian tradition sometimes saw them as the souls of drowned sailors, or even minor fallen Angels, cast out from Heaven but not wicked enough for Hell. A less romantic modern belief is that mermaids were real animals – dugongs, manatees, or sea cows: sea mammals without the mermaid's legendary beauty, but with human-like breasts that caused sex-starved ancient mariners to take them for sea-women. Others say they were optical illusions caused by atmospheric distortion in freak weather. Sightings date from ancient times: Roman naturalist Pliny recorded a shoal of dead mermaids stranded on a beach in Gaul (France). Columbus saw three off Guyana, and 17th century navigator Henry Hudson described one seen by his crew: from the waist up a white-skinned woman, with long, black hair; from the navel down with "the tail of a porpoise, speckled like a mackerel." And in 1977 a South African newspaper reported a mermaid found in a storm sewer. There are many accounts of the capture of mermaids, dead or alive, but no specimens seem to have reached the showmen of freaks and wonders. Thus, in the 16th-19th centuries fake mermaids – small, ugly curios, far from the myth of beauty – were in demand and were usually made by sewing the shaved top half of a monkey onto a fish's tail.

Mermaids abound in church carvings – not as pagan ornaments but as emblems of a moral lesson. To medieval churchmen, the mermaid who lured sailors to their deaths symbolized the fate of those tempted into sexual sin.

The manatee is said to have inspired the mermaid legend. It is hard to believe any sailor, however long at sea, could have seen it as a lovely woman!

Folklorists interpret the romantic mermaid of legend as the perfect and unattainable woman of men's dreams.

The mermaid supporters of the coat of arms of Boston, England, add imagery that refers to the town's growth as port and fishing center.

When a mermaid falls in love with a mortal man, the outcome is almost invariably tragic, for the lovers cannot enter each others' worlds.

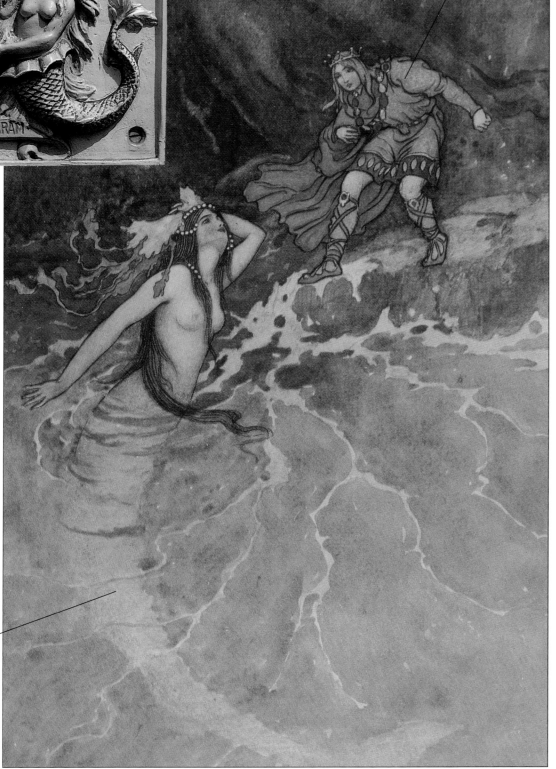

❏ "Sea people" include the Siren of classical myth, half woman, half bird, whose enchanting song lured ships onto reefs; and the Selkies, or seal people, of Scottish legend, who have human shape on land but become seals in the sea. Folktales tell of love affairs, often tragic, between Selkies and mortals – and some old Scottish families still boast of Selkie blood in their ancestry.

❏ Benin (modern Nigeria) was once ruled by a merman. Wily 14th century King Chen cheated tribal laws that condemned ailing rulers to death. When paralysis struck his legs, he announced that his lower limbs had become those of a mud fish, proving him the incarnation of a sea god – and continued to reign.

❏ Not all mermaids belong to the sea. Some are river dwellers, the most famous being the Lorelei of Germany's Rhine River. She lured boatmen to their deaths by singing sweetly from a rock.

❏ In the 1820s crowds watched a mermaid that sang nightly from a rock in the sea off Cornwall, England. On her last appearance she burst unexpectedly into "God save the King" before plunging into the sea, never to be seen again. Eccentric local minister and practical joker Robert Hawker had grown bored with posing in a seaweed wig and a tail made of oilskin.

Nessie and her cousins

Reports of a monster in Loch Ness, Britain's largest lake, go back to 563, when St. Columba is said to have saved a fellow monk from its jaws. British folklore swarms with lake beasts: Welsh *afancs* (fierce giant beavers), Irish and Scottish water-horses, and English monsters ranging from "Jinny Greenteeth" to "Rawhead-and-Bloody-Bones." But only Nessie has slithered from legend into modern popular belief, with more than 3,000 sightings since 1933 – and many blurred photographs, dismissed by skeptics as distorted views of otters playing, floating logs, or freak water conditions. Belief that Loch Ness holds a beast (or beasts) unknown to science – a long-necked seal, a giant sea slug, or, most popular, a plesiosaur (aquatic dinosaur) – has inspired costly expeditions with small submarines and/or electronic echo finders. All attempts have failed to prove or disprove Nessie's existence. Many other lands boast lake monsters – some (cynics think all) blatantly invented as tourist attractions, others of greater antiquity. Scandinavia boasts several, such as the beast of Lake Storsjön, Sweden, renowned since 1820 and said to be shown on an ancient runestone on the lake island. North America, where Native American legends have been supported by modern eyewitnesses, claims more lake monsters than any other region. Longlived favorites include Ogopogo of Lake Okanagan, British Columbia – said by one witness to look like a telegraph pole with a sheep's head – and the serpentine Champ of Lake Champlain, New York-Vermont. Most of these cousins of Nessie have been photographed, but the pictures are ambiguous. One theory is that lake monsters occupy a different plane of existence – which is why photographs of them are never clear.

Scientists argue over Nessie photos: fakes, mistakes, or genuine? This one was taken in September 1983 by a woman on a cycling vacation near Loch Ness. It has a marked resemblance to Anthony Shiels's 1977 picture, opposite.

In 1987, Operation Deepscan pursued Nessie underwater, combing the loch systematically with sonar from a line of boats, but to little effect.

Anthony Shiels was one of the luckier monster hunters. He scored this Nessie snapshot in May 1977 on only his second visit to the loch.

Loch Ness is large and deep enough to hide several monsters and so clouded with the peat swept in by 50 streams that a diver could swim right by Nessie without spotting her.

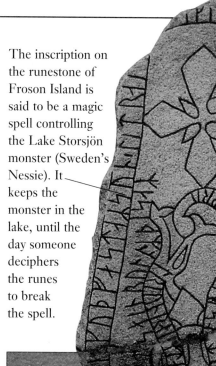

The inscription on the runestone of Froson Island is said to be a magic spell controlling the Lake Storsjön monster (Sweden's Nessie). It keeps the monster in the lake, until the day someone deciphers the runes to break the spell.

Giants of the snows

In 1832 the British Resident Officer in the Himalayan kingdom of Nepal reported that a hairy demon had chased his porters. Local peoples had long believed wild men inhabited the snowy Himalayas, but this was the West's first encounter with the Abominable Snowman, or Yeti. Mountaineers and local Sherpas reported more sightings of a giant, hairy, apelike beast, walking on two legs, and in 1951 climber Eric Shipton's photographs of huge footprints – 13in (33cm) long and 8in (20cm) across – in the snows of Everest inspired explorers and zoologists to serious Yeti-hunting. The quest goes on: more footprints have been found; mountain monasteries' holdings of Yeti scalps, bones, and skins have been examined. Skeptics dismiss local people's reports as failure to distinguish between reality and religious beliefs

According to legend, Abominable Snowmen sometimes venture down from their mountain hideouts to raid cultivated valleys, such as this one near Pokhara, Nepal, for food or even human prey.

The hairy relic displayed by the chief lama (priest) at a Tibetan monastery is said to be the scalp of a Yeti. No complete or even partial body has yet been found.

and Westerners' sightings as glimpses of known animals (bears, wolves, foxes, langur monkeys, or snow leopards) or wandering holy men, or as hallucinations caused by oxygen starvation at high altitude. Footprints may be animal or human tracks distorted by melting snow: it has been said that Shipton's photographs show superimposed tracks, expanded by melting, of the fore and hind feet of a large snow leopard. Yeti scalps examined by Western scientists have proved to be aged goatskin hats. If the Yeti does exist, what is it? Some think it is a large ape as yet unknown to science; others, a surviving descendant of Gigantopithecus, a prehistoric giant ape thought to be long extinct. Similar in appearance to the Yeti – and thought by some to be a surviving race of Neanderthal Man – is the Alma, reported many times this century from Mongolia's Gobi Desert to the Caucasus Mountains. Siberia also has a similar being in its Chuchuna ape man.

"Yeti tracks" found by British mountaineer Eric Shipton in 1951 extended c.900yd (820m) along Nepal's Menlung Glacier.

Shipton photographed a 13in x 8in (33cm x 20cm) footprint (with ice ax to show scale). Tracks were at an altitude of about 19,000ft (5,800m).

❑ Australia's man-beast is the Yowie, seen in New South Wales and Queensland. One witness saw a creature 6ft (1.8m) tall, with black fur, bulging eyes – and "the stink of a badly-kept public lavatory." Japan's version, the Hibagon, has the same problem with body odor. A 1974 witness commented, "He must have bathed in a septic tank."

❑ In 1961 the Nepalese government introduced licenses for Yeti hunters: $640 per Yeti.

❑ During a visit to the Himalayas in 1986, Anthony Wooldridge photographed a Yeti which cooperated by standing still. Some naturalists said that his photographs proved the existence of a big, unknown primate. But further research in 1989 showed that Wooldridge's subject was only a large, Yeti-shaped rock.

❑ In 1941 the Soviet Army caught a man-beast in the mountains of Daghestan. Colonel V.S. Karapetyan, who saw it before its death, said it was c.6ft (1.8m) tall, entirely human in shape, covered with shaggy, dark brown hair, and with the eyes of an animal.

❑ Sherpas say that Yetis are meat-eaters and, when starved, even man-eaters who raid villages for victims. In 1948 a Norwegian prospector in the Himalayas claimed to have been mauled by a Yeti.

Missing link in the American wilderness?

The ancient Greeks and Romans believed that forests were the domain of a goat-footed god (Pan or Silenus) and his hairy henchmen, the satyrs. From the Middle Ages come tales of the wodewose, a wild man of the woods, sometimes described as a club-wielding, flesh-eating ogre. These were Old World monsters; as the great forests of Europe were felled, so the wild men faded into extinction. Not so in the New World, where tales of a forest giant, called Wendigo by the Algonquins, Sasquatch by other Native U.S. peoples, were taken up by European settlers in the early 19th century. Modern reports of the North American wild man, now usually called Bigfoot, center on the forests of British Columbia, Canada, and the U.S. northwest, the wilderness regions of the Rockies and Cascade ranges in Oregon, Washington, and northern California. Many informed observers, including scientists and naturalists, now accept that there is very strong evidence of wild men dwelling in these forests. From hundreds of well-documented sightings, including footprints, photographs, even movie footage, it seems that Bigfoot may stand up to 10ft (3m) tall and weigh about 300lb (136kg). An overall covering of reddish-brown hair, huge chest and shoulders, and non-existent neck, give an ape-like impression – but Bigfoot walks upright like a man. Skeptics speak of hoaxes (although it would take a very determined joker to fake the trail of c.1,100 well-defined footprints traced in Washington State in 1969) or over-imaginative sightings of grizzly bears. Others believe that the missing link in the evolutionary chain may walk America's surviving wildernesses.

The trail of Bigfoot: this 16.5in (42cm) long footprint was one of more than 1,000 prints traced in snow at Bossburg, Wash., in 1969.

Concrete evidence? The cast of a huge footprint found at Bluff Creek, Calif., in 1964.

The late Roger Patterson was one of the first to produce hard evidence.

Striking movie footage shot by Roger Patterson at Bluff Creek, Calif., October 1967, shows Bigfoot, very ape-like in appearance, walking upright like a human. (Photo Patterson/ Gimlin, © 1968 Dahinden.)

A 16th century German artist's impression of a wodewose, the fabled wild man of Europe's forests. The hairy, green giant wields a young tree (note the unfortunate human) as a club.

❏ Credible Bigfoot sightings in the Northwest have triggered more imaginative reports from all over the United States. In 1973 a short-lived sensation was the Murphysboro Mud Monster, a huge being, its long fur matted with foul-smelling mud, that was seen along the banks of the Big Muddy River in southwest Illinois.

❏ The Minnesota Ice Man of 1968-69 (above) was accepted as genuine by zoologist Dr. Bernard Heuvelmans. This Bigfoot frozen inside a block of ice was exhibited by carnival showman Frank D. Hansen, who claimed to have found it floating in the Sea of Okhotsk, Siberia. Few believed him; fewer still credited a young woman who claimed to have shot it in self defense – her story appeared under the tabloid headline: "I was raped by the Abominable Snowman." A Disneyland technician has claimed to have modeled the Ice Man from foam rubber and expanded polystyrene.

Do dinosaurs walk the Earth?

Dinosaurs died out some 65 million years ago – or did they? Reports from both native peoples and explorers of dinosaur-like monsters in remote areas have led to theories that some dinosaurs may survive; especially since several animals "known" to be extinct have resurfaced in recent years. One of the best-known living dinosaurs is Mokele-mbembe, a giant, long-necked reptile that may live in the swamps of the Congo River in Africa, a region with an ecology comparatively little changed since the dinosaurs' era. It is said to be a harmless vegetarian. Several expeditions have claimed sightings, backed by some dubious photographs. Firm evidence seemed forthcoming in 1959, when Pygmies were said to have caught a specimen – but then it was reported that they had eaten it! In 1932 a carnivorous dinosaur was reported in Central Africa by a plantation overseer who described a huge lizard some 42ft (13m) long, which he had seen eating a rhinoceros. As well as dinosaurs, monster-hunters have found traces of prehistoric mammals. One candidate is Kenya's Nandi Bear. Africans describe a giant, flesh-eating, bear-like beast. This may be a case of mistaken identity – a large hyena or baboon – but some believers favor a Chalicotherid, a large, long-extinct, vegetarian mammal. Moving much farther north, there are stories of woolly mammoths (which died out more than 12,000 years ago) roaming the Siberian taiga, an unexplored forest covering nearly 3,000,000sq mi (7,770,000sq km). Accounts dating as far back as the 16th century may stem from discoveries of deep-frozen mammoth carcasses; but in 1918 a Russian hunter (who, it was established, had never heard of mammoths) described an encounter with two huge, hairy elephants with curved tusks.

A 1919 report of a horned dinosaur resembling this *Triceratops* in the then Belgian Congo led the Belgian government to protect it by law. It disappeared from record shortly afterwards.

Could a huge carnivorous dinosaur escape human notice?

Witnesses have reported pterodactyl sightings not only in unexplored Africa but in populous areas of the United States.

This giant carnivore, called *Albertosaurus*, flourished in North America some 70 million years ago. Here it is feasting on the carcass of a ceratopsian.

Naturalist Ivan Sanderson, who saw an African mystery monster in 1932, was convinced Africa had "room in it for all manner of things as yet unknown."

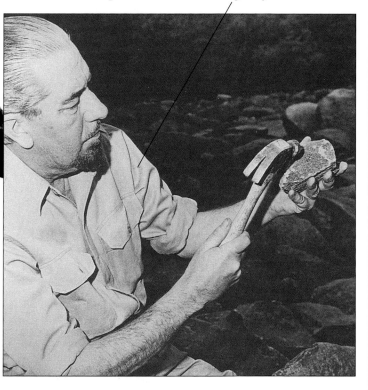

FACT FILE

❏ A "living fossil" recently rediscovered is the Chacoan peccary, a South American wild pig. It was thought to have died out 8,000 years ago – but in 1975 Paraguayan hunters revealed its existence to an American zoologist. The "extinct" peccary was well known to Indians, who for years had sent its hide to New York furriers, to trim hats!

❏ In the 1890s explorer Ramon Lista reported a mystery beast in Patagonia. Huge, longhaired, and armored, it sounded like a giant ground sloth – a species that disappeared in the late Ice Age. Then fragments of apparently fresh ground sloth skin were found in caves in Argentina. The survival of the ground sloth seemed proven, until carbon dating showed the skins were 10,000 years old.

❏ 19th century explorers thought they had discovered surviving woolly mammoths (above) in Alaska, assuming that Inuits' recent drawings of mammoths were made from life. The truth was that earlier explorers collecting fossil mammoth ivory in the region had drawn a mammoth for the Inuit, who liked the picture and made many copies.

183

New wild beasts and undiscovered animals

"There is little hope of discovering new species," said naturalist Baron Cuvier in 1812. He was wrong. More than 100 new mammals have been found this century, including the elusive "jackalope" of Vietnam's remote mountainous forests, whose existence was announced in 1993. Combining characteristics of the goat, cow, and horse, it has horns like an antelope and weighs about 220lb (100kg): rumors of others merit serious investigation. Some native myths have proved true: the Atti, striped donkey of the Congo region, became known to science as the Okapi in 1901. Still unproven are Australia's dog-like Yokyn (a feral dog; perhaps a mainland race of the Tasmanian wolf) and Bolivia's Mitla, half-dog, half-cat. In 1920, Swiss geologist Francis de Loys claimed to have met apes in South America – where there are none. His photograph of a dead specimen is dismissed by most zoologists as that of a common spider monkey, distorted by decomposition, its scale deliberately falsified, and its tail (which no ape has) concealed. Less dubious are reports since 1961 of the Thylacine (Tasmania's marsupial "wolf"), presumed extinct since the 1940s but now thought to survive in small numbers. Some mystery beasts can be easily explained: a hairless, lion-headed monster roaming Britain's Isle of Wight in 1940 was an aged fox with severe mange. Displaced animals – real beasts seen in unlikely places – remain a puzzle: zoo escapes, popular hysteria, or genuine mysteries? U.S. cities reportedly teem with big cats, kangaroos, and sewer alligators – and in 1979 an elephant in Brooklyn. Britain favors phantom big cats (often black, but usually called pumas): the Surrey Puma achieved fame in the 1960s.

184

In 1902 the mystery antelope or donkey said to haunt the unknown forests of the African Congo left myth to enter zoology under the name of the Okapi.

Pygmies described the Atti as zebra-striped.

Source of heated argument since 1920: Francis de Loys's photograph of a mystery South American ape – probably a decomposing spider monkey.

"The Nondescript," a cheerful hoax, was made in 1824, probably from a howler monkey's rear end, by puckish British naturalist Charles Waterton.

A rare photograph of the Surrey Puma, taken in August 1966 by two ex-police photographers who were sure it was no ordinary cat.

❑ Since c.1870 witnesses have described a large, fierce, striped marsupial "tiger" in the Queensland jungles of Australia. The only solid evidence for the Queensland tiger is a sketch of a footprint. In 1895 a Queensland hotel displayed what was said to be a stuffed specimen – but some saw it as an Assyrian wolf, a mongrel bloodhound, or even a deformed calf.

❑ When a strange cheetah – blotched and striped instead of spotted – was found in 1926, zoologists thought it a new species, even a cheetah-leopard hybrid. But in 1981 a King Cheetah born at a South African research center proved that it was just a rare color variant. But scientists think the mutation, fitting nocturnal forest-dwellers, may eventually produce a new race of cheetahs, distinct from existing daytime savannah hunters.

❑ In 1974 a driver saw a "most peculiar animal" in her headlights. She was certain it was a Thylacine (Tasmanian wolf) (above) – but the encounter took place on the other side of the world, in southern England.

185

Giants in the sky

Like the sea, the air has its monsters: strange flying creatures nicknamed Unidentified Flapping Objects. Some are impossibly huge birds, seen worldwide but especially associated with the United States, where Native American legends of the Thunderbird may have a basis in fact. In 1895 a giant-bird was reported to have carried off a 10-year-old girl in West Virginia. The 1970s brought many "big bird" reports from the Texas-Mexico border, where legends of monster birds are longstanding. Witnesses described huge, bat-winged, cat-faced birds. Skeptics said these had to be pelicans, blue herons, or oversized barn owls, but some giant-bird spotters believed they had seen living pterodactyls: prehistoric flying lizards that died out with the rest of the dinosaurs – or did they? Modern reports of pterodactyls have come from Africa, New Zealand, South America, and elsewhere. Some think African peoples' legends of giant bats prove pterodactyl survival; others see them as tribal memory of prehistoric life – or a real, unknown, giant bat. Another species of flying monsters is the winged humanoid. In 1877, New Yorkers told of a man with bat's wings and frog-like legs flying over Brooklyn and Coney Island. More recently, the West Virginia Mothman was frequently sighted in 1966. Witnesses said he was more than man-size, armless, with no apparent head but glowing red eyes, and with a wingspan of about 10ft (3m). The Mothman kept pace with an automobile at 100mph (160 kph) and squeaked like a big mouse. The Owlman of Cornwall, England, seen in 1976-78, had pointed ears, big red eyes, and feet like pincers. Two sisters who saw it wrote the local newspaper: "Our mother thinks we made it up because we read about these things. That is not true. We really saw the bird man."

The Thunderbird of Native American tradition, carved on a totem pole. Were giant bird sightings inspired by the Thunderbird legend or could it be vice versa?

The 1838 report of an eagle that carried off French five-year-old Marie Delex is not unique, although scientists estimate an eagle's maximum load at c.12lb (5.4kg).

"It was like something in a horror film . . . Red eyes. Black mouth. It was very big with great big wings and black claws." A child witness's drawing of the Owlman. This apparition took place in Cornwall, England, in 1976.

The potent image of the giant bird appears again, 100yd (90m) long, in one of the mysterious Nazca lines, huge drawings in the Nazca desert, Peru. Visible only from above, it seems to have been drawn for the eyes of the gods alone.

❑ According to the *Tombstone Epitaph* of April 26, 1890, two Arizona cowboys found a winged monster in the desert: a huge alligator-headed snake with skeletal clawed wings spanning 160ft (49m). Apparently sick or wounded, it flew only a short distance before sinking to the ground, where the cowboys promptly shot it. The report may have been one of the hoaxes popular in the press of the time – but perhaps not.

THE JERSEY DEVIL

❑ In January 1909 a winged monster known as the Jersey Devil (above) terrorized New Jersey. Witnesses told of a "what-is-it" with wings, four legs ending in hoofs, reptilian skin, and a horrible cry. One man thought its head like that of a horned ram; another said it had a horse's face on a collie dog's head! Within a few days it had been seen in more than 30 towns and left hoofed footprints in the snow – before vanishing as mysteriously as it had appeared.

Werewolves and their kin

For all their reputation, flesh and blood wolves rarely attack people. Zoologists ascribe most verified attacks to rabid animals or wolf-dog hybrids: most wolves have more to fear from humans than vice versa.

Worldwide belief in shape-changers – people who can take the form of animals – may stem from the totem animals mystically associated with tribal groups. Most shape-changers are malevolent, often cannibalistic. In Africa *gluka simba* (man-lions) feast on human flesh, and Leopardmen, dressed in leopard skins with metal claws, committed ritual murder until recent years. Old Mexico had a similar cult based on the jaguar; in Asia maneating tigers were thought to be men in tiger shape. Native Americans and Canadian Inuits tell of Werebears and Werewolves. In Europe the Werewolf has ancient origins: Rome's founders, Romulus and Remus, traditionally suckled by a she-wolf, may have belonged to a Werewolf cult. In the Middle Ages Werewolves were dreaded as servants of the Devil. In its human form, a Werewolf might be betrayed by eyebrows that met, crooked fingers or claw-like nails, pointed ears, hair on the palms of the hands, a vestigial tail, or hair on the inside of the skin (some suspects died under examination for this sign). In wolf shape, he or she might be extra large and savage or of unusual color. The plainest proof was to wound a wolf, then find a human with the same injury: in many stories a hunter cuts off a wolf's paw – and later finds his wife trying to hide her severed hand. Defense against a Werewolf included naming Christ; calling it three times by its baptismal name (French-Canada); or, as all "creature feature" buffs know, shooting it with a silver bullet. But not all Werewolves are wholly evil. Giraldus Cambrensis (1147-1220) tells of a Celtic priest who in pity gave the sacrament to a dying Werewolf; medieval tales of King Arthur feature Werewolves such as the knight Bisclavret and King Gorlagon as heroes.

In the 1760s, a wolf nicknamed the Beast of Gevaudan, which killed at least 60 people in France, was thought to be a Werewolf until an ordinary bullet ended its reign of fear.

A more positive image of the wolf, the she-wolf suckling Rome's legendary founders, Romulus and Remus, may be a relic of an early Werewolf cult.

Unlike Hollywood Werewolves, which retain a basically human appearance, the medieval version in wolf form looked just like the real thing.

❏ A person might become a Werewolf by wearing a magic wolf skin; using an ointment; eating wolf flesh or using a cup made from a wolf's skull; eating the herb wolfbane; or rolling naked in sand at the full moon. The change might be involuntary: Werewolf blood might be inherited, or acquired as a curse when one offended the gods (or, later, a saint); or accidental: drinking from a stream where a wolf had drunk, or being bitten by a rabid wolf. Direct transmission of the taint by a Werewolf's bite – as in horror movies – is a fairly recent addition.

❏ Doctors recognize a rare medical condition, lycanthropy (or zoanthropic paranoia), in which the victim imagines himself to be an animal (typically a wolf) and has an appetite for human flesh.

❏ The Vikings – ''sea wolves'' to victims of their raids – were familiar with shape-changers. Sorcerers were held to take on animal form: one was the 9th century warrior Kveld-Ulf, whose name means ''Evening Wolf.'' The term ''berserk,'' now used for anyone who runs amok, was applied to Viking warriors who fell into a killing frenzy in battle: it meant ''bear-shirt'' and signified one who became like a savage bear.

❏ A Norman chronicle claims that unpopular King John of England (reigned 1199-1216) was not only a bad king but also a Werewolf.

Risen from the tomb

Legends of the "un-dead," who rise at night from their tombs to feast on the blood of the living, are common to all ages and cultures. Most Vampires of folklore are female. Ancient Greeks and Romans feared the Lamia, half woman-half snake; the Aztecs whispered of Itzpapalotl, a blood-hungry butterfly; and the Langsuir of Malaysia and Bruxas of Portugal are woman-headed birds. The Jigar-khor of India is a witch who eats human livers, while Denmark's Mara is a beautiful sorceress who seduces male victims. Medieval Europeans believed Vampires were the risen corpses of suicides or murderers, and as late as the 19th century such persons were often buried at crossroads and "staked down" in their graves. Irish novelist Bram Stoker (1847-1912) based his classic *Dracula* (1897) on European legend. He took the name from 15th century Walachian (Romanian) ruler Vlad IV Dracula (son of the dragon), said to have executed some 26,000 persons by impaling them on sharp stakes, and drew also on tales of Hungarian Countess Elizabeth Bathory, who tried to preserve her youth and beauty by bathing in the blood of virgin girls. Condemned in 1614 for 60 (some accounts say 600) murders, she died of slow starvation after being walled up in her castle. Dracula and its many spinoffs have formed our modern image of the Vampire: a strangely attractive male with hypnotic powers, who may be able to change shape to that of a bat. He fears the crucifix, garlic, and running water, and can be destroyed only by staking with wood or iron, beheading, or exposure to sunlight. Has the legend a base in reality? It may date from medieval plagues that caused catalepsy (a trance state resembling death). Sufferers may have escaped from shallow graves to the terror of the living. More recently, a rare medical condition has been found to give some persons a taste for blood.

Prince Vlad Tepes, "Vlad the Impaler" (from his favored method of torture; in background) enjoyed watching his enemies chopped into pieces.

British actor Christopher Lee, "tall, dark, and gruesome" (the title of his autobiography), seen here in *The Scars of Dracula* (1970), is famed for his portrayals of the Count.

Bram Stoker, writer and theatrical impresario, said that his novel *Dracula* was inspired by a nightmare caused by a seafood supper.

The vampire bat (about 3.5in/9cm long) uses its sharp incisors to feed on mammals' blood. It is a carrier of rabies.

FACT FILE

❏ When Demetrious Myiciura, a Polish immigrant in England, was found dead in bed in 1973, a police surgeon reported he had choked to death while eating a pickled onion. But neighbors testified that the elderly East European had been terrified of Vampires. His room was littered with salt and garlic, and further examination showed that he had choked while sleeping with a garlic clove in his mouth, for added protection against the threat of the un-dead.

❏ One of the most effective portrayals of Dracula was that of Hungarian-born Bela Lugosi (1882-1956). His stage performance in New York in 1927 was said to be so scary that medics stood by to treat members of the audience, and he played the part in movies in 1931-48. His later life was a tragedy of drug abuse. When he died, he was buried in the black cloak, lined with scarlet satin, that he had worn in his most famous role.

❏ An American girl called Theodosia Goodman (1890-1955) became the world's best-known Vampire in the 1910s-20s. As a star of silent movies, she was hyped as a man-eating sex goddess, with the screen name Theda Bara (anagram: "Arab death"). The word "vamp" (short for "Vampire") entered and has remained in the English language to mean the kind of character she portrayed.

Zombie: the walking dead

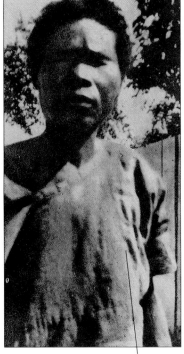

This photograph of Zombie Felicia Felix-Mentor was taken at a Haitian hospital in 1936 – 29 years after her death and burial in 1907.

In contrast to the cunning, "un-dead" Vampire, the Zombie of Haiti is the "walking dead," a human robot. It is claimed that Haitian *bokors* (Voodoo sorcerers) can call fresh corpses from the grave, after taking possession of their souls at the moment of death, and make them mindless slaves. It may be done for revenge (the *bokor* might reanimate a woman who has spurned him) or for profit from cheap labor. Like other aspects of Voodoo, a belief that arose among black slaves brought to the Caribbean, the word comes from Africa. Zumbi was the python-god of Dahomey: in Haiti the snake-god Damballah is called on to help raise the corpse. The Zombie, recognizable from its blank face, staggering walk, and halting speech, has neither memory of the past nor knowledge of the present: those who recognize Zombies as former relatives or friends are unable to evoke any response. Only if it is allowed to taste salt will it realize its fate – and return to its grave. When belief in Zombies was strongest in Haiti, elaborate precautions were taken against graverobbing *bokors*.

The rich built strong tombs and paid for the grave to be guarded until the corpse had decayed beyond raising; the poor often deliberately mutilated or dismembered corpses before burial. Now Zombies are sometimes faked for tourists, but there is too much evidence to dismiss them all as a myth. Some say they are the product of drugs. The *bokor* secretly administers a poison – datura, a plant extract, and tetrodotoxin, from fish, are specified – that causes serious brain damage and puts the victim into a deathlike trance. After burial he is dug up and revived with another drug (a stimulant secreted by the New World toad *Bufo marinus*), which gives great physical strength.

Like Vampires, Zombies have featured in many horror movies. Here, one of the walking dead struggles up from his grave in the British feature *The Plague of the Zombies* (1966) – set, surprisingly, not in Haiti, but in rural England.

The fire burning in a cemetery at Port-au-Prince, Haiti, has been lit by a *houngan* (Voodoo priest) to summon Baron Samedi (also called Ghede), god of death, to help him in healing a worshiper.

Those who take part in Voodoo ceremonies may be possessed by powerful spirits. Here, a devotee gripped by fire god Ogoun (derived from Nigerian deity Ogun) wallows in mud.

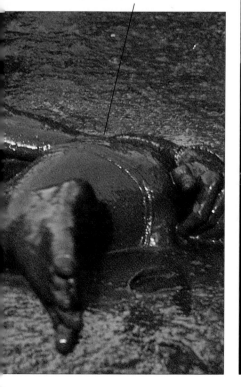

FACT FILE

❏ Some say that to achieve power a *bokor* must undertake to supply the forces of evil with an agreed number of souls (by making Zombies) each year. Should he fail to fill his quota, he himself becomes a Zombie.

❏ Voodoo mixes Christian and pagan beliefs, and its temples feature images of Christian saints (above). The serpent-god Damballah is often represented by St. Patrick – who according to legend drove all snakes out of Ireland.

❏ Tetrodotoxin, a drug said to be used in making Zombies, is found in the tissues of the blowfish. In small doses it is a potent anesthetic; in large ones, it causes out-of-body experiences, brain damage, and eventually death. In Japan the blowfish (*fugu*) is considered a gourmet delicacy and a sexual stimulant. Specialist *fugu* restaurants employ expert chefs and charge huge prices – but every year several cases are recorded of patrons paralyzed or killed by the deadly treat.

Man-made monsters

We need monsters, even if only to give harmless expression to the darker side of our personalities. Thus, as well as the real (or possibly real) monsters described elsewhere in this book, fiction writers and, more recently, movie makers, have been tireless in inventing new ones. Perhaps the most famous is the nameless, humanoid, "undying monster" built by Victor Frankenstein from human spare parts. Like the Golem of Jewish legend – a huge clay figure brought to life by inscribing the Hebrew word *emeth* (truth) on its forehead; deactivated by removing the letter "e" to leave *meth* (he is dead) – Frankenstein's creation is what we now call an android. *Frankenstein: or The Modern Prometheus* (1818) is a book almost everyone knows of but few read, for the prose style of Mary Wollstonecraft Shelley (1797-1851) is not to modern taste. But it is a milestone in horror fiction, uniting two factors that still dominate such works: distrust of scientists who aim at godlike powers; and sexual unease ("I shall be with you on your wedding night," the monster warns Frankenstein – and makes good the threat). Mary Shelley has Frankenstein inspired to create artificial life by reading the 16th century scientist Paracelsus, who claimed to have grown a homunculus (miniature human) from human semen, first buried in a magnetized jar, then unearthed and nourished with human blood. Another memorable humanoid monster, a triumph for Hollywood's makeup experts, is the Gill Man of *Creature From the Black Lagoon* (1954). Non-human, but far more sympathetic than the humanoid horrors, is the giant ape *King Kong*: the 1933 movie stands out in being both a spectacular "creature feature" and a touching cross-species love story.

The Hebrew letters on the scroll on the Golem's forehead will either set it in action or stop its movement.

194

In his most famous role, actor Boris Karloff (1887-1969), as the "undying monster," menaces Mae Clarke, playing his creator's bride, in the 1931 movie *Frankenstein*.

Mary Shelley wrote more weird tales – including *The Last Man* (1826) about a worldwide plague – but *Frankenstein*, written at 21, remains her most famous work.

An invocation bound to the handle of an awl indicates that the skull is intended to work evil. The clay Golem beside it is a tiny figure: such "robots" are traditionally giants.

Medieval magicians tried to "grow" homunculi (tiny humans). They failed – unlike the "mad scientist" (actor Ernest Thesiger) in the movie classic *The Bride of Frankenstein* (1935).

An Australian Aboriginal bark painting shows strange creatures of the "Dreamtime."

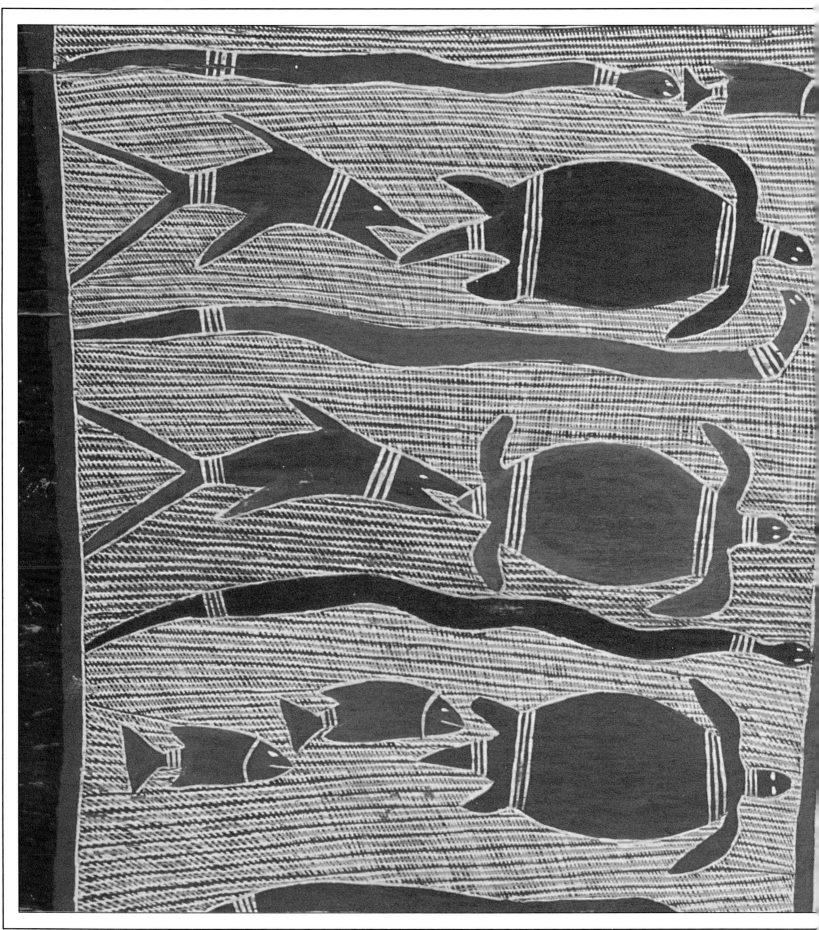

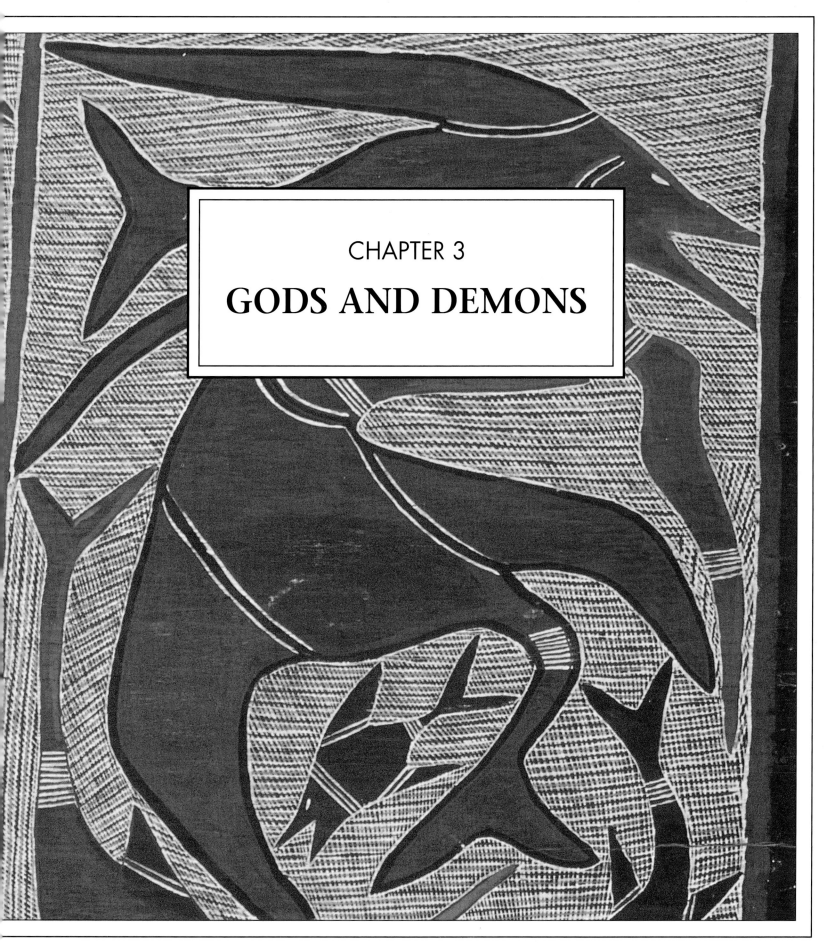

CHAPTER 3
GODS AND DEMONS

Religious mysteries and miracles

To some readers it may seem strange, even wrong, that the first part of this chapter should deal with some of the beliefs of Christianity and other religions. The answer lies in examining the original meaning of the word "mystery." It derives from the Greek words *mystos* (keeping silence) and *myein* (with closed eyes or lips). In the ancient world – in Babylon, Egypt, Greece, Rome, and elsewhere – the gods were worshiped through "mysteries": groups of worshipers who formed secret societies to preserve the purity of their

beliefs. "Mystery" came also to mean the truth of religious belief itself: the inner, central truth, which humans can never fully understand intellectually, but can know only through divine revelation. It is these "mysteries" that the first part of this chapter examines.

Christianity is a late comer among the world's great religions, senior only to the Islamic faith. And just as Islam adopted some aspects of Christianity, such as belief in the Hebrew prophets and in Angels, so Christianity was influenced by the beliefs of the ancient world. It is not to belittle Judeo-Christian beliefs that I have tried to show the connections between, for example, Persia's Ahura Mazda and Christianity's God the Father; between Mesopotamian and Babylonian heroes and the Biblical Noah. Rather it is to show that all religions that seek to raise up humanity tend towards similar "mysteries."

The peoples of the ancient world were closer than modern ones are to nature, so it is not surprising that their gods often represented the most powerful natural forces they knew, from the Sun, Moon and other heavenly bodies to such strong or supposedly wise animals as the bull or serpent. This chapter explains some of their beliefs, and although some of the more peculiar aspects

The people of ancient Babylon feared Lilitu (who later appeared in the *Old Testament* as Lilith), a female demon who, as her attendant owls suggest, flew through the night sky to whip up storms and work evil.

of their many cults are described, this does not mean that they should be mocked. But while preserving respect for all religions, the chapter shows how some, like those of Egypt and Greece, tended to let the outward mysteries – the cults and legends – obscure the inner, spiritual ones.

The ancient Egyptians identified lion-headed Sekhmet, wife of the god Ptah, with the merciless heat of the Sun and made her a goddess of war and conquest.

Demons tear out the eyes of the damned: a 14th century artist's vision of Hell – a very real place for most Christians until very recent times.

Our Lady of Czestochowa, southern Poland, traditionally painted from life by St. Luke, is among the most famous of the world's many miracle-working Black Madonnas.

Miracle cures have occurred at the shrine of St. Cecilia at Trastevere, Rome – although she is now considered a legendary rather than real martyr of the early Church.

In examining the beliefs that their ancestors held on such subjects as Angels and demons, readers must remember that their faith was simpler, and perhaps deeper. To them Heaven and Hell were real places, that could be described in detail and even mapped. Modern readers may think of them as superstitious – yet many people still believe in miracles, as the examination of modern Madonna cults and stigmatics shows. And what harm is there even in disputed miracles, such as the famous Turin Shroud or Our Lady of Knock (both of which skeptics dismiss as tourist attractions), if they help to focus our attention on spiritual rather than material things?

Wise folk and witches

In contrast to the universal aspects of religious belief covered in the first part of this chapter, the second part begins with an examination of more localized beliefs and practices. They range from the old Druidic religion of the Celts of Western Europe to the mystical beliefs still held by some Aboriginal peoples in Australia; from the often bloody cults of the Vikings of Scandinavia and of Central and South American peoples before the European conquest to the animistic (based on nature) beliefs of traditional Japan and of Native American societies.

Western witches were said to use poppets (French: *poupée*; doll), like this 19th century British example, to call down curses on the people in whose images they were made.

A shaman (witch doctor) performs a ceremony. Such traditional healers and seers are found in many lands: this "wise man" is at work in the Republic of Suriname, northeast South America.

Again, while not neglecting what are (to us) the stranger, and sometimes repellent, aspects of these beliefs, this chapter tries to show how much genuine religious feeling they embodied. Until quite recently it was common for so-called educated or advanced people to dismiss the shamans (wise men and women; prophets and healers) of such groups as the Inuit, Native Americans and, especially, the peoples of Black Africa, as medicine men or witch doctors – terms that carry with them the suggestion of primitive superstition or trickery. Today, people are becoming aware that the traditional wisdom, in particular herbal lore, and meditation and mind expansion techniques, preserved by such societies may help cure some of the evils of "advanced" societies.

A leading exponent of New Age ideas, actress Shirley MacLaine (b.1934) is also well known for her writings on reincarnation and out of body experiences.

Meditating in the Lotus posture, a girl seeks oneness with the universal spirit through the ancient Indian discipline of yoga (Sanskrit: *yog*; union).

An Aztec mask based on a human skull, overlaid with a mosaic of turquoise. This gem stone symbolized water and sky; only jade was more highly prized.

power of the Devil. But in the wrong hands, or in the wrong circumstances, the most innocent belief may be perverted. Germany's Nazis made use of occult beliefs and symbols in their climb to power; modern tyrants such as Haiti's Papa Doc Duvalier and some African dictators have held power by exploiting the religious beliefs of their peoples. Farther back in history, as is shown in the final part of this chapter, Muslim and Hindu cults were transformed to mass-murder movements, while in Europe and North America it was partly a reaction against free thinking, against harmless eccentrics who were judged to be a danger to society, that led to the execution of thousands of persons accused of witchcraft and the worship of Satan.

Some of this reevaluation of wisdom once ignored by the sophisticated West has been triggered by the growth of the New Age movement, ushered in, its enthusiasts tell us, by the dawning of the Age of Aquarius, a new period of spiritual growth. There is much to admire in New Agers' advocacy of respect for the Earth (Mother Gaia), in their true concern for the environment, and in their willingness to explore alternative medical techniques.

Taken to the extreme, however, New Ageism leads to an exaggerated respect for the weird and way-out – simply because it is weird and way-out. New Ageism tends towards cultism. There are, of course, many harmless modern cults: Wicca (modern "white" witchcraft) has, so far as is known, harmed no one; modern Satanism probably owes more to tabloid journalists than to the real

Fairies, sprites, and spooks

"All argument is against it; but all belief is for it." That was the view of the supernatural taken by the great 18th century thinker Dr. Samuel Johnson (whose investigation of a ghost with the splendid name of Scratching Fanny features with other ghostly tales in the last part of this chapter). He was, probably, right in thinking that most people wish to believe in the supernatural – but since Johnson's time the work of psychic researchers has provided many more arguments in

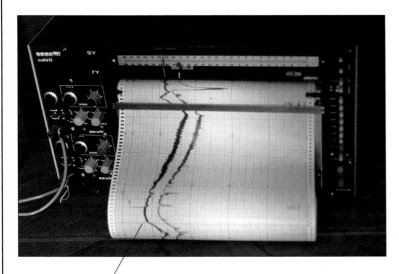

Hunting ghosts with modern technology: inexplicable changes in temperature were recorded when this machine was used to monitor an apartment plagued by poltergeists in Mulhouse, France.

favor of such belief.

With the mass of evidence gathered, it is hard to deny the existence of poltergeists: unseen but noisy spirits, perhaps created by pyschic energy released by troubled teenagers or disturbed persons, whose pranks sometimes take a sinister turn. The traditional ghost of Gothic fiction – the white-sheeted, moaning, chain-rattling spook – has become a comic cliché, but too many rational men and women have reported ghostly experiences for all such accounts to be dismissed as products of imagination.

Ghosts may be divided into two major categories: "hauntings" and "apparitions." Hauntings are appearances of persons known to be dead. They may be repeated many times over a period of years, even centuries, but tend gradually to fade with time. Some believe they are caused by mental imprints of violent events and great emotions; that such things are somehow "recorded" and may "play back" from time to time. Certainly, among the most commonly reported hauntings are the appearances of suicides, murder victims, and soldiers killed in battle.

More common, and perhaps more easily credited, are apparitions: single supernatural appearances of people who may be either dead or

still alive. Typically, the figure of a person at the point of death appears to tell a close relative or friend of the event, or to deliver a warning or message. Apparitions of the living, sometimes interpreted as unconscious telepathic messages that take on physical shape to the mind of the receiver, usually appear to loved ones at times of crisis.

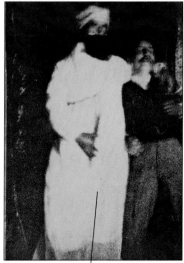

A photograph taken in 1878, at a Spiritualist séance where a medium called Eglington claimed to have materialized this figure in Arabic dress.

A headless "ghost dog," unseen by the photographer at the time, appeared in a picture taken by a retired British police inspector around 1916.

Joe Groombridge, while a member of the British army, had a typical experience of an apparition of a living person. Early in World War II, he was a tank driver with an armored unit in the North African desert campaign. In a skirmish near Tobruk, Libya, his tank was hit, and he was wounded and knocked unconscious. He came around to hear a voice calling: "Wake up, Dadda; you must wake up!" Through the driver's eye slot he saw the figure of his 4-year-old son Richard urging: "Get out, Dadda; get out quickly!" Joe dragged himself from the tank – a few seconds before it was hit again and erupted into a flaming ball of fire. As Joe said, it was probably his subconscious that told him that a stationary tank under heavy shellfire was no place to be; but he was certain that he had seen and heard Richard – who has absolutely no memory of the event.

God the Father: God the Mother

Humankind created gods in its own image. Perhaps the oldest portrayals are Stone Age Venuses, stylized statuettes of pregnant women with huge breasts, bellies, and thighs: the Mother Goddess at her most basic. From this crude image of maternity sprang the queenly goddesses of the ancient world: Phoenician Astarte, Phrygian Cybele, Babylonian Ishtar, Thracian Bendis, Cretan Rhea, and Egyptian Isis. Deities not just of fertility but of sexual love, most are models of female beauty, like Aphrodite of Greece. But the Goddess may also be super-feminine (many-breasted Diana of the Ephesians); part masculine (bearded Ishtar of Assyria, "lady of battles"); or even multiple (the Celtic trinity of Mothers). In many later cultures the Mother was forced to yield place as Supreme Being to a male Creator. But often the divine Father remained a background figure, while people gave more active worship to gods of fertility or war. Thus Mesopotamia's central deity was Baal (Lord), the young, virile rain god, not the aged, all-knowing supreme god El, while the Celts' "all-father," the Dagda (Good God), was a shadowy, even comic figure – a fat, greedy man. In Europe the sky god Dyaus Pitar (Divine One) replaced the Mother as Creator from about 2000 B.C. As Greek Zeus or Roman Jupiter he displays very human characteristics: ancient myths tell how the father of men often visited mortals – usually to seduce their women. In Northern Europe, the all-father was the wind god Odin. Like Zeus, Odin traveled among men; but this sinister, one-eyed figure, in great gray cloak and slouch hat, was an inconstant lord who often betrayed his followers. More enduring than any were the faceless gods of two religions that forbade the portrayal of Godhead: the Jews' Jehovah, and the Muslims' Allah.

In the Classical world the love goddess (Greek Aphrodite or Roman Venus) was an ideal of female beauty far removed from maternity – and a wanton, jealous, and vengeful deity who brought strife among gods and mortals alike.

The Israelite leader Moses saw God, not as a physical presence but represented by a burning bush. His people were among the first to conceive of a God without bodily form.

Christianity never quite destroyed the cult of the Celtic Mother Goddess. Across Britain, country churches feature her ugly yet powerful images, unrepentantly pagan and sometimes rampantly sexual.

This early bronze bust of a Canaanite fertility god (probably Baal) depicts Godhead via a simple phallic shape rather than as an image of human beauty.

Farmers in Canaan relied on the rain god Baal to fend off Mot, deity of death and sterility.

The life everlasting

"Don't mourn for me now, don't mourn for me never: I'm going to do nothing for ever and ever." The hardworked housewife's epitaph depicts Heaven simply as a place of rest. Many religions have held much the same view, seeing Heaven as a land of ease in reward for virtue and as compensation for life's hardships. For Ancient Egyptians it was a farmers' paradise, a fertile Land of the Blessed where nature's abundance meant no need to labor; Native American peoples looked to the Happy Hunting Grounds, a hunters' Heaven. The Islamic peoples of the arid Middle East saw Paradise as a perfect oasis garden, with rivers of pure water, milk, wine, and honey, where blessed souls relaxed in silken robes, served by beautiful maidens. Warlike Vikings aspired to Valhalla, Hall of the Slain: the ultimate banquet hall, with warm fires, unlimited pork and mead, and daily battles – from which the dead rose each night to join their slayers at the feast. Some religions took a more spiritual view. Buddhism and Hinduism see Heaven not as an end in itself but as part of the cycle of rebirth through which the soul passes. Indian Buddhists believe that souls progress through 26 Heavens. The lower ones offer sensual rewards: golden palaces equipped with every luxury from divine food to dancing girls. From these pleasures, souls graduate to higher Heavens of worship and meditation. The Heaven of Christianity is meant to be another spiritual one, of everlasting bliss in God's kingdom; but at various times it has been described in terms of more earthly rewards. Although Christians have never been offered concubines or alcohol in heaven, one of the delights they were promised by the medieval church was that of gloating, in most un-Christian spirit, over the pains of sinners in Hell below.

The Christian Paradise: an enchanted garden where men and women – and animals – return to the primeval innocence of Eden.

The Eight Immortals of China: sages who, Confucianists and Taoists believe, won the goal of the virtuous – not Heaven, but unity with Heaven and Earth as a perfected Immortal.

Far from the bustle of earthly life, perfected souls are freed from the curse of labor laid on Adam and Eve and their descendants.

Heaven rewards the just. Here the Prophet Muhammad ascends to a warm welcome in Paradise, greeted by Angels laden with gifts, fine clothing, and banquet dishes.

Viking heroes expected to pay for afterlife hospitality in Valhalla by backing the gods in a cosmic battle at the end of the world.

They faced no ordinary foes, but the monstrous wolf Fenrisulfr, his brother the World Serpent, and a rampaging mob of fire giants.

Angelic hosts of Heaven

Gods such as Zeus and Odin had human characteristics, and often took earthly forms to interact directly with mortals. Not so the unseen deities of Judaism and Islam, Jehovah and Allah, who spoke to men through divine spirits called Angels (from the Greek word for messenger). *The Bible* tells how God sent Angels to halt Abraham's sacrifice of Isaac and to announce the coming of Jesus to Mary. Angels also form the Heavenly court, worshiping at God's throne. As pure spirits, they lack bodies, although convention depicts them in beautiful human form, with wings and white robes. The medieval Christian Church evolved an elaborate Angelology: its scholars, addicted to classifying and counting, worked out a pecking order of ranks and functions. Most agreed on nine angelic orders: Seraphim, Cherubim, Thrones, Dominions, Virtues, Powers, Principalities, Archangels, and Angels. Highest ranking were Angels of the Presence, God's attendants: lower ranks tended to human affairs.

A blast on a trumpet by an Angel (Gabriel say Christians, but Muslims favor Israfel) will herald the Day of Judgment.

Theologians described a civil war in Heaven, when the Angel Lucifer led a rebellion against God – and was cast out, to become Satan. We are told that Angels visited early Christian saints and the Prophet of Islam, Muhammad. But today Angel visits are rare. The last major angelic intervention in human affairs was reported in 1914 in the London *Evening News*, which told (with eyewitness reports) how Angels appeared to hearten British troops in the desperate action at Mons, Belgium, early in World War I. Years later, author Arthur Machen revealed that it had been a propaganda stunt based on his short story telling how the spirits of bowmen from Agincourt (Britain's great victory in France in 1415) had come to fight alongside their descendants. But even soldiers who had themselves fought at Mons credited the story and later swore that they had seen Angels.

Modern ideas of Angels as graceful, winged beings largely stem from paintings by masters such as Simone Martini, who portrayed the Archangel Gabriel in this *Annunciation* of c.1333.

The Archangel Michael appears in The *Bible's* *Old* and *New* *Testaments.*

❏ A famous naturalist calculated that an Angel the size of a man, with a body weight of around 160lb (73kg), would need wings with a total span of about 16ft (5m) in order to fly. To keep aloft it would need to beat these wings once every second, which would call for pectoral (chest) muscles at least three times stronger than those of the average weightlifter.

❏ Of Christianity's seven Archangels, only Michael and Gabriel (above) are mentioned by name in The *Bible*. Raphael appears in the *Apocrypha*, the books added to some editions. The names of Uriel, Chamuel, Jophiel, and Zadkiel were assigned by early theologians following ancient Hebrew usage.

❏ The servants of the Norse god Odin were not Angels but animals: his information-gathering ravens Huginn and Muninn (Thought and Memory), and his eight-legged horse Sleipnir. But he also had his messengers to men: warrior-maiden Valkyries (Choosers of the Slain) whom he sent to battlefields to pick out those of the dead who merited a place in his hall.

Michael, traditionally the "captain of the heavenly host," is seen weighing out human souls on Judgment Day in a 15th-century painting.

Angels in an old Persian manuscript: the Muslim faith shares with Christianity a belief in Angels, who visited the Prophet Muhammad.

The Blessed Virgin is at first alarmed by the angelic messenger's news that she is to bear the Son of God.

The legions of the damned

The Devil we know – horned, hoofed, smelling of sulfur, and black as Satan – was designed by Pope Gregory the Great (c.540-604). But his roots are much older, going back to Ahriman (Destructive Thought), Persian god of evil and forebear of Judaism's Satan. Unlike Ahriman, Satan was no equal rival to God, but an adversary temporarily tolerated as part of the divine plan. Christianity inherited and developed this idea, giving the Evil One attributes from a range of pagan gods. Pope Gregory borrowed the horns and hoofs of the Greek god Pan, Roman Vulcan's lameness and Saturn's blackness, and Norse Thor's beard and sulfuric smell. Other gods, mostly those of Old Testament times, such as Beelzebub, Asmodeus, and Astaroth, provided the names for Satan's demon followers. Satan himself was identified with the rebel Angel Lucifer, who led a war in Heaven and was cast out to Hell with his followers. By the 14th century he was seen as the Archenemy of God and man, aided and abetted by demons "as numerous as bees" (calculated variously by medieval Catholic churchmen as between 7,405,926 and 133,306,668) ranked in a hierarchy which aped the Church's. His portrait was expanded with lurid details of his anatomy and habits meant to frighten people into virtue. This could work the wrong way: the powerful image drew some to devil-worship and witchcraft. Many tales tell how magicians strove to control demons, or signed pacts with the Devil, trading their souls for worldly wealth. Satanic cults still exist, though only a minority takes them seriously. To the Church, Satan's role, tempting mortals to sin and overseeing the torments of Hell, is simply part of God's plan: "The demons are our Lord's bailiffs, whom he hath set apart to exercise men," explained St. Francis of Assisi (1181-1226).

Many magicians have tried to call up demons to aid them. "Lucifuge Rofocale," as this medieval style illustration suggests, was invoked by those who hoped to find buried treasure.

Horrific demons and monsters people Hell in the fearsome vision of Pieter Breughel the Elder (c.1525-69).

A 12th century carving at the Church of San Zeno, Verona, Italy, shows Saint Zeno (d.c.372) exorcising a woman possessed by a demon – which is leaving by way of her mouth.

An Angel in medieval armor, presumably Archangel Michael, traditionally the leader of the heavenly host, heads the battle against the demons.

The painter meant these grotesque figures to represent the fallen Angels, cast into Hell for their revolt against God.

It is in this form, as the Sabbatic Goat, that the Devil is said to have joined witches at their meetings (Sabbats). The picture is based on a drawing by the famous French occultist Eliphas Lévi (1810-75).

The terrors of Hell

Many ancient religions never troubled to design elaborate afterworlds, but taught of an existence after death that can only be described as deathly dull. Their lands of the dead – like the ancient Greeks' Hades, or the old Hebrews' Sheol – were sad, dull, shadowy places where souls wandered aimlessly and endlessly. Later, more sophisticated creeds developed the idea of a place of punishment for souls. Late Judaism introduced Gehenna, a place of "gloomy fire always burning," named after the spot where Jerusalem's garbage was burned. Hinduism and some forms of Buddhism go much farther. Hindu scriptures tell of 100,000 Hells, each specifically made to punish a particular crime with horrid torments: souls are ground between millstones, cast onto knives, and so on. Buddhism also has many Hells equipped with fearful tortures: it is said that merely to describe them would take 100,000 years. But both Hinduism and Buddhism see existence as a never-ending cycle of rebirth; so punishment after death is severe, but not unending. When the soul has served its sentence, it is freed, to be reborn in a lower life form. Islam too promises sinners torment in Hell – but with an escape clause: Allah the All-Merciful pardons the sincerely repentant even in the midst of Hell. It was Christianity that took the horrors of Hell to their ultimate by making them eternal. The true Christian Hell is the spiritual agony of exile from God; but during the Middle Ages it was elaborated in ever more sadistic and grotesquely realistic terms. Then the Church aimed to terrorize people into virtue, and much of the artistic and literary ingenuity of the Middle Ages was devoted to picturing the cruelest afterworld of any world religion.

Mounted on a winged demon, the damned soul of a sinful woman is carried down to Hell: a grim warning from the Italian painter Luca Signorelli (1441-1523).

The damned souls are condemned to eternal torment. Hellfire was a real terror for most medieval people, and artist Hans Memling (c.1430-94) was probably no exception.

Bérenger Saunière (d.1917), the priest who designed this demon figure for his church at Rennes-le-Château, France, was said to have found a great treasure – perhaps with unholy aid – and to have died a millionaire.

Merciless demons, one in the form of an ape, inflict the punishment decreed by God. Such horrific pictures were intended to terrify people into good Christian behavior.

This bestial demon is from the *Infernal Dictionary* of French demonologist Collin de Plancy (1793-1887), an expert in the field.

Taloned hands and feet, tail, and leopard's head characterize the minor demon Flauros.

FACT FILE

❏ The ancient Greek underworld (below), realm of Hades, was a desolate land ringed by five rivers, including the (mythical) Styx and (real) Acheron. The dead were buried with a coin to pay the ferryman – or they would wander the banks of Acheron forever. By classical times, Hades incorporated judgment after death: the good were rewarded by bliss in the Elysian Fields; the sinners punished in Tartarus.

❏ Norse warriors believed that souls not chosen to enter Valhalla went to a desolate land ruled by the goddess Hel. The destination of a person's soul did not depend on living a virtuous life, but on how the person died. Death by violence – in battle or as a sacrifice – was the way to Valhalla. Death from sickness or old age led the soul to Hel's bleak realm.

❏ Medieval clerics studied Hell's geography. A German divine stated that 100 billion souls, packed tightly, would fit into a cubic mile. Perhaps the Jesuit Cornelius à Lapide used similar figures to work out that Hell was only 200 Italian miles wide.

Holy Mother and Holy Son

Although Church authorities are reluctant to endorse them and skeptics speak of mass hallucinations, there are many well-attested reports of apparitions of the Virgin Mary and of miraculous images of her. Weeping, bleeding, or moving Madonnas are reported worldwide, ranging from icons in ancient European churches to plaster statuettes in U.S. mobile homes. Her most famous appearances have been in 1858 at Lourdes, France, where she revealed healing waters to St. Bernadette, and at Fátima, Portugal, in 1917. There, although only three peasant girls saw her, about 70,000 persons witnessed a meteorological phenomenon (dance of the Sun) she had promised. It is said that the Virgin of Fátima made a revelation, for the Pope's ears only, foretelling global catastrophe and that in 1960 Pope John XXIII told Vatican officials it made him "weak with horror." Manifestations of the Virgin's Holy Son include the stigmata (Greek: brands), wounds like those of the crucified Christ, that appear on some holy persons. Padre Pio (1887-1968), an Italian monk, bled from hands, feet, and side from 1918 until his death – when the wounds vanished. Sister Elena Aiello

The holy love of the Mother for her Child is so miraculously portrayed by artists like Botticelli that it is no wonder millions have sought the Blessed Virgin's aid.

(d.1961), another Italian monastic, bled from her hands. Blood spots on the wall of her room formed a face of Christ that itself exuded blood that tests showed to be human. It has been suggested that stigmata are caused by autosuggestion, from within the stigmatic's own mind: in the case of monastics, from their long contemplation of Christ's agonies. Skeptics say that just as most apparitions of the Virgin are to young girls, who describe her conventionally as a young, beautiful woman in blue robes, so stigmata appear on the palms and soles – where Christ is traditionally shown as being nailed – rather than on wrists and ankles, where the nails would have been driven in a Roman crucifixion.

The hands of Antonio Ruffini (seen here in 1987) have borne stigmata since he had a vision of the Virgin near Rome in 1951.

Believers worldwide say that many images of the Virgin, like this one in Brooklyn, N.Y., 1984, have wept for sinful, suffering humanity.

A Brazilian Black Madonna. In Europe, some dark-skinned images of the Virgin are said to be miracle working.

Teresa Neumann of Bavaria, Germany, received the stigmata after a vision in 1926. Every Friday until her death in 1962 she bled from hands, side, feet, and forehead.

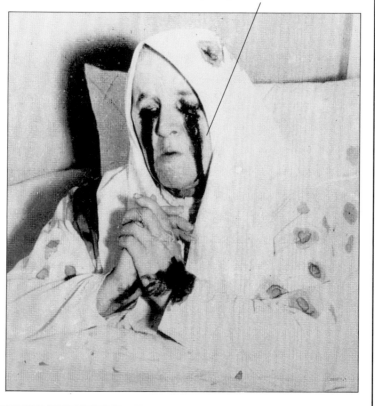

❑ Worried by huge crowds flocking to Padre Pio (above) and by large sums sent him by admirers (he was released from his vow of poverty, but gave all donations to charity), the Catholic Church twice suspended Padre Pio from religious duties. As well as a stigmatic, he was a clairvoyant and healer. Tests showed that in trance state his body temperature rose to 118.4°F.(48°C.). Calls for his canonization are opposed by some Church authorities.

215

Gods of ancient empires

Pazuzu, a demon feared by the Assyrians, who dominated the area of Mesopotamia in c.1300-600 B.C. They worshiped the goddess Ishtar.

Like the demons of traditional Christian belief, Pazuzu is shown with claws, wings, and horns.

Historians call Mesopotamia's Tigris-Euphrates Valley the cradle of civilization. It saw the first farmers in c.8000 B.C., the earliest towns, and, by c.3500 B.C., the sophisticated Sumerian Empire. The development of writing in Sumer allows us knowledge of some of humanity's first gods, handed down by Sumer to the successive empires of Akkadia (after c.2300 B.C.) and Babylon (from c.1990 B.C.). The deities are those of a farming culture dependent on rivers and honor the powers of nature. At the center of the ancient empires' pantheon were neither Mother Goddess nor Sky-Father – but gods who, tiring of tilling the soil and digging canals, created mortals to do it for them. A huge family of gods was ruled by three great ones: heaven-god An; air-god Enlil; and mother-goddess Ninhursag. Enlil ruled the land where people worked: his chief gift to humanity was the pickax, the tool that built canals and cities. Babylon kept Sumer's basic theology, but made a local god Marduk (bull calf of the sun) its chief deity. Sumer's Creation Myth was expanded into Babylon's epic *Poem of Creation* (known from its opening as *Enuma elish*; When on high) in which Marduk became the Creator who slew the ocean-dragon to form Heaven and Earth from her body. Its importance is apparent from the large number of copies surviving, dating from c.900-200 B.C. Mesopotamian myths have intriguing parallels with the *Old Testament*. The tale of the water god Enki, cursed by the mother goddess for eating forbidden plants in Dilmun (Paradise), recalls Adam's fall in Eden. Another myth tells how the gods punished humanity with a worldwide Flood and how the virtuous Ziusudra, warned by Enki, built a boat and preserved his family, like Noah.

Marduk, champion of the gods, is seen in combat with Tiamat, whom he slew, in an illustration based on an ancient Assyrian carving showing the story of the Creation.

Symbols of sun god Shamash, moon god Sin, and another Mesopotamian deity are at the head of a Babylonian stele (memorial tablet) of around the 9th century B.C.

Tiamat, the fearsome, female dragon of Babylonian myth, lived in the salt water of the ocean. The people of Mesopotamia recognized this as the original source of all life.

Babylonian script: the art of writing was first developed in Mesopotamia c.5,000 years ago.

Fish-tailed Dagon was the sea god of the Philistines from c.1200 B.C. He is sometimes quite wrongly identified with the Mesopotamian fertility god, Dagan.

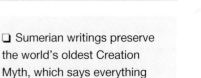

FACT FILE

❑ Sumerian writings preserve the world's oldest Creation Myth, which says everything sprang from the ocean. Scientists today also believe life began in the seas, but they speak of a "primal soup" of chemical elements rather than Sumer's sea goddess Nammu or Babylon's monstrous ocean-dragon Tiamat.

❑ Mesopotamia's gods were generally depicted in human form. An exception was the Babylonian water god Ea – part man, part fish – who came from the sea to teach people farming, writing, laws, and crafts. His fish aspect may stem from the Sumerian water god Enki, whose priests wore fish costumes.

❑ Sumerians and Babylonians, like later peoples, saw the natural dwelling place of gods as mountains. Faced with the flat plains of Mesopotamia, they tried to make the gods feel at home by raising ziggurats (above): temples on platforms of mud bricks.

Gilgamesh, the first superhero

In 1857 scholars cracked the code of Babylonian cuneiform ("wedge shaped writing," from its symbols) and began to read texts from ancient Mesopotamia. Soon they deciphered clay tablets of the 7th century B.C. from the Assyrian royal library of Nineveh and rediscovered the world's first bestseller, the *Epic of Gilgamesh*. Gilgamesh was king of the Sumerian city of Uruk, c.2700 B.C. Tradition says he rebuilt Uruk – probably true, since he reigned in Sumer's great age of temple-building – and the survival of his name alone tells us he was a ruler whose works and personality were extraordinary. There history ends and myth begins. The mythic Gilgamesh is no mortal king but the most glorious of the heroes; the epic, far from factual biography, explores the ageless theme of man's dread of death. Gilgamesh is a superhero, son of a goddess and a mortal man. At the outset he has yet to control his semidivine nature: he slays young men and ravishes women. He is transformed when the gods create a fit companion for him: Enkidu, the wild man, who must be tamed to become the hero's inseparable friend. Together they perform great feats, destroying the giant Humbaba and the monstrous Bull of Heaven. Then death claims Enkidu. Gilgamesh, alone again, realizes, "What my brother is now, that shall I be when I am dead," and sets out on a quest for immortality. He almost succeeds: at last, and inevitably, he fails. Returning to Uruk, he recognizes that death is the destiny for all: the only immortality is fame, by which a person's name lives on. The story of Gilgamesh's heroic yet doomed quest spoke directly to Mesopotamia's embattled peoples. It was retold through successive empires, over more than seven centuries: versions survive in Sumerian, Old Babylonian, Hittite, Hurrian, Akkadian, and Assyrian.

Sumerian superman Gilgamesh, hero of the world's first great epic, carries a lion in an 8th century B.C. carving from the palace of Sargon II, at Khorsabad, modern Iraq.

Gligamesh was ruler of Uruk (modern Erech, Iraq) in c.2700 B.C. This gold dagger from nearby Ur dates from around the same period.

An intricate scabbard provides a fitting sheath for so precious a weapon.

A gold bull's head with beard of lapis lazuli, found at Ur, is mounted on a reconstructed stringed instrument of the time.

Court musicians at Uruk and other Sumerian cities used instruments like this lyre (harp), carved with gods and heroes, to sing the praises of Gilgamesh and other rulers.

Goddess Ishtar (Astarte), seen here on an 8th century B.C. relief, was angry when Gilgamesh refused her offer of love and set the monstrous Bull of Heaven on him.

❏ Biblical scholars were astounded to find in the *Epic of Gilgamesh* a Flood myth comparable to that in *Genesis*. Utnapishtim, parallel to Biblical Noah, tells Gilgamesh how the gods punished mankind with a Flood and how he was warned by the god Enki to build an Ark (below) to save himself and his family. The story's details match those of *Genesis*: historians believe both reflect ancient tribal memory. But the conclusion differs: instead of God's covenant with his servant Noah, there is a dispute among the gods.

❏ Some scholars see the story of Enkidu as an allegory of human progress from savagery to civilization. He begins as a wild man, living with beasts. When frightened locals engage a city harlot to seduce him, the animals reject him. Gradually, he enters the world of men, first as a shepherd, finally entering the city of Uruk to become a hero. But on his deathbed he looks back to his old, wild life and curses those who educated him.

Egypt's cult of the dead

"Die not a second time" was a popular slogan on ancient Egyptian coffins, and no culture has invested more in the afterlife. The resolve of Egyptians not to miss out on life after death created a vast embalming industry, a handbook for departed souls (the *Book of the Dead*), and the world's most famous tombs, the Pyramids. Egyptians believed that the spirits of the dead needed their bodies as a kind of base camp: hence mummification (a statue or portrait was used if the corpse was lost). An inspirational cult was that of the god Osiris, murdered by his brother Seth, then restored to become judge and ruler of the dead. The funeral of Osiris, carried out by jackal-headed Anubis, was the model for complex burial rites, including the ceremony of Opening the Mouth to allow dead persons to use their bodily senses in the afterlife. They were buried with protective amulets, food and household goods, and the *Book of the Dead* – a guide for the journey to the afterworld, containing spells to help surmount the many obstacles on the way and to ward off demons. For the corpse's greater security, royal tombs evolved in the Old Kingdom period (c.2475-2134 B.C.) into pyramids of increasing size and splendor, culminating in the Great Pyramid of Cheops (Khufu), one of Seven Wonders of the Ancient World. It took 50,000 workmen all 23 years of Cheops's reign to build – for it used some 2,300,000 limestone blocks, weighing from 2.5 to 15 tons. But despite the effort to safeguard their rulers' bodies, some Egyptians either disbelieved the whole thing or cared nothing for the fate of the pharaohs' souls. Most pyramids were soon looted – by the laborers who built them or by professional tomb robbers – and the carefully prepared mummies stripped and smashed.

Enduring for millennia, the pyramids of Egypt are a lasting reminder of the ancient civilization's cult of the dead.

A bronze figure from Bubastis (near modern Zagazig), center of her cult in ancient Egypt, shows the Moon goddess Bastet as a cat.

The *Book of the Dead*, laying down what must done to ensure life after death, was buried with every notable person.

Ram-headed Sphinxes line an avenue in the great temple complex at Luxor (Al Uqsor; ancient Thebes). Sphinxes (Stranglers) were guardian figures in ancient Egypt.

Anubis, jackal-headed god of funerals, supports a pharaoh's mummy case as his wife, daughter, and servants look on in adoration.

❑ Mystics have theorized that the dimensions of the Great Pyramid foretell the future. One pyramidologist "read" its Grand Gallery as a record of the history of Christianity, with emphasis on the British Church – since, he said, it was built by a lost tribe of Israel, ancestors of the British race. Others claim pyramids have preservative powers, keeping bodies undecayed and food fresh. Scientists deny "pyramid power," but believers sit in model pyramids (above) to cure toothaches or calm the mind. In 1991 it was reported that members of the royal family had tried this New Age therapy.

❑ Expert mummification was a 70-day job: removing organs for separate burial in jars, drying the corpse with natron (a kind of rock salt), and cosmetic treatment that included mud packs under the skin to plump it out. Then the mummy was wrapped in up to 1.5mi (2.5km) of linen bandages. Later embalmers grew slipshod. Fine packaging often hid a body so ill-preserved it had fallen apart and been reassembled with pieces from other corpses.

Soap opera on Mount Olympus

The gods of ancient Greece and Rome were immortals with very human personalities – so human that classical myths read like divine soap opera. On Mount Olympus, the king of the gods, Greek Zeus or Roman Jupiter, headed a bickering family addicted to intrigue and adultery. Their interference in mortals'' affairs was arbitrary: aiding favorites; persecuting those who offended them. The Greeks hit a delicate balance between their humanized gods and religious belief. They enjoyed stories of sex and power, like that of blacksmith god Hephaistos catching his wife Aphrodite, goddess of love, in bed with her lover Ares, god of war. But they solemnly worshiped the same gods at temples, local shrines, and oracles. At last soap opera and faith proved incompatible. When Greek philosophers began to set reason against myth, even the death sentence passed on Socrates for impiety could not wipe out the influence of that "midwife of men's thoughts." In Rome the state religion became a political tool. It boosted Roman superiority over subject peoples by making the emperors gods – usually after their deaths, although the insane Caligula deified himself. But for those who sought something deeper, there were mystery cults, reserved for initiates. In Greece these included the secret rites of the agriculture goddess Demeter and the orgiastic feasts of wine god Dionysos, whose female followers, Maenads (wild women), were said to tear wild animals and even men to pieces. These uninhibited rites shocked Rome into banning the Dionysian cult in 186 B.C. and executing thousands of worshipers. But Rome had its own mystery religion, Mithraism, a cult of soldiers, for whom it was a secret society much like modern Freemasonry. Others in Rome turned to a new religion that also offered personal salvation: Christianity.

A statue of c.100 B.C., shows Aphrodite (Roman: Venus), goddess of love, as the period's ideal woman.

God of sexual love: Eros (Roman: Cupid), Aphrodite's son. Seen as a winged child, he is often shown with a bow and "arrows of desire."

A goat's legs and horns mark lustful Pan, god of pastures and herds. Angered, he struck humans with sudden fear: "panic."

❑ Animal sacrifices to the gods were made regularly, with special offerings in thanksgiving for special favors. This caused the Athenians some embarrassment after their victory at the battle of Marathon (490 B.C.). Before the battle, they promised the goddess Artemis as many goats as they slew Persians. The slaughter was so colossal that they did not have enough goats and had to pay off the goddess at the rate of 500 goats each year.

❑ The cult of the god Mithra (above), who brought fertility to the world by slaying a divine bull, came from Persia – brought to Rome, says historian Plutarch, in 67 B.C. by captured pirates. Lord of battles, Mithra had a special appeal to Roman soldiers, who spread his cult across the Empire. Mithraism had much in common with Christianity in both ethics and rituals – and seemed to Christians a Satanic travesty of their faith. Christianity won, but a Mithraic echo lingers in the date of Christmas Day: December 25 was the feast of Mithra's birth.

Poseidon (Roman: Neptune) was the god of the seas, armed with a magical trident made by the Cyclopes, a race of one-eyed giants.

Sky father Zeus (Roman: Jupiter), king of the gods and master of the weather, is portrayed as a handsome, mature man in this noble sculpture dating from the 5th century B.C.

A mosaic from the Roman city of Pompeii, destroyed by an earthquake in A.D. 79, portrays Demeter (Roman: Ceres), the goddess of Earth's fruitfulness.

The bull as god and monster

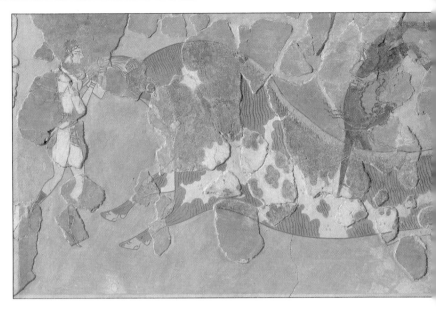

Our ancestors saw gods at work in the forces of nature. In many parts of the world they developed a cult of the bull: a beast whose strength and sexual potency impressed hunters and farmers alike. Its image figures much in Stone Age cave paintings in Europe and was immortalized on the walls of Babylon in 600 B.C. Slain by the god Mithra, it became the symbol of the Mithraic faith – equivalent to Christianity's Cross. In Egypt the bull was supreme among sacred animals – particularly the Apis bull, which was held to be the god Ptah incarnate and was housed royally in a temple at Memphis, with human servants and a harem of concubine cows. When it died, its successor was recognized by its markings. Another bull cult inspired the Greek myth of the hero Theseus and the Minotaur: a bull-headed monster, unnatural offspring of Pasiphae, wife of King Minos of Crete, by a bull. Minos kept this brute in an impenetrable maze, the Labyrinth, and demanded an annual tribute of 14 young Athenians to feed it. Theseus, son of King Aegeus of Athens, resolved to end the slaughter and went to Crete as one of the sacrificial victims. He killed the Minotaur, escaped from the maze, and sailed home triumphantly. Sadly, on his journey back he forgot to raise a signal to tell his father of his success. Aegeus, believing his son dead, killed himself before Theseus landed; Theseus succeeded him and is credited with founding Athenian democracy. In 1900, a historical basis for the legend emerged when British archeologist Sir Arthur

Evans discovered a vast Bronze Age palace at Knossos in Crete. Its rulers – perhaps including Minos himself – had left abundant evidence of a major bull cult, suggesting the origins of the mythical Minotaur, while the palace itself, with its maze of corridors and rooms, may well have been the original Labyrinth. Today, the bull cult endures only in bullfighting.

Generations of Apis bulls were worshiped by the ancient Egyptians as manifestations on Earth of the god Ptah. Here, an Apis bull carries the mummy of a deceased notable to the Hall of Judgment.

This wall painting from Knossos, center of the Minoan civilization of Crete, shows the famous bull leaping rites, in which youths and girls performed gymnastic feats over the backs of huge, sacred bulls.

Athens sent an annual tribute of human sacrifice to the Cretan Minotaur – until the hero Theseus slew the monster, as seen on this vase.

Legend tells how the god Poseidon, angry at King Minos, cursed his wife Pasiphae with unnatural love for a great bull sent by the god from the sea. She gave birth to the Minotaur, half man and half bull.

Europa of Tyre attracted the desire of Zeus, king of the gods. He carried her off to Crete, where he fathered on her Minos, founder of the Minoan civilization.

Zeus often took animal form to further his love affairs with mortals. To abduct Europa, he became a bull.

FACT FILE

❏ The Apis bull of Memphis was the greatest of Egypt's sacred bulls. Others included the Buchis bull of Armant – said to change color every hour – and the Mnevis bull of Heliopolis. Both were linked with the sun god Re (Ra). Feted in life, in death the bulls were embalmed and buried with the same pomp as pharaohs, with gilded heads, artificial eyes of stone or glass, and gilded crowns. The cows that bore the sacred bulls were also allotted special cemeteries.

❏ The symbol of the labyrinth appears in early European rock art of c.1000 B.C.; in Pompeii's graffiti; in early Christian iconography; and in medieval English turf mazes (above), used for races and games until the 19th century. British tradition knows the labyrinth symbol as Troy Town and links it with classical antiquity; some modern scholars regard it as a much older image of the maze of life.

❏ Bull leaping was long held to be an actual Cretan ritual with highly trained athletes and specially bred bulls; but modern rodeo experts say bull-leaping as portrayed in the art of Knossos is just not humanly possible.

225

Hercules: Superman of the ancient world

The Greek view of what made a god was elastic, stretching to include several mortal heroes who became demigods. Among them were Theseus of Athens; Perseus, who slew snake-haired Medusa the Gorgon; Jason, who led the quest for the Golden Fleece; Bellerophon, rider of the winged horse Pegasus; and Hercules (Herakles), the ancient world's Superman. Son of Zeus by a mortal, Hercules was blessed with superhuman strength – but cursed with the enmity of Zeus's wife, the goddess Hera. As a baby he thwarted her first attempt on his life, strangling the snakes she sent to kill him. He grew to be a matchless warrior, and Hera struck again, inflicting on him a fit of madness in which he killed his wife and children. As penance he had to perform 12 tasks: the Labors of Hercules. He had to kill or capture monsters such as the nine-headed Hydra and maneating Stymphalion birds and to obtain fabulous trophies. One was the girdle of Hippolyta, queen of the Amazons, a female warrior nation. She gave it to him willingly, but then Hera stirred up the Amazons so that Hercules had to fight them, and kill Hippolyta. In his last task – seizing Cerberus, the underworld's three-headed guard dog – Hercules defeated Hades, king of the dead, and so won immortality. When his mortal life ended, he joined the gods and was at last reconciled with Hera – as her divine son-in-law. The Classical world honored Hercules as a demigod, raised temples in his name, and spread his cult across the Roman Empire. Portrayed with his war club and Hera's serpents, he was also identified with several Celtic deities, including Ogmios, god of eloquence and poetry. His name appears at Romano-British shrines, and some scholars think Britain's huge, carved hill figures, such as the Cerne Giant, are representations of Hercules.

The last of the 12 labors of Hercules was to abduct Cerberus, three-headed guard dog of the Underworld. His defeat of its master, Hades, king of the dead, won him immortality.

Hercules' first labor was to kill the savage Nemean lion. Finding that even magical weapons could not wound the beast, he strangled it with his bare hands.

The Cerne Giant, cut into a hill in England, may be an ancient fertility symbol. It is said to resemble a picture of Hercules found on a piece of Romano-British pottery.

Mighty Hercules prepares for combat. His mortal life ended tragically: his wife Deianira was tricked into killing him by means of a tunic smeared with the poisonous blood of an enemy.

Hercules (Herakles) remains the best known ancient hero, many times portrayed in movies. Lou Ferrigno, seen here in *Hercules* (1983), was well cast: he had formerly played the Incredible Hulk.

❏ Hercules' 11th labor was to gather the golden apples of the Hesperides, garden of the gods. No mortal could go there, so Herakles sent the giant Atlas in his place – and meanwhile took over Atlas's task of supporting the world on his shoulders. Centuries later, Shakespeare's Globe Theatre in London took its name from its sign: Hercules carrying the globe of the Earth.

❏ The mad Roman Emperor Commodus (161-192) made his subjects worship him as *Herakles Secundus* (the second Hercules). In his role of heroic warrior, he was both fight promoter and gladiator. But his idea of amusement was to arrange fights between physically handicapped people – and the 1,000 gladiators he boasted of killing were allowed no weapons.

❏ Long before the women's liberation movement, Greek myth created the Amazons: a race of women who spurned men, using them only to sire children. Baby boys were killed or sent to their fathers. Girls were raised as warriors, their right breasts burned off to allow freer use of weapons (Amazon: breastless). The Amazons were said to have built the temple of Diana at Ephesus, one of the Wonders of the Ancient World. Later, explorers gave their name to the Amazon River because of tales of a female warrior tribe.

227

Good versus evil – the cosmic battle

Persia (modern Iran) is a land of contrasts – mountain and valley, summer heat and winter cold – and its great prophets were inspired by another contrast: good and evil. Persia's earliest gods and demons were personified virtues and vices: Hospitality and Victory, Wrath and Procrastination. Tradition says that about 600 B.C. (historians now favor 1500-1000 B.C.) the prophet Zoroaster (Zarathustra) adapted these to his vision of a cosmic battle between good and evil. The spirit of light and wisdom, Ahura Mazda (Wise Lord), became Supreme Being, Creator of all good, waging perpetual war with Ahriman (Destructive Thought), source of all evil. Ahura Mazda created Persia as an earthly paradise: Ahriman spoiled it by inventing heat, cold, disease, and so on. Ahura Mazda urged men to virtue and heavenly rewards as followers of truth: Ahriman tempted them to sin – and Hell. "Every gift I have given mankind," said Ahura Mazda, "has been counterbalanced by an evil present from Ahriman . . . author of unrest, misfortune, and death." But good was destined to triumph: Zoroaster's revelation of the Good Religion heralded the last round of the battle, in which Ahura Mazda would triumph and the world would be perfected. Later teachers expanded Zoroastrianism: one spinoff faith, Zurvanism, held that Time (Zurvan) was the ultimate Being, source of both Ahura Mazda and Ahriman. A later Persian prophet, Mani (c.A.D. 215-276), blended Zoroastrian dualism with Christianity and Buddhism. The Church condemned Manicheanism as heresy, but it lingered into the 13th century. Despite centuries of persecution, Zarathustra's teachings endure as a religion with about 150,000 followers, notably the Parsees of Bombay.

A Zoroastrian prays at Ahura Mazda's holy fire. He wears the *kusti* (cord, or belt) and *sudra* (shirt), sacred to all followers of Zoroaster.

Under Persia's Sassanid rulers (c.A.D. 226-641) – among them Shapur I, seen here in a carving of c.A.D. 260 – Zoroastrianism was the unifying religion of a powerful state.

A winged sun disk forms an appropriate setting for a portrayal of Ahura Mazda (sometimes called Ormazd), lord of light and wisdom. This relief carving dates from the 9th century B.C.

Envoys from conquered lands carry tribute to Persia's kings of the Achaemenid dynasty (c.500-331 B.C.): a detail from the fine carvings on their palace at Persepolis, near modern Shiraz, Iran.

229

Priests of the sacred grove

A popular view of Celtic religion in pre-Christian Europe relies on Roman reports of barbarous rites in forest glades spattered with human blood. Celts, said the Romans, raised no stone temples, but worshiped via natural features: water, hilltops, and trees. In fact, the Celts built wooden shrines and earthworks, but their altars were wells, rivers, bogs, and pits, seen as channels to the gods below, which received offerings of treasure (we still drop coins in a wishing well for luck) and human sacrifices. Their temple was the forest *nemeton* (sanctuary): a sacred grove, often of oaks; their priests were Druids, whose true role is obscure because Celts held it improper to make written records of religious matters. Roman authors dwelt much on human sacrifice (a practice Rome had only recently abandoned), reporting that Druidic diviners read omens in human entrails or in a stabbed victim's death throes and sacrificed captives by shooting them with arrows, impalement, or cramming them into huge wickerwork figures to be burned. But although the warrior Celts were headhunters and venerated severed heads, Druids dealt with more than bloodshed. They formed a living reference library, a store of their people's religious, legal, and practical knowledge, and had advanced astronomical and calendrical skills. This aspect took the fancy of 18th century scholars, who credited Druids with a "Natural Religion" derived from Abraham, all kinds of magical skills – and the erection of pre-Celtic monuments such as Stonehenge. British antiquarians revived the Druid cult, and today modern Druids claim to perpetuate ancient Celtic wisdom, performing mystic rites on Midsummer Day and other pagan festivals.

The human head played a most important part in Celtic religious beliefs and rites.

This Celtic stone head, perhaps carved for ritual purposes, was found beneath a Roman temple in Britain. The Romans may have purposely built their temple on a sacred site of the pagans they despised.

An 18th century picture sums up the popular idea of a Druid: a sage uses a sickle to cut mistletoe in a sacred grove at Stonehenge, then thought to be a Druidic temple.

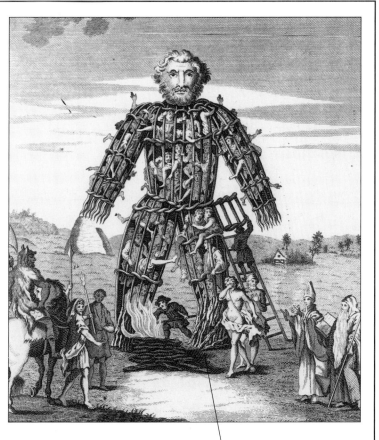

Like Stonehenge, most of Britain's 40 or more stone circles – like this one in Yorkshire – were formerly said to be Druidic temples. Most are older than Druidic rites, which perhaps began c.500 B.C.

Julius Caesar, conqueror of Britain in 54 B.C., wrote that the Celts made human sacrifices in this way – burning their captives alive in giant wickerwork figures.

Ax age, sword age

Heroism, fatalism, and black humor, hallmarks of Viking society, color Norse mythology. If classical myths are divine soap opera, Norse myths are sword-and-sorcery with a generous dash of comic strip. The gods are a motley crew to suit the needs of every individual. The practical man would worship thunder god Thor, Old Redbeard, a mighty brawler with his great hammer Mjöllnir. The more mystically minded turned to Odin, sinister lord of war and sorcery, who gifted his followers with elated states of mind inspiring both poetry and battle rage. His counterpart for women worshipers was fertility goddess Freyja, inspiration of seeresses and associated with *seidr*, a kind of witchcraft concerned mainly with divination. Her twin, the more earthy fertility god Freyr, looked after the crops and the marriage bed. Other gods included Mimir, the wise; Heimdall, the watcher; Njord, sea god and lord of ships; and trickster god Loki, a sinister comedian. Central to Norse myth is the belief that the gods themselves are doomed and that Loki is fated to set in train the events leading to Ragnarok, "twilight of the gods." Other nations have predicted the world's end, but the Norsemen included even the gods in their Armageddon. Ragnarok will begin with Fimbul-winter, a three-year freeze when civilization collapses into war, treason, incest, and fratricide: "Ax age, sword age, shields are sundered; wind age, wolf age, before the world crumbles," promises a 10th century Icelandic poet. Then comes battle between the gods, aided by warrior souls, against cosmic monsters – the World Serpent and the great wolf Fenrisulfr – and fire giants riding in a ship made of dead men's fingernails. But all are fated to fall in the battle, and Heaven and Earth are destroyed by fire.

In Norse mythology, the world is held by the great ash tree Yggdrasil. But the World Tree is under constant attack from cosmic animals like this stag that gnaw away at it.

The name of the popular god Thor lives on in Scandinavian personal names, place-names in Scandinavia and England – and, of course, in Thursday.

Odin will lead the gods to battle at Ragnarok, his raven on his shoulder and his spear Gungnir in his hand. But he is doomed – to be devoured by monstrous wolf Fenrisulfr.

Small bronze statuette of Freyr (Lord). The fertility god, with his twin sister Freya (Lady), belonged to a group of gods called the Vanir, said to predate Odin, Thor, and the rest (the Aesir).

❑ In a Swedish fertility rite each fall, a wagon carried Freyr's image, with a priestess, the god's ''wife,'' to bless the fields. An Icelandic saga says that when Norwegian exile Gunnar Helming fled to Sweden, he used this ritual to his advantage, stealing the idol's clothes and impersonating Freyr. His performance was a hit: locals were impressed by a god who joined in their feasts and preferred offerings of goods and money to human sacrifices – and when Freyr's ''wife'' became pregnant, Gunnar returned to Norway a rich, married man.

❑ A crude and richly comic story tells how Loki's tricks were punished when he was raped by a stallion. But the story has a sting in its tail. The progeny of the monstrous mating were Sleipnir, Odin's eight-legged horse (above); Hel, dread goddess of the underworld; Jormungandr, the World Serpent that will emerge from the seas with poisonous floods at Ragnarok; and Fenrisulfr, the destroying wolf destined to cause the death of Odin himself.

Arthur: once and future king

Arthur fights a giant in this 16th century woodcut. The Virgin Mary watches over him: Welsh tradition says he carried her image into battle, probably painted on his shield.

The story of King Arthur, Britain's legendary hero, has inspired his countrymen for 14 centuries. Welsh warriors of the Dark Ages strove to match his victories; Tudor kings justified their claim to the English throne by faking descent from him; and writers from the 9th to the 20th centuries have created libraries of Arthurian literature. The Arthur of popular fantasy is king of a medieval-style court and leader of the Round Table of knights who, like modern comic strip heroes, roam the land righting wrongs. Among the best-known tales are the tragic love affair between Arthur's faithless queen Guinevere and his best knight Lancelot and the Quest for the Holy Grail (a chalice holding drops of Christ's blood). All this is fiction, the work of medieval romancers (some not even British: Lancelot is a French creation). But most scholars agree Arthur existed – not as a king, but as a 6th century guerrilla fighter against Saxon invaders. He may have not even have been named Arthur: early chroniclers call him only *dux bellorum*, "battle leader." The myth-makers not only crowned him but made him immortal: the "once and future king" who sleeps with his men in a hollow hill and will return in his country's hour of need. Storytellers transformed his military base (some Celtic hill fort) into the sophisticated court of Camelot, and the patchwork of petty Dark Age kingdoms into a glorious land called England, Logres, or the "adventurous kingdom." Here the mythical Arthur ruled an idealized world of chivalry, peopled with knights errrant busy with wars, tournaments, and quests in search of holy relics or damsels in distress. In this glorified form the theme of Arthur and his court became a national epic renowned as the Matter of Britain.

The Round Table at Winchester is a famous fake Arthurian relic from medieval times. Legend says Arthur made his table round to give each knight a seat of equal status.

Legend says Arthur was born here at Tintagel Castle, in Cornwall, England. But these dramatic ruins mark the site not of a castle, but a monastery.

A 19th century Arthur shown as an idealized, noble youth; a far cry from the guerrilla of history's Dark Ages.

The Holy Grail perhaps began as the sacred cauldron of pagan Celtic religion, but is now firmly Christianized.

FACT FILE

❏ Arthur's legendary mounted knights may have some basis in fact. Britons in the 6th century fought mainly on foot or from chariots: native ponies were not up to warriors' weight. But early historians credit Arthur with battles so farflung as to suggest he may have introduced cavalry. Perhaps novelist Alfred Duggan was right: his fictional Arthur is a rustler who steals the necessary war-horses from the departing Romans.

❏ The promise that Arthur would return was taken seriously. Some claimed that Philip II of Spain was only permitted to wed Britain's Queen Mary in 1554, if he swore to resign the kingdom to Arthur if necessary.

❏ Camelot was invented by a 12th century French poet, but that did not discourage a quest for Arthur's base. Most of Britain's major ruins, from Caerleon's Roman fortress to Tintagel's Celtic monastery, have staked a claim. From 1542 the favorite has been the 5th century hill fort of Cadbury, Somerset (above). Local legend said Arthur and his men slept under the hill — and excavations in 1966-70 showed it had been a major military base in Arthur's supposed time.

Shinto: way of the gods

The magnificent Todai-ji Temple at Nara, Japan, where ancient Buddhist and Shinto shrines stand together, emblematic of the close ties between the two faiths.

Shinto (Chinese: divine way; the Japanese is *Kami-no-Michi*, way of the gods), Japan's ancient faith, originated in worship of divine spirits (*kami*) in natural objects or forces – mountains, trees, winds, and the like. Of more than 8,000,000 *kami*, the greatest is the sun goddess Amaterasu. Japan, says Shinto myth, was the world's first nation, born of sexual intercourse between gods (the afterbirth formed other nations). Amaterasu's grandson Ninigi came to Earth, where his great-grandson Jimmu Tenno (*Tenno*: Emperor) became first ruler of a united Japan in 660 B.C. From Jimmu the imperial rulers, who are both gods and men, descend in an unbroken line through 125 generations to Emperor Akihito (b.1933). For centuries Buddhism was Japan's more vital faith, but after Emperor Meiji's restoration of imperial power in 1867, Shinto was seen as a more valuable tool of nationalism.

Seen here in a 15th century print, sun goddess Amaterasu is the greatest of the many Shinto deities and is claimed to be the ancestress of Japan's imperial line.

Kokutai (State) Shinto was decreed to be not a religion but a national ethic to which all must subscribe. It taught absolute dedication to Emperor and nation (as one and the same thing). In 1937-45, Kokutai Shinto inspired Japan's wars of conquest, and even led some soldiers, survivors of isolated Pacific garrisons, to refuse to surrender into the 1970s. In 1945, Allied occupation authorities forbade Kokutai Shinto and Emperor Hirohito renounced his divinity. Today, Shinto is a loose organization of more than 80,000 shrines. But its most sacred objects remain the mirror, sword, and jewels associated with Amaterasu. Tokyo's Meiji Shrine and Ise Shrine, near Kyoto, traditional centers of the imperial cult, remain its major sanctuaries. On his accession in 1989, Emperor Akihito revived an ancient ceremony of "sleeping with the goddess" (he kept an all-night vigil in a Shinto shrine) that some allege was a step towards reaffirming his divinity.

State Shinto helped inspire some Japanese soldiers, such as Shoichi Yokoi, seen here after his capture on Guam in 1972, to refuse to surrender until long after World War II's end.

Shinto's sacred mountain, Fujiyama, an extinct volcanic peak near Tokyo, is said to be the home of the ancient creator god Kunitokotachi.

❏ Japan's *kamikaze* suicide squads of World War II were assured by Shinto belief of a place as demigods at Tokyo's Yasukuni Shrine. A common farewell between all Japanese servicemen before an attack was: "See you at Yasukuni."

❏ Out of Japan's present population of about 125,000,000, some 118,000,000 people claim to be Shintoists (belonging to around 130 different sects) and about 90,000,000 say they are Buddhists. Except for the period of Kokutai Shintoism, it has always been possible to be both Shintoist and Buddhist.

❏ An offshoot of modern Shrine Shinto is Sukyo Mahikara (True-Light Supra-Religious Organization), founded in the 1960s. Its *miko* (shamans), almost all women, are said to have magical powers, including the ability to mend broken microwave ovens.

❏ An erotic highlight of Japan's red light clubs is a striptease act called *tokudashi*. Clients are given flashlights and magnifying glasses for close-up viewing of the performers. The participants deny this degrades women – for it has religious significance. According to Shinto legend, the sun goddess Amaterasu once denied her light to the world – but a striptease dance by the goddess Ama-no-Azume made the other gods applaud, and Amaterasu came out to see the show.

Lord Jaguar and the Long Count

Turquoise mask portraying the god Quetzalcoatl – a historical priest-king who became the "plumed serpent" to whom thousands were sacrificed.

From ancient times until European conquest in the 16th century, Central America saw a succession of priest-dominated societies whose subjugation to fierce gods produced a strange blend of primitive and sophisticated culture. They failed to develop wheeled vehicles, but in the service of the gods they evolved writing, astronomy, and advanced math. They built pyramidal, stone temples in cult centers so vast that Western explorers thought them cities. Their gods demanded not only conventional worship but also human sacrifice. This rite the Aztecs took to its limits: 15,000 men a year were shot with arrows, flayed, decapitated, burned, or had their hearts cut from their living bodies. Priests and worshipers did not spare themselves, but offered their own blood from pierced tongues or ears. The gods who demanded such service were often portrayed as part wild animal: above all, the jaguar, the Americas' most striking great predator, became a living image of divine power. Its worship began with the Olmecs – termed "jaguar psychotics" by a modern zoologist. Their temples are dominated by jaguar mosaics, masks, thrones, and "werejaguars," figures part human, part jaguar. They even molded their babies' heads to resemble the jaguar's flattened skull. Later cultures, the Zapotecs and Maya, also knew the jaguar god. But the Maya shifted the emphasis from religious rituals to the calendar developed to schedule them. Their obsession with the measurement of time produced the Long Count calendar: a mathematical masterpiece, covering not only days of the year but vast cycles of years within an infinity of time. It was so precise that its computation of the solar year differs by no more than 0.0008 of a day from modern reckoning.

A massive reclining figure at the Temple of Warriors in Chichén Itzá holds a platter for sacrificial offerings – of human hearts.

A pyramid temple at the great Mayan center of Chichén Itzá, on the Yucatan Peninsula.

Even the stairs honor the Long Count. Four great staircases total 364 steps: the platform makes 365 – the number of days in the year.

Such altar-statues, or *Chac Mools*, were used by both the Toltecs and Maya.

Mayan gods demanded endless blood sacrifice. In this carving of c.750 A.D. a worshiper makes an offering of his blood by drawing cactus spines through his tongue.

❏ Some scholars see the Olmec "werejaguar" (below) as a stylized portrayal of a child with congenital skull deformities – perhaps caused by spina bifida. If such children were born to the ruling family, they would have been thought to prove direct descent from the sacred jaguar.

❏ The great Mayan center of Chichén Itzá in Yucatan had two wells. Only one was used as a supply of water. The other, 60ft (18m) deep, was for the gods. Into it were thrown offerings of jade, gold, incense, and, on special occasions, human sacrifices. Flung in at dawn, victims were checked at midday to see if they were dead. Any who survived both the fall and the hours in the water were fished out, on the assumption that the gods had sent them back with a message for the living.

Golden hoard and green hell

The Inca Empire in the Andean region of South America was destroyed in the 1530s by gold-hungry Spanish conquerors. From survivors of their massacres they learned of El Dorado (Spanish: the Gilded), variously interpreted as a Golden City or a Golden Man. For many years European expeditions sought El Dorado throughout South America, not knowing the Spaniards had probably destroyed it (or him) in 1536, when they looted the Chibcha people of Bolivia. The Sun-worshiping Chibcha revered gold as "sweat of the Sun," and every year their chief, coated in gold dust, led his people in a sacrifice in which gold and jewels were thrown into Lake Guatavita (near modern Bogotá). Although they did not recognize this rite as the true source of the El Dorado legend, the Spaniards learned of the lake – and killed thousands of Indian slaves in attempts to drain it. More

modern, less greedy Europeans sought the lost cities of the Incas – and one, British explorer Colonel Percy Fawcett (1867-?1925), sought the Incas themselves. Fawcett had spent many years in the Mato Grosso, the vast Amazon jungle – "I love that green hell," he wrote – and believed it concealed vast ruined cities where lost remnants of the Inca peoples still lived. From an account supposedly written by a Portuguese explorer in 1753, Fawcett learned of City X deep in the Mato Grosso and in 1925 set out with two other Europeans to find it. They disappeared, but for decades travelers told of meeting an old European wandering in the jungle, or of encountering forest Indians who claimed to have killed Fawcett's party – or who said he had found City X and stayed there. An Irish medium claimed to be in clairvoyant contact with Fawcett from 1935, when he told her he had found an "Atlantean settlement," until his death in 1948.

A gold and turquoise god of the Chimu civilization, which flourished in north Peru and the Andes from c.A.D. 1000.

The figure's base forms the blade of a ceremonial knife. The Incas, who conquered the Chimu about 1470, valued such work for its beauty – the later Spanish conquerors loved its gold.

Hidden among Andean peaks, Machu Picchu perhaps was a temple complex.

The Spaniards never found the lost city of Machu Picchu, but the U.S. explorer who discovered the Inca stronghold in 1911 found no gold there.

A golden man, probably made as a religious offering. Happily, some of the Incas' magnificent artifacts escaped the Spaniards' melting pots.

This golden model of priests on a raft, found near Bogotá in 1969, was probably made by the Muisca people of the Chibcha civilization to mark their annual ceremony at Lake Guatavita.

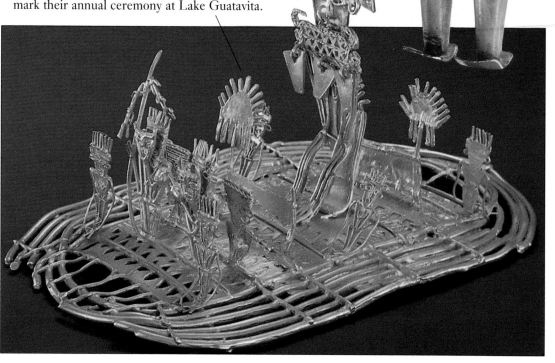

❑ One of the early Spanish explorers, Barco Centenara, reported in about 1600 that he had found a ruin lit by "a column surmounted by a moon" and described what has been interpreted as an electric or neon light. Fawcett (above), on his many explorations in South America, noted that none of the ancient buildings he saw bore the marks of smoke from oil lamps and agreed that the Incas may have had a form of artificial lighting "based on the ultraviolet ray" (i.e. solar energy).

Native American dreamers and dancers

Today conservationists contrast white settlers' misuse of North America's natural resources with the "green" approach of Native Americans, whose religious beliefs taught respect for nature. The Great Spirit was present in all things: animals were seen as the original owners of the land and as the ancestors of both modern animals and humans. Protective spirits or demigods included many animals, such as Raven and Blue Jay, as well as the Sun, thunder, corn, and flint. Evil spirits also abounded and must be pacified by special rites. Medicine men – visionaries who could enter the spirit world in trance state – mediated between humanity and the spirit world. But spirit visions were not reserved for these shamans alone: adolescent boys underwent solitary fasts to contact the guardian spirits who would give them their adult name; war leaders sought guidance in prophetic dreams. Rituals often took the form of mass dances, many lasting for days. Plains tribes held a Sun Dance each year to ensure the renewal of nature. In its mildest form it was a test of endurance: braves danced for days around a sacred tree, without sleep or food. Some tribes, such as the Cheyenne, extended this ordeal: dancers had skewers thrust into their chests, which were tied to the tree, and danced backwards until their flesh tore through. In the 1880s another ritual dance arose when Wovoka, a Paiute, had a vision of the end of the "white man's world" and of a Native American savior who would then establish an earthly paradise. His followers gained ecstatic glimpses of the promised utopia in the frenzied Ghost Dance. When white officials fearing unrest sent troops to suppress the dances, the Sioux rose. The Messiah War, the last major Indian War, ended with the infamous massacre of the Sioux at Wounded Knee in December 1890.

Demigod Raven presides over a totem pole, erected to honor the dead and carved with animal spirits linked with the dead man's ancestors.

Paintings cover the rock face at Newspaper Rock, Utah. The image of the mounted huntsman shooting a stag is an example of sympathetic magic: the artist painted a successful hunt to make it happen.

The horned figure represents the shaman or medicine man, who acts as a living bridge between the worlds of spirits and humans.

Warriors act out sighting an enemy in the Discovery Dance. Special dances attended every important aspect of life, as rituals to bring guidance and success.

Today Native Americans, such as this modern medicine man in his traditional regalia, seek to preserve their ancestors' knowledge and customs.

Shamans of the north

One of the oldest surviving religious traditions is the shamanism of northern Europe and Asia, which may date back to the Stone Age. From North America to Finland and Siberia, shaman cultures believe in a spirit world separate from but affecting that of humans. Disharmony between the worlds causes human troubles, from famine to individual illness. Only the shaman – a figure between priest and witch doctor – can enter both worlds and restore the balance between them. Aided by ritual dancing and drumming, meditation, or hallucinatory drugs, he or she enters a trance state in which the soul leaves the body and travels to the Otherworld for spirit guidance. The shaman is a seer, with prophetic skills; a social worker who seeks spiritual reasons and remedies for his community's problems; and above all a spiritual healer. To become a shaman requires both a divine call and a rigorous apprenticeship, culminating in an ordeal of symbolic death, dismemberment, and rebirth. This passage through death equips the soul to visit the upperworld of spirits and the underworld where the souls of the sick await rescue. The shaman is guided in his journeys by a totemic spirit, sometimes an ancestor but often an animal. An Inuit shaman whose totem was the wolf-being Amarok said he became kin to wolves as a 5-year-old, when his father took him to a wolf den where for 24 hours he played unharmed among the beasts. He claimed to understand wolf "language" – and staggered a Canadian zoologist with translations of howls (as inter-wolf reports on the movements of both prey animals and men) that events proved correct. Such close contact with the animal world enables shamans to guide hunters, ensuring food for the people.

Siberian shaman in impressive traditional costume, with his medicine bag of amulets and his indispensable sacred drum.

The shaman's drum, made of hide and decorated with magic symbols. It is the key with which he unlocks the door to the spirit world, beating on it with a spoon-shaped drumstick until he falls into a trance, aided by hallucinatory drugs.

The magic drum is common to all shaman cultures. This is an Inuit example, made of hide and wood, from the Northwest coast of America

By ritual dancing and drumming, these Yakut shamans from eastern Russia seek to free their spirits from their bodies to enter the spirit world or realm of the dead.

Dressed in animal skins, horned and tailed, the shaman enters the animal kingdom in spirit. The spirit hunt he carries out enables his people to carry out a successful real hunt.

❏ The Inuit of Alaska say human sins form dirt in the spirit world. This clogs the hair of the Sea Woman, angering her into a refusal to give mortals her seals, walruses, and whales. To save the people from starving, the shaman's spirit must go under the sea to comb the Sea Woman's hair clean. Only then will she give good hunting.

❏ The Vikings' *völva*, or seeress, derived from shaman tradition. A Norse saga describes how the *völva* was consulted. Clad in animal skins (including calfskin boots and catskin gloves), she ate ritually of animal hearts before entering a trance, while a helper summoned the spirits with song. Then she reported what the spirits had told her.

❏ In Mongolia, land of horsemen, the shaman's horse was not, as might be expected, the best mount available. Burials reveal that many were lame – crippled with arthritis. They may have been kept into old age because of special markings. But some authorities think their lameness was not the effect of age, but the identifying factor of a shaman horse, related to the ritual deformity of the Lame King of some mystic cults.

❏ Many shamanistic cultures believe both mortal and spirit realms are supported by a vast World Tree. Sometimes the shaman's drum is said to be made from its wood.

Dreaming down under

The first Europeans to study the Aboriginal peoples of Australia concluded they had no religion at all – and the Aborigines were equally shocked by what they saw as the irreligious attitude of European Christians. The Europeans had failed to see the woods for the trees: native Australian religious belief is so closely interwoven with daily life and social structure that the newcomers simply could not distinguish it. Where many faiths look to the future, in a life after death, Aboriginal belief looks back to the time of creation: the Dreamtime. In that age ancestor spirits such as kangaroo-men and bowerbird-women lived on Earth. They shaped its hills, rocks, waterholes, and trees; created humans; and taught them how to live on and with the land. So to the Aborigines the entire land is a temple; the priesthoods of other faiths are replaced by a tradition in which everyone is an equal inheritor of religious knowledge; and living by the moral laws of the ancestor spirits is the major part of worship. Those who break these laws may be literally cursed to death by "pointing the bone." The executioner prepares a sharpened bone (or stick) and "loads" it with psychic energy before pointing it at the condemned man. The victim is now regarded by his people as dead – and his own belief in the ritual ensures his death within a few days. Dreamtime laws and legends are passed on through generations by song-cycles, and are reenacted in song and dance at "corroboree" ceremonies. At other times people may go "walkabout" as pilgrims to sacred landmarks associated with Dreamtime events, guided by Songlines, a psychic map accessed through ancestral chants. Today the modern world has broken down much of the Aborigines' traditions and their link with the land; yet a few groups strive to preserve their ancient values, beliefs, and ceremonies.

A 20th century bark painting of a kangaroo (a clan totem animal) is decorated in traditional cross-hatched style.

Even today, Aborigines celebrate the events of the Dreamtime in song and dance at "corroboree" ceremonies, their bodies painted with age-old designs and decked with foliage.

This bark painting depicts a Creation myth. Both people and animals share ancestor-beings who were part animal, part human.

Aborigines honor the spirit shared by the kangaroo-men's issue, human and animal alike.

Bark paintings – an art-form unique to the Aborigines – not only have ritual significance but form teaching aids by which elders explain tribal myths to the next generation.

The whole landscape is a memorial to and a living link with the events of the Dreamtime, and landmarks such as mighty Ayers Rock are sacred sites to this day.

❏ Since 1969, Alan Webb has been one of the few Aborigines to survive the curse of "pointing the bone." An Australian court cleared him of manslaughter charges, ruling that his killing of a fellow tribesman acidental, but tribal elders disagreed and condemned him to death. Despite Webb's "white" lifestyle, he believed implicitly that he would die once the killing-bone pointed at him. So he fled and began a life on the run. Years later, his would-be executioners were still trying to find him.

❏ Binbinga Aborigines tell how, back in the Dreamtime, humans were unable to catch the large bats (flying foxes) that had been provided for them to eat. Snake ancestor-spirit Bobbi-Bobbi came to the rescue. He tore out one of his own ribs to make a throwing weapon – and thus invented the boomerang (below).

Killers for faith: Assassins and Thugs

Appearing in the terrifying form of Durga (Devi), wife of Shiva, Hindu goddess Kali, patroness of the Thugs, wears a necklace of skulls and a belt of severed heads.

The word "assassin" dates from the 12th century. It is from *hashishiyun* (hashish smokers), Arabic name of a Muslim sect founded about 1090 by Hasan ibn Sabbah (c.1033-1124), called the Old Man of the Mountain from his fortress at Alamut in the Elburz Mountains of Iran. He sent suicide squads, inspired by visions of Paradise gained by smoking hashish and promised eternal bliss if they died in action, to cut down opponents of his heretical sect – orthodox Muslims and Christians. He claimed 70,000 followers, including his killer elite the *fedayeen* (devoted ones; a name still used by Muslim extremists), linked by a "magical" intelligence network: carrier pigeons. The Assassins' reign of terror in the Middle East ended after 1256, when Mongol conqueror Hulagu took Alamut – but legend says some Assassins escaped to India, to become worshipers of the Hindu goddess Kali, the Black Mother, and establish the caste of hereditary murderers called Thugs (Hindi *thag*: Deceiver) or *Phansigars* (Stranglers). Certainly, Hindus and Muslims were united in Thuggee – but Hindu tradition traces the cult back to about 800 A.D. Thugs are said to have killed about 1,000,000 persons in central India in the 17th-19th centuries. They operated in gangs up to 150 strong. *Belhals* (spies) located parties of travelers; *bhartotes* (killers) ambushed and murdered them by strangling with a *rumal* (kerchief); *lughahs* (diggers) gutted and dismembered the bodies, using a sacred pickax (Kali's tooth), then buried them. From about 1800 to 1845, Thuggee was stamped out by India's British rulers. Sir William Sleeman (1788-1856) masterminded a campaign to turn Indian villagers against the Thugs and recruited undercover agents to hunt them down.

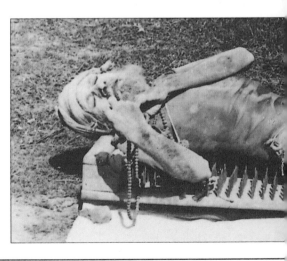

Thugs carry off the bodies of murdered travelers for ritual mutilation and burial in a remote place.

The *rumal* (kerchief; strip of twisted cloth) with which a victim has been strangled is still tight around his neck.

The Hindu goddess Lakshmi, as benevolent as Kali is terrible, rides with her husband, the powerful Vishnu, on Garuda, king of all birds.

Some Westerners may regard this feat of endurance as an equivalent of the rope trick, but this devotee of Kali is lying on a bed of nails as a penance, to humble himself at one of the goddess's shrines.

Ancient wisdom of Africa

The traditional beliefs of Africa, vast cradle of the human race, are as various as its peoples. Most have in common a deep belief in the spirit world, whether the spirits venerated are those of ancestors, natural forces, or totem animals. Many peoples, such as the Zulu of South Africa, also believe in a great spirit, whom the Zulu call simply Unkulunkulu (the Chief). In the past, most white settlers scorned African peoples' beliefs and dismissed their priests, prophets, and healers as witch doctors. Now it is acknowledged that Africa's ancient wisdom, in particular the herbal lore of its healers, has much to offer. Although most black Africans now profess to follow Christianity or Islam, traditional beliefs retain their hold. This is not always for the good: in internal wars in modern times, rebel leaders have enlisted "witches" to terrorize peaceful villagers into supporting them (as did the Mau Mau in Kenya in the 1950s), or to persuade their troops that fetishes (charms) or magic potions could make them bulletproof. The Simba guerrillas in the Congo (Zaire) in the 1960s believed this and were massacred by white mercenaries. In the 1970s tyrants such as Field Marshal Idi Amin of Uganda and Emperor Bokassa of the Central African Republic buttressed their power by exploiting their peoples' traditional beliefs. In the 16th-19th centuries native West African beliefs were exported via the slave trade. Some melded with the Christianity forced on the slaves to form new faiths – among which at least two still have many followers. The Voodoo of the Caribbean islands blends African magical lore with Roman Catholicism. The Macumba cults of Brazil unite rites originating with the West African Yoruba people with both Spiritualism and older European cults, including white and black magic.

Ashanti craftsmen (Asante; modern Ghana) carved fetish figures like this "antelope man" for religious purposes. They are still sometimes used in fertility ceremonies.

A Nigerian healer at work: his medicine is in a water buck's horn lying across the patient's afflicted part. Such traditional healers were once dismissed as witch doctors.

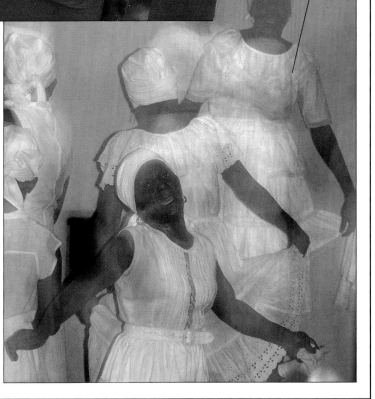

Although, like other black African peoples, many Zulu of South Africa are now nominally Christian, the *sangoma* (shaman) still plays a part in their traditional way of life.

Long hair braided with beads into the style known as dreadlocks (and now mainly associated with West Indian Rastafarians) is also a mark of distinction among the Zulu people.

Voodoo worshipers in Haiti seek to call up a spirit. Voodoo blends traditional West African beliefs with Christianity. Its name is said to come from an African word for a spirit: *voudou*.

FACT FILE

❏ Traditional belief almost destroyed the Xhosa people of South Africa in 1856-57. Obeying a prophetic vision by Nongquase, teenage niece of a witch doctor, the Xhosa destroyed their crops and killed their cattle, believing their ancestors would return to build an earthly paradise. About one-third of the Xhosa starved to death; the remainder had to give up their lands and become laborers for the white settlers. But the Xhosa recovered to become leaders in South Africa today: Nelson Mandela (below) is a Xhosa.

❏ Although witch doctors were powerful in Africa in the 19th century, white colonial powers often exaggerated their "barbaric" practices for political ends. French and British wars of conquest in Dahomey and Asante (Ghana) respectively were justified by the need to suppress rites of human sacrifice. The British claimed that Asante customs regularly involved the sacrifice of enough persons so that their blood would fill a pool on which the ruler could paddle his canoe.

251

Mirade men of Tibet

Most Eastern religions teach believers to look inward and cultivate in themselves the powers of the mind. Yogis (holy men) strive to school the mind to master the body, thus achieving such supernormal powers as levitation, telepathy, and (by controlling the metabolism to produce suspended animation) the ability to survive long periods of living burial. An especially mystical form of Buddhism evolved in Tibet, cut off from the outside world by the Himalayas. Tibetan lamas (holy men) seek enlightenment through spiritual exercises that include prolonged contemplation of religious symbols (mandalas) and endless repetition of words or phrases (mantras). Their creative visualization is said to endow them with the powers of teleportation (moving themselves or objects from place to place by mind power); invisibility; producing *tulpas* (creatures of their thoughts that become real beings); and *tumo* (control of body heat that enables the adept to endure long periods of naked contemplation in the Himalayan snows). Tibetan Buddhism was little known in the West until the late 19th century, when travelers' tales of lamas' amazing feats attracted much attention – and inspired some Western mystics to incorporate Tibetan elements into their creeds. Notable was Russian-American Helena Petrovna Blavatsky (1831-91), whose worldwide travels included Tibet. In New York City in the 1870s, she founded a cult called Theosophy, which she claimed was based on spirit guidance from Hidden Masters in Tibet. Blavatsky was denounced as a fraud by the Society for Psychical Research and others, but Theosophy flourished, especially in India, where Mahatma Gandhi is said to have been influenced by it. Many Westerners have since adopted outward forms of "Eastern wisdom" – from yoga exercises to incense sticks.

A bronze figure of Tara, the great goddess of Tibetan Buddhism. Like her husband, the *bodhisattva* (Buddhist saint) Avalokitesvara, she is seen as a savior, a deity full of love and compassion.

The Potala, palace of the exiled Dalai Lama, at Lhasa, Tibet. Legend says secret tunnels link it to Chang Shambhala, an earthly paradise like the fictional Shangri-La.

Lord Mara, chief tempter of the Buddha and archdemon of Buddhist theology, is the enemy of all who seek *nirvana* (supreme enlightenment).

Mara holds the Tibetan Wheel of Life. Its six palaces symbolize the cycle of death and rebirth, and the temptations along the way.

Although Lamaism, the Tibetan form of Buddhism, has been persecuted since the Chinese invasion of 1950, some monks are still able to pursue lives of prayer and contemplation.

❏ Exiled from Tibet since the Chinese takeover in 1950, the present Dalai Lama, Tenzin Gyatso (b.1935) (below), 14th reincarnation of the first holy man to hold the office of Tibetan priest-king in the 17th century, has suggested that he may also be the last in the line; that he himself will not be reincarnated.

❏ In the 1960s, "hippies" seeking enlightenment sometimes tried trepanation: a hole is drilled in the skull and, in theory, lets in more oxygen to "expand the brain." This novel surgery was popularized in the bestselling books of "Tibetan lama" T. Lobsang Rampa (in fact, an English handyman who never visited Tibet), who claimed he had undergone the operation to "open a third eye."

The man who talked with Angels

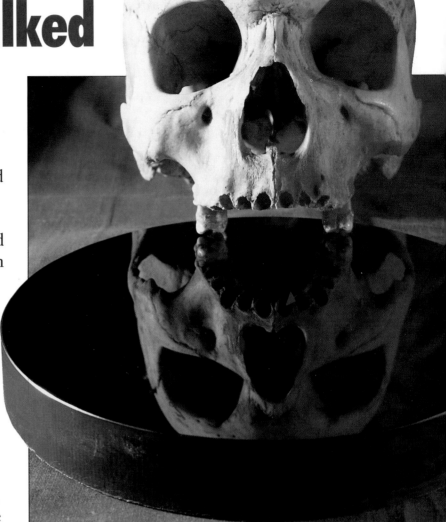

In the England of John Dee (1527-1608) most people saw little difference between science and magic. Dee was among the best astronomers, mathematicians, and geographers of the time; his mapmaking won him the friendship of New World explorer Sir Walter Raleigh. But he was looked on as a magician – and regarded himself as one, devoting as much effort to alchemy and astrology as to conventional learning. As an astrologer he was consulted in turn by King Edward VI (1537-53) and Queen Mary I (1516-58), but was accused of plotting the latter's death by magic when he cast a favorable horoscope for her then imprisoned half-sister Elizabeth. On Bloody Mary's death, Queen Elizabeth I (1533-1603) made Dee her Astrologer Royal. He was often sent abroad: officially on scientific research; secretly as a spy for the Admiralty. On one trip he acquired a "scrying glass": a magic mirror in which he expected to see visions. But no visions came – until Edward Kelley (1555-95) offered himself as a medium. Kelley, whose ears had been mutilated as punishment for forgery, had an unsavory reputation as a necromancer (one who works magic through corpses). But when he claimed that Angels spoke to him through the mirror in the Enochian language of Heaven, Dee believed him. The two toured Europe, where noblemen entertained them royally – until they realized that the angelic messages never seemed to be of practical use. A seven-year partnership ended when Dee married a young and pretty wife – and Kelley announced that the Angels commanded a wife swap. Kelley stayed abroad, where he died in an attempted jail break in Prague. Dee went home to England, where at last only a lonely, poverty-stricken death saved him from facing charges of sorcery under witch-hunting King James I.

Painted at the age of 67, Dr. John Dee seems in a pensive mood, perhaps regretting the trouble his reputation as a magician brought him.

Dee and Kelley probably used a disk of polished obsidian (black glass) like this as a "scrying glass." Gazing long into the reflective surface concentrates the seer's spiritual powers.

Protected by a magic circle, necromancers raise from a grave in England, the corpse of a man believed to have left a concealed treasure.

Edward Kelley conjures with spell book and staff in an 18th century print of one of the foul deeds attributed to him.

A practical ruler reputedly the intellectual equal of most men of her time, England's Queen Elizabeth I nevertheless appointed Dee as her Astrologer Royal.

❏ Dee's "scrying glass" was described at the time as being of polished obsidian (black volcanic glass) and was said to be an Aztec artifact looted from the New World by Spanish conqueror Hernando Cortés in the 1520s. The British Museum, London, now displays a sphere of pinkish crystal that is sometimes identified as the magic mirror, although by other accounts this sphere was given to Dee by Uriel, Angel of light.

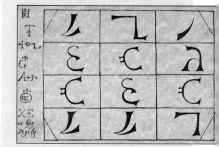

❏ Say *"Ils d ialprt, soba upaah chis nanba zixlay dodsih,"* and you might have a heavenly visitor. It is a bidding call in the Enochian language (from the patriarch Enoch, who, according to some interpretations of the *Book of Genesis*, was bodily taken up to Heaven) used by Kelley and Dee, who tried to codify it (above), to talk with Angels.

❏ Some say Dee was the model for Shakespeare's Prospero in *The Tempest*. It is more likely that mighty magician was based on physician and astrologer Simon Forman (1552-1611), whom several associates of Shakespeare are known to have consulted.

The witches of the West

Two witches were hanged in 1618 for killing by magic Henry, son of the Earl of Rutland, whose image stands on the witchcraft tomb in England.

Witches appear in Egyptian papyri, Greek myth, and the Old Testament, but Western Europe's great witch craze did not occur until comparatively modern times. On witchcraft, people in the so-called Dark Ages (c.A.D. 500-1000) were more enlightened than their descendants. In the 9th century the Church forbade belief in witchcraft – but not its practice, because, great theologians said, that did not exist. But from the 14th century Church and State began to equate heresy (religious unorthodoxy) with witchcraft. Catholic and, later, Protestant authorities saw witchcraft as a great conspiracy to win Europe for Satan. This was partly an expression of the Churches' traditional anti-feminism: most accused witches were women – some, such as Joan of Arc (considered both witch and heretic), were women whose refusal to conform to traditional stereotypes made them political and social undesirables. In the witch-hunters' heyday, the 16th-17th centuries, it was generally believed that witches regularly anointed themselves with devil's grease that enabled them to fly to Sabbats (meetings) where they had sex with demons and worshiped Satan (who appeared as a giant goat or toad) with obscene rites. In fact, the great majority of those who confessed (often under torture) to witchcraft were people on the fringes of society who were made scapegoats for sudden misfortunes, from crop failure to plague – or persons suffering from religious mania. Modern witches claim as many as 500,000 witches were judicially burned or hanged: the actual figure may be close to 30,000. At Bamberg, Germany, notorious as Europe's center of witch-hunting, only about 900 trials were held from 1610 to 1635, when the mania was at its height. A witch was legally burned at Glarus, Switzerland, in 1782 – but by that time the scientific rationalism of the 18th century had ended the witch craze.

A great, horned goat – the Evil One himself – presides at The Witches Sabbath nightmarishly portrayed by Spanish artist Francisco Goya (1746-1828).

❑ The word Sabbat perhaps did not derive from the Hebrew word for the "seventh [holy] day" (as anti-Semites liked to believe), but from the French *s'esbettre*, to fling oneself about, a reference to the witches' orgiastic revels.

❑ Witch-hunters in the 17th century said witches had "international conference centers" where they held huge Sabbats on such major festivals as Walpurgis Night (April 30; also called Beltane) and All Hallows Eve (October 31; Halloween). Among the most important were the Brocken peak in Germany's Harz Mountains; the Blåkulla plain in Sweden; and La Hendaye, in southwest France – where 12,000 witches were said to gather.

❑ If the same authorities are right, English witches were the best fed. At the Sabbat, they said, German witches feasted on sliced turnips cut to resemble the sacred Host; French witches on the flesh of infants; Spanish witches on stolen corpses; Swiss witches on bat stew. But English witches were known to feast on roast beef and ale.

❑ All witch-hunters agreed that witches had sex with Satan – but via incubi (male demons) for women, and succubi (female demons) for men. For women the act was not pleasant.

Some of England's Lancashire Witches, tried in 1612, are seen in a print of the time. Of 20 people accused, 8 women and 2 men were hanged.

A demon, supposedly the "familiar" servant granted to witches by Satan, flies in formation with a male and female witch as they ride the wind on broomsticks.

The five-pointed star called a pentagram is one of the most powerful symbols used in magical rituals. Witches were said to use it reversed – single point downward.

Matthew Hopkins, Witch-finder General

England's Civil War (1642-51), in part a religious conflict between Puritan Parliamentarians and "high church" Royalists, saw the nation's major witch scare and its most infamous witch-hunter. In 1644 lawyer Matthew Hopkins alleged that witches in Manningtree, Essex, had sent a demon in the shape of a bear to attack him. He had 29 people arrested: 4 were hanged – others perhaps bribed him to drop charges. Scenting riches, Hopkins styled himself Witchfinder General. He toured Puritan eastern England, exposing witches for some £20 (then some two years' pay for a laborer) per conviction – plus generous expenses. Most of his victims were old, poor men and women, bullied into confessions by Hopkins and his searchers. Moles and blemishes on suspects' bodies were declared "paps" – nipples from which demons fed; probing with needles discovered insensitive spots said to be "Satan's seal." The accused might be shut in a room with one tiny entrance, where any living creature that penetrated, even a fly, could be denounced as a "familiar," a disguised demon serving the witch. Denied sleep and food, suspects were run, beaten and hustled about, then "swum": thrown into water with thumbs tied to the toes of opposite foot. If they sank, they were innocent (but might drown or die from shock); if they floated (easy for witch-finders to ensure, by allowing air to be trapped in their clothing), they were guilty. Of some 1,000 witches legally hanged in England (the last in 1685), about 200 were Hopkins's victims. But his reign of terror was short, ending when Puritan clergy (although not denying the existence of witches) attacked his methods and motives.

Tradition says that in 1647 Hopkins himself was convicted of witchcraft and hanged – but he is also said to have died peacefully or to have fled to New England.

Matthew Hopkins, the self-appointed Witch-finder General, profited only briefly from England's last serious outbreak of witch mania.

Hopkins's victims are forced to name their "familiars," devilish servants in the form of animals: cat, dog, rabbit, weasel – and horned greyhound.

258

A witch feeds her familiars, including two huge toads. Some alleged the demonic beasts fed from extra nipples on the witch's body.

A written curse is pinned to an image of the person to be harmed. This curse doll, or poppet, may date from the 18th century.

If she drowns, she is innocent: if she floats, guilty. A treatise of 1613 illustrates the cruel ordeal of "swimming" for a suspected witch.

FACT FILE

❏ Like Red-hunting Senator McCarthy in the 1950s, Hopkins gained credibility by publicly displaying secret documents; in his case, what he claimed to be the Devil's List, written in code by Satan himself, naming all of England's witches.

❏ Those who hanged witches were themselves breaking England's witchcraft laws, the mildest in Europe. They forbade torture, and the Witchcraft Act of 1563 prescribed death only for those guilty of murder by sorcery. No English witches were burned: that penalty was reserved for heretics and traitors.

❏ During the English Civil War, Parliamentarians alleged that Prince Rupert of the Rhine (above), the Royalist cavalry leader also noted for his scientific experiments and inventions, was a witch, and that his poodle Boy (who rode into battle on his saddle and was at last killed in action) was his familiar. Royalists replied that Oliver Cromwell had a pact with Satan – and had been seen taking tactical advice from a demon before his victory at the battle of Naseby in 1645.

259

Witch mania in Massachusetts

Eminent Boston clergyman Cotton Mather wholeheartedly backed the Salem witch trials, but later admitted that he had been wrong.

The "bewitched" children of Salem: a scene from the 1957 movie *The Crucible*, based on Arthur Miller's play equating the trials with 1950s' McCarthyism.

In North America's first documented witch trial in 1648, Margaret Jones was condemned at Plymouth, Mass. Some 20 more New England witches were hanged before America's greatest outbreak of witch mania began in Salem, a village near Boston, in 1689. It was a result of childish make-believe. After hearing West Indian Voodoo tales from a black servant, Tituba, minister's daughter Betty Parris (9), Abigail Williams (11), and other girls claimed that evil spirits were tormenting them. Rev. Samuel Parris and physician William Griggs decided they were bewitched, and the girls, having gone too far to back down unpunished, named the witches responsible: Tituba, Sarah Good, and elderly invalid Sarah Osburn. Afraid for her life (she was spared, but sold into slavery to pay trial expenses), Tituba confessed that she and others in the community had made pacts with Satan. The girls gave more names: soon some 150 persons from Salem and nearby were jailed. At their trials the girls had hysterics when touched by the accused; saw yellow birds bring messages from Satan; and swore that they were threatened by the witches' astral bodies. Many witches confessed – for most who would not were sentenced to death. Two people died in jail; 19 were hanged. But now the Salem girls began to finger prominent persons: Rev. Samuel Willard, President of Harvard; Lady Phips, wife of the Governor. Assisted by Boston divine Increase Mather (1639-1723) – whose more credulous son Cotton Mather (1663-1728) had helped fuel the witch mania – Governor Phips ensured that magistrates ceased to accept "spectral evidence." Of 52 people accused in 1693, only 3 were condemned (and later pardoned). The witch-hunt ended – and by 1736 accusation of witchcraft was a criminal offense in Massachusetts.

A British woodcut from the time of the Salem trials shows witches presenting their infants to the Devil, either for unholy baptism or human sacrifice.

Uproar in court: George Jacobs kneels, pleading for his life, as his own granddaughter accuses him of witchcraft. He was hanged on August 19, 1692.

❏ Sarah Good was hanged on July 19, 1689. On the gallows she was urged to confess by witch-hunter Rev. Nicholas Noyes. She cried: "I am no more a witch than you are a wizard, and if you take away my life, God will give you blood to drink." In 1717, Noyes died after a hemorrhage, choking to death on his own blood.

❏ 80-year-old Giles Cory, whose wife was convicted and hanged, refused to plead at his trial. To loosen his tongue he was subjected to pressing beneath heavy stones, an ordeal dating from medieval Europe, and died under the torture.

❏ Many at nearby Andover were accused of witchcraft by the Salem girls, among them the town's chief magistrate, who fled the colony. They also accused two dogs, which were hanged. But the girls left Andover abruptly when a "worthy Gentleman from Boston" whom they attempted to finger swore out a warrant for slander and demanded damages of £1,000 (perhaps $250,000 today).

❏ Cotton Mather's *Memorable Providences Relating to Witchcrafts and Possessions* (1689) said an unsupported confession "after due examination" (i.e., after denial of food and sleep and after threats of torture) was enough for conviction: "What needs now more witness or further Enquiry?" he asked.

White witches and black magic

British warlock Aleister Crowley may have designed this seal for his own use as grand master of a modern magical cult. "Baphomet" was one of his many aliases.

Modern practitioners of witchcraft – which many call Wicca (Anglo-Saxon: witch) – disassociate their "neo-Pagan religion" and its "white" magic from the "black" practices of Satanism. Wicca owes much to anthropologist Margaret Murray (1863-1963), whose *Witch Cult in Western Europe* (1921) and later books taught that medieval witchcraft stemmed from a pre-Christian, matriarchal, fertility religion. Although most scholars now deny the existence of this old religion, with a Mother Goddess and Horned God (not Satan, but a nature spirit like the Green Man), Murray's beliefs are accepted, for different motives, by many New Age cultists and some feminists. A witchcraft revival surfaced in the 1950s under the leadership of British witch king Gerald Gardner (1884-1964). He called it "a religion of love, pleasure, and excitement," and his instructional manual, *The Book of Shadows*, attracted many. At his death it was estimated there were 5,000 witches in Britain – and Wicca is now said to have up to 50,000 practitioners in the United States. But Gardner's enemies said he accepted too many of the teachings of black magician Aleister Crowley, a major influence on modern Satanism. Crowley was obsessed by sex magic, and it is claimed that many Satanists use their religion as a cover for sexually degrading activity. The practices of Anton Szandor LaVey (now "retired"), who founded the California-based Church of Satan in 1966 and attracted as many as 25,000 disciples, were fairly mild. He declared the sinister sacrifices of the Black Mass outmoded. Real danger may come not from organized Satanism but from the climate of belief it creates. In the United States and elsewhere an increasing number of crimes are committed by people claiming to be possessed by Satan or his demons – and by killers who claim that their victims are agents of the Devil.

"Skyclad" (naked) witches dance at midnight around a bonfire in Ireland in 1981. They hope to invoke the power of a monster inhabiting a nearby lake.

Portrait of Anton LaVey, founder of California's Church of Satan in the 1960s. He appeared as Satan in the movie *Rosemary's Baby* (1968).

A red witch candle, its color signifying that the spell being attempted concerns health or sex, and a reflecting stone.

❏ Although there were no witch trials in Britain after about 1750, witchcraft remained a criminal offense there until 1951. Then, the Witchcraft Act of 1736 was replaced by the Fraudulent Mediums Act, aimed at those who worked scams by pretending to have magical powers.

❏ Perhaps the most successful modern witch was British-born Sybil Leek (1923-83), active in the United States from the 1960s. She made many T.V. appearances (usually with her pet jackdaw, ''Mr. Hotfoot Jackson'';) and wrote some 60 books on magic. At the time of her death she was said to be a millionaire.

❏ Anton LaVey's followers included movie star Jayne Mansfield (above). Her attorney Sam Brody quarreled with LaVey, who cursed him – and in June 1967 warned Mansfield of danger if she continued to see Brody. A few days later the car in which Brody and Mansfield were driving hit a truck, and both were killed.

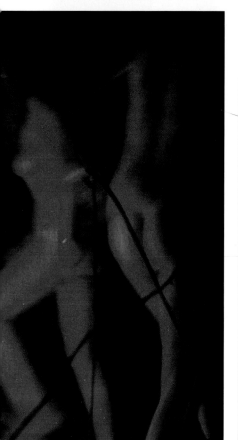

Magical ingredients on sale at a witch doctors' market, La Paz, Bolivia. New Age interest in magic has seen stores like this flourish in North American and European cities.

Magic and the Third Reich

Along with "Adolf Hitler is alive and well and living in California," a favorite tabloid sensation since 1945 has been "Hitler was a black magician." But Hitler's potent and deadly magic lay solely in his own evil genius. He was prepared to pervert and exploit ancient occult lore, not to believe in it. The swastika emblem, originating in the Middle East before about 3000 B.C., was for millennia used worldwide (from ancient Egypt to the Navaho of North America) as a symbol of good fortune. In Nazi hands the *hakenkreuz* (hooked cross) became, Hitler said, a symbol of "the struggle for victory of the Aryan man." The emergent Nazi Party took advantage of an upsurge in occult interest after World War I. It exploited alchemy, helping Munich alchemist Franz Tausend set up Company 164 to change base metals to gold. In 1931 the project collapsed. Tausend went to jail; the party banked a small fortune extracted from investors in the scam. Astrology was seen as a black propaganda tool (fake horoscopes were used by both Axis and Allies), and Karl Ernst Krafft, often named as Hitler's astrologer, may never have met the *Führer*. Hitler's deputy Rudolf Hess may have been a believer: after his flight to Britain in 1941 astrologers thought to have influenced him were imprisoned; Krafft himself died in a concentration camp. One of Hitler's attempts to pervert an ancient mystery may have backfired. In 1938, he had the Holy Lance, supposedly the spear with which a Roman soldier pierced the side of the crucified Christ, removed from Vienna to Nuremberg. It was said to have been carried by the great Germanic leaders Charlemagne and Frederick Barbarossa – both, legend said, had died after mislaying it. On April 30, 1945, U.S. troops took possession of the Lance: hours later Hitler killed himself in Berlin.

The serviceman who wore this paid dearly for his swastika emblem: the Wound Badge in gold was awarded only for five or more wounds.

Although many had good reason to regard him as the Devil incarnate, Hitler had no personal belief in the occult.

Much of magic is ritual – and the Nazis were masters of ritual. Brownshirted stormtroopers' banners flank a rostrum with a giant swastika; Berlin, 1938.

As a mosaic decoration in an old Roman villa in Cyprus, the swastika means good luck. The Nazis made it a badge of shame.

Hitler's magical oratory made evil seem good to many Germans. Here, he speaks at a prewar May Day rally.

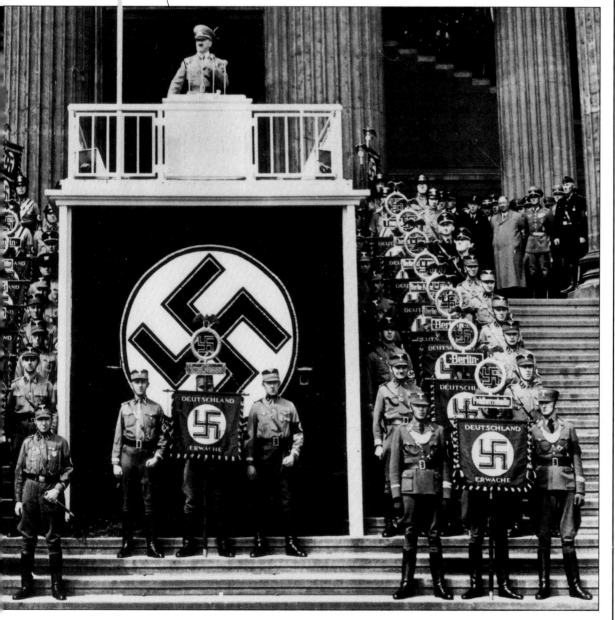

❑ English black magician Aleister Crowley helped spread pro-German propaganda in the United States before U.S. entry into World War I in 1917. He later claimed to have advised future Nazi leaders to adopt the magical swastika emblem (used by his own occult group, the Order of the Golden Dawn, from around 1890). Other sources say the emblem was suggested to Hitler by his dentist.

❑ Hitler's attitude toward astrology, in his own words (recorded by Martin Bormann on July 19, 1942), was: "The horoscope . . . is another swindle whose significance must not be underestimated. Just think of the trouble given to the British by the publication by a well-known astrologer of a horoscope foretelling final victory for Germany!"

❑ German naval intelligence once theorized that the Allies were locating German submarines by "pendulum dowsing" on a map of the Atlantic. German occultists were ordered to predict the movements of Allied ships by similar means. They failed.

❑ The Viennese Holy Lance was only one of four such relics acclaimed in the Middle Ages. There were rival claimants in the Vatican, Rome; in Paris (said to have been brought by King Louis IX (St. Louis; the Crusader) (1215-70) from the Holy Land; and in Cracow, Poland.

Fairy tales

Today, we dismiss fairies as the stuff of children's stories. It was not always so. As recently as the 19th century, fairies held much the same position in popular belief as space aliens do today: many people were skeptical, but a fair number believed. Earlier, even learned men accepted fairies' existence – but not as the pretty, winged, "little people" of traditional book illustrations. Fairies came in even more shapes and sizes than modern aliens: there were delicate elves, misshapen dwarfs, elusive leprechauns, savage trolls, and many more. Most were feared as a powerful, even dangerous people midway between humans and devils – sometimes said to descend from fallen angels not bad enough for Hell, but not good enough for Heaven. They lived underground, sometimes visiting the human world (usually invisibly) from hills or old grave mounds. Though they rewarded good treatment (those who put out a nightly bowl of milk for the sprites might find chores done in return), they were often mischievous or malignant. It was risky even to speak their name – people spoke instead of the "good people," "fair folk," or "men of peace" – and many mysterious misfortunes were blamed on them. Rheumatism or cramps came from fairy blows and pinches; horses found off-color in the morning had been ridden by fairies overnight. If a child ailed, its parents knew the fairies had stolen their healthy baby and left a substitute, or changeling – for they often took mortal children to raise as their own, or to sacrifice, in place of one of themselves, as the seven-yearly tribute they paid to Hell. Even adults were not safe. A sudden death might indicate a fairy kidnapping: the victim had been stolen away, and his or her apparent corpse was a dummy left in its place.

The Dandelion Fairy.

In the 20th century, fairies, once seen as sinister, became pretty sprites in children's tales, as in this illustration from around 1920.

Found in the Pedro Mountains, Wyoming, in 1934, this 14in (36cm) tall mummy was once said to be proof of an ancient race of "little people." In fact, it is the body of a Native American infant.

General Tom Thumb (1838-83) and his wife Lavinia Warren (1841-1919) in 1863: some have theorized that people of restricted stature were the original little folk.

Fairies and gnomes look on as a craftsman elf goes to work: a fantasy illustration of the 1980s. Modern people like to escape into Fairyland, but their ancestors feared it.

❑ When a Scottish laborer found a cache of 84 Norse chessmen on the Isle of Lewis in 1831, he dropped his spade and fled in terror, taking the still figures to be sleeping fairies. His tougher wife sent him back to get them – and the Lewis Chessmen (below) are now displayed in London's British Museum. But the museum's guard dogs apparently agree with the finder: tradition says this is one exhibit they refuse to pass.

❑ The line between fairies and the souls of the dead was sometimes blurred. Tin miners in the Cornwall section of England spoke of friendly goblins called Knockers, who led them to rich seams of ore. Perhaps these originated as nature spirits, but the miners said they were the souls of Jews, punished for their rejection of Christ with endless labor in the mines.

❑ World War II airmen with engine trouble turned, like their ancestors, to the supernatural for an explanation. Any mysterious problem was blamed on Gremlins – modern goblins specializing in technological sabotage.

Sherlock Holmes in Fairyland

Few Englishmen of his time were more popular than Sir Arthur Conan Doyle (1859-1930), creator of the great detective Sherlock Holmes. A master of imaginative writing, he desperately wanted to believe in the paranormal – he was a leading supporter of Spiritualism and psychic research – but his bewitchment by the "Cottingley fairies" brought him widespread ridicule. In July 1917, 16-year-old Elsie Wright of Cottingley, Yorkshire, took a photograph that appeared to show her 10-year-old friend Frances Griffiths with four tiny, winged fairies. Frances photographed Elsie with a grotesque gnome. Their parents assumed the girls had faked the pictures with cutouts from books; the girls insisted that the stream near their village was indeed alive with little people. Mrs. Wright showed the photographs (five were taken in 1917-21) to psychical researchers – who pronounced them genuine. A medium sent by Doyle to investigate also saw fairies at the stream (but failed to photograph them) and decided the girls were natural mediums who enabled elemental spirits to materialize. Although even Elsie Wright's father said the great writer was "bamboozled," Doyle proclaimed in the *Strand Magazine* that the fairies were proven fact and published a full account in *The Coming of the Fairies* (1922). The kindest press comment on his credulity was that to attack such beliefs was like "killing Santa Claus with statistics." The sensation died, to be revived in the 1960s-70s when journalists rediscovered elderly Frances and Elsie. Elsie admitted that they had faked the photographs with cutouts – but only after failing to take genuine photographs of the real fairies. In a T.V. interview in 1976, Frances denied that the photographs were faked.

Many people noticed that the "Cottingley fairies" closely resembled the dancing sprites in this contemporary advertisement.

William Marriott produced this fake to discredit the Cottingley hoax: a photograph of the Night Light fairies is superimposed on one of Conan Doyle.

Price's Night Lights

Frances Griffiths and the leaping fairy, one of the later photographs in the series. Elsie Wright claimed that she took this photograph from a distance of about 3ft (1m) in August 1920.

Popular fairy paintings like this – an illustration from a children's book of 1914 – may have originally inspired the Cottingley girls' prank.

Does it look convincing? Taken in July 1917, the first Cottingley photograph shows 10-year-old Frances with dancing fairies.

Doctor Johnson's strangest case

A hard-nosed realist but by no means a knee-jerk skeptic, Dr. Samuel Johnson, one of the most learned men of his time, proved an ideal "ghostbuster."

In 1759, English businessman William Kent and his mistress Frances (Fanny) Lynes took rooms in the house of Richard Parsons on Cock Lane, in London. Their stay ended in a quarrel when Parsons failed to repay a loan from Kent. The Kents moved nearby, and, in February 1760, Frances died suddenly, officially from smallpox. Parsons claimed to have a vision of her as she lay dying, and very soon his 11-year-old daughter Elizabeth was plagued by a scratching, banging spirit. "Talking" by a knocking code with Methodist minister John Moore, it identified itself as Fanny Lynes – poisoned by William Kent. Kent himself was made to come and hear, and angrily yelled: "Thou art a lying spirit!" Fashionable London flocked to Cock Lane to hear Scratching Fanny, whose knocks, it is recorded, went on even when Elizabeth Parsons was put under restraint. A Committee of Gentlemen was formed to consider whether Kent should be indicted for murder. It was headed by the age's most respected intellect, Dr. Samuel Johnson (1709-84). Fanny promised to prove her bona fides by knocking on Frances Lynes's coffin in the crypt of

The interior of the rectory at Epworth in Lincolnshire – now a museum to the founder of Methodism – where John Wesley and his family experienced poltergeist activity in 1715-16.

St. John's Church. The committee went there, Kent with them, and heard nothing. Johnson's opinion was that Elizabeth Parsons "has some art of making or counterfeiting particular noises, and that there is no agency of any higher cause." Then Elizabeth was caught in bed with a board on which she made knocks and scratchings. The child was spared punishment, but Parsons and his wife were imprisoned for conspiracy, and Moore heavily fined. But many still believed in Scratching Fanny – and when what was said to be Frances Lynes's coffin was opened in 1803 the body showed no trace of smallpox, but was in a condition of adipocere (a sign of arsenic poisoning).

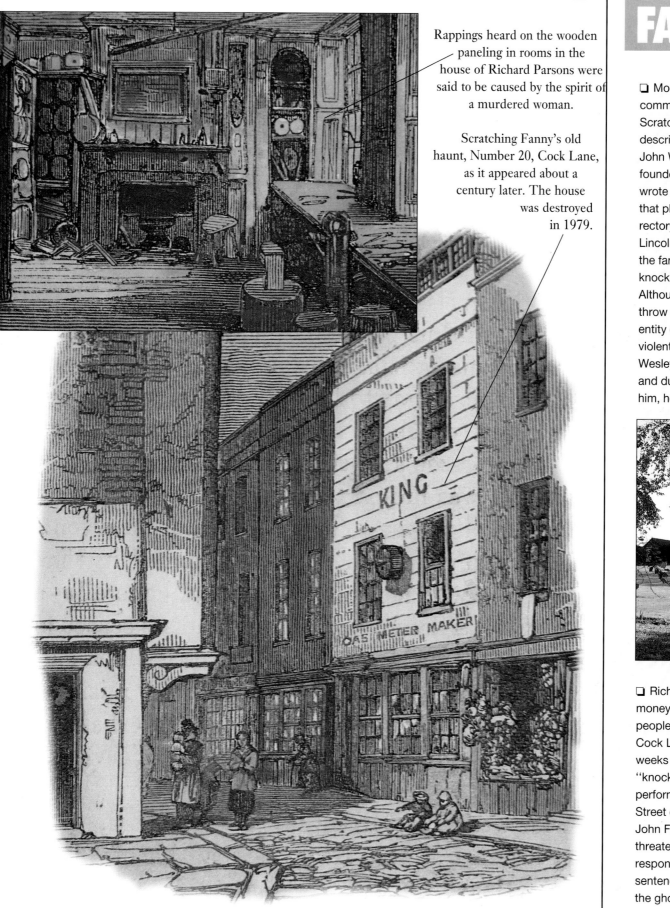

Rappings heard on the wooden paneling in rooms in the house of Richard Parsons were said to be caused by the spirit of a murdered woman.

Scratching Fanny's old haunt, Number 20, Cock Lane, as it appeared about a century later. The house was destroyed in 1979.

❑ Moore's way of communicating with Scratching Fanny was like that described by Johnson's friend John Wesley (1703-91), founder of Methodism. Wesley wrote an account of a spirit that plagued his father's rectory (below) at Epworth, in Lincolnshire, in 1715-16, when the family heard loud knockings by Old Jeffrey. Although noisy and liable to throw objects around, the entity only once became violent: when the Rev. Samuel Wesley challenged the "deaf and dumb devil" to confront him, he was shoved aside.

❑ Richard Parsons made good money from fashionable people who came to hear the Cock Lane knockings. Within weeks of his trial, another "knocking ghost" began performances near the Bow Street court of magistrate Sir John Fielding. When Fielding threatened that those responsible would be sentenced to hard labor in jail, the ghost swiftly fell silent.

The real ghostbusters

Hereward Carrington, among the S.P.R.'s leading researchers in 1900-20, made a special study of "projection of the astral body."

When Lady Palmer photographed her friend Miss Townsend in a chapel at Domrémy, France, in 1925, two "phantom priests" appeared in the background.

Scientific investigation of the supernatural began in 1882, when Frederick Myers, Edmund Gurney, and other academics at Cambridge University founded the Society for Psychical Research (S.P.R.). An American S.P.R. was formed in 1884 under Harvard philosopher-psychologist William James (1842-1910). Early research focused on Spiritualist mediums, but soon widened to include ghosts and – with the work of Professor J.B. Rhine at Duke University in the 1920s-30s – "parapsychology": a word coined by Rhine to embrace E.S.P. and other "wild talents." Throughout their history the S.P.R. and A.S.P.R. have been attacked from all sides. Believers claim their preoccupation with scientific proof, which has always relied much on the camera and now uses state-of-the-art electronics, is inimical to such a sensitive subject. Skeptics say they too readily accept evidence that may be faked (and in that category might include the "ghost" photographs reproduced here). The top U.S. psychic research body today is the Parapsychological Association, founded in 1957 and in 1969 affiliated to the American Association for the Advancement of Science. The major organization of ghostbusting skeptics is the Buffalo-based Committee for the Scientific Investigation of Claims of the Paranormal, which claims supernatural phenomena either have a scientific explanation or are fraudulent.

"It may well be the most genuine ghost photograph we possess," said an S.P.R. spokesman. The Brown Lady of Raynham Hall in England – an apparition reported many times – was captured as a misty, veiled figure by a photographer in 1936.

If, as many experienced psychic researchers believe, this picture is genuine, it ranks among the classics. The ghostly nun materialized at a séance in Lisbon, Portugal, in 1918.

A phantom hand clasps the waist of Vernon D'Cruz of Adelaide, Australia, in this 1975 photograph. His family later said the picture was a hoax – but no one has yet explained how it was done.

❏ Many mocked the academics who founded the S.P.R. Famous scientist Thomas Henry Huxley said: "The only good that I can see in a demonstration of the truth of 'Spiritualism' is to furnish an additional argument against suicide. Better live a crossing-sweeper than die and be made to talk twaddle by a 'medium' hired at a guinea [then about $6] a sentence." When Gurney died in 1888, it was said he had committed suicide on realizing the futility of his researches. Enemies said Myers's main motive in investigating mediums was the chances it gave him to molest girls in darkened rooms.

❏ William James (above) promised A.S.P.R. colleague Professor James Hyslop he would communicate with him after death. Hyslop waited years; then two Spiritualists wrote him from Ireland that "someone called William James" was monopolizing their séances with demands they pass an urgent message to Hyslop (whom it had taken them a long time to trace). The message was "Do you remember the red pajamas?" – a reference to an old, personal joke that convinced Hyslop of its authenticity.

Harry Price, ghost-hunter

Harry Price (1881-1948), Britain's top ghost-hunter, took a scientific approach: he pioneered the use of remote control movie cameras to record phenomena and in 1926 established a National Laboratory of Psychical Research in London. But fellow S.P.R. members criticized his objectivity – and to skeptics he was often a figure of fun. His association with Austrian mystic Baron von Schrenk-Nötzing (nicknamed "Shrink-from-nothing") was said to prove his credulity; so was his attempt, with eccentric philosopher C.E.M. Joad, to turn a white goat into a man by means of magic rites on Germany's haunted Brocken Mountain in 1932. In 1936 he attracted more derision by appearing to endorse "Gef, the talking mongoose," when a family on the Isle of Man claimed their daughter's imaginary pet had materialized and entertained them with conversation and song. Price's major investigation was of England's most haunted house: Borley Rectory in Suffolk, built in 1863 on the site of a much older building. For decades its owners, clergymen and their families, reported hauntings: sounds of bells, voices, footsteps, knockings; sightings of a phantom coach and horses, a headless monk, a spectral nun; and many poltergeist incidents. Price recorded as many as 2,000 "happenings" in 1930-35 alone, when the house was occupied by the Rev. Lionel Foyster and his wife Marianne. In 1937-38, Price himself lived in the rectory and decided that the disturbances were caused by the spirit of a 14th century nun who had been strangled at the site. In 1939 the rectory was destroyed by a fire caused, according to its new owner, by a poltergeist throwing books at an oil lamp. In 1943, Price claimed to have unearthed part of a woman's skull in the ruins, and it is said that when this was reverently buried in 1945 Borley's ghosts ceased to walk.

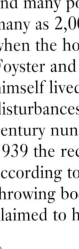

British psychic researcher Harry Price, seen here with one of his gadgets, pioneered the use of electronic aids for ghost-hunting.

Price left his collection of 17,000 occult volumes to London University. The Harry Price Library is now a Mecca for researchers.

England's most haunted house, Borley Rectory, is seen just after it was wrecked by a fire, said to have been caused by a malevolent poltergeist, in March 1939.

Human remains found at Borley in 1943 – said by Harry Price to be those of a nun murdered there – are given Christian burial in 1945.

Harry Price (right) and philosopher Cyril Joad (1891-1953) prepare to work ritual magic on Germany's Brocken Mountain, 1932. The much derided experiment may have simply been a stunt to publicize Price's more serious work.

FACT FILE

❏ For his Brocken ritual (which he said was derived from an ancient magical text), Price needed a "pure maiden;" a potion of soot, honey, rust from church bells, and bat's blood; and a full Moon. The maiden was soon found – but it proved hard to catch bats, and the Moon obstinately remained veiled in mist. The rite failed, and Price and Joad claimed that they had only tried it to show that ritual magic did not work.

❏ In 1979, 80-year-old Marianne Foyster, widow of Rev. Lionel Foyster, told members of the S.P.R. that although some truly supernatural things had happened, her husband had faked many of the poltergeist incidents recorded by Price at Borley Rectory. At the time, Price himself had suspected that "disturbed" Marianne Foyster might be faking phenomena, including spirit messages to her that appeared on the Borley Rectory walls (below).

Marianne Please help get

❏ London University ignored Price's plea to establish a psychical research fellowship, but he left it his collection of 17,000 books on the occult.

Poltergeists, the unquiet spirits

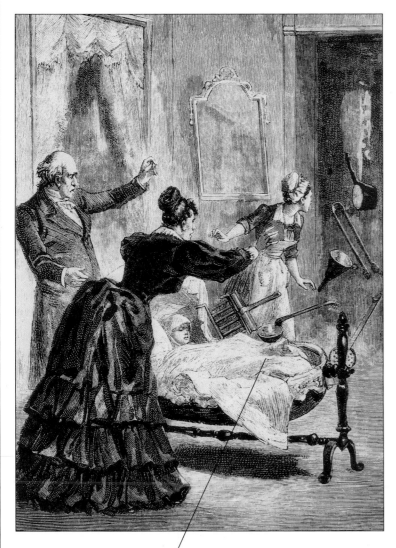

Poltergeist disturbances often involve teenagers. The uproar at a French farm in 1849 ceased after 14-year-old maidservant Adolphine Benoit was subjected to exorcism.

The most common of all ghosts, reported worldwide for many centuries, are those known as poltergeists (from the German words for noisy spirits). It is an apt name, for poltergeists most often manifest themselves in noise-making activities: loud scratchings or knockings; sounds that may be interpreted as human speech; or the violent displacement of objects. They may be simply mischievous, breaking a vase or scribbling on walls; but sometimes seem malevolent, throwing heavy furniture, setting fires, or wrecking houses (as in the celebrated case of the Martin family of Methuen, Mass., driven from two houses in 1963 when poltergeists caused flash floods in their rooms, even when water mains were turned off and pipes drained). Do these activities sound rather like those of delinquent children? Some experts believe this is just what they are, theorizing that psychokinetic forces generated by disturbed youngsters (particularly by the latent sexual energy of adolescents) are linked to such disturbances. The activities of the most famous American poltergeist, the Bell Witch of Adams, Tenn., centered on teenage Betsy Bell in 1817-20. Hundreds claimed to have heard or witnessed the insults and pranks of a spirit that identified itself as Old Kate, most aimed at Betsy's father, John. Matters took a sinister turn when John died – and his family claimed that medicine prescribed for him had been switched for poison by the spirit. Later researchers have suggested that John (whom most contemporary accounts describe as a good man and loving father) perhaps may have treated Betsy cruelly, and that, consciously or unconsciously, she summoned up Old Kate to punish him.

As well as throwing household goods around, poltergeists may use fire or water to achieve their destructive ends. This damage to a home in Brazil was caused by a fire perhaps started by a poltergeist.

In 1985, when this home England was wrecked by alleged poltergeist activity, its occupants received messages via computer from a man who had lived in the 16th century.

Poltergeists infesting a home in France in 1978-81, supposedly produced these graffiti on a piece of paper inside a sealed camera from which the film had vanished.

England's screaming skulls

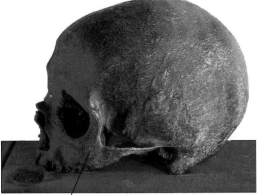

If the skull of Ambrose Barlow, a Roman Catholic priest martyred in 1641, is removed from Wardley Hall, England, screams and thunderclaps are heard.

Ancient peoples kept severed human heads in their homes as war trophies; sometimes as family relics, as we keep photographs of kinfolk; and often to ward off evil. Some English houses still hold guardian skulls that legend says have a life of their own. Bettiscombe Manor, Dorset, has one of the most famous, a skull said to shriek "like a trapped rat" when moved, to rattle by night in ghostly bowling games – and to have heralded World War I by sweating blood. Several owners tried to scrap the grim relic: some reinstated it when local disaster ensued; others were thwarted by the skull itself, which returned whether thrown into a pond or buried deep in the ground. Legend variously says that it is the skull of a murdered girl, or of an 18th century black slave whose master failed to return his body to Africa for burial; scientists say it is prehistoric. The screaming skull of Burton Agnes Hall, Yorkshire, truly belongs there. Anne Griffith, whose father built the hall around 1590, so loved her home that on her deathbed she asked her family to keep her head there – and haunted them with dreadful noises when they tried to disobey. The skull (nicknamed Old Nance) screamed horribly if removed, and Anne's ghost walked the house to guard the relic – until, in 1900, the owners allayed her fears by building it into one of the walls. Theophilus Brome (d.1670) was equally determined to keep his skull at his house, Higher Chilton Farm, where it remains. As a Puritan he may have been motivated less by love of his home than the wish to thwart Royalists, who celebrated the Restoration of King Charles II by digging up dead opponents to exhibit their heads on stakes. Long after such risk was past, Brome's skull is said to have made "horrid noises" when anyone made an attempt to move it.

Some people now fear the skull because it reminds us we all must die; in former times people kept ancestral skulls as venerated relics.

Burton Agnes Hall, in Yorkshire, England, still looks as stately as in this view of 1879. Since 1900 one of its walls has entombed the skull of "Old Nance."

At his own wish, the clothed skeleton of philosopher Jeremy Bentham (d.1832) is now kept on display at University College, London – where his ghost is said to walk in times of trouble.

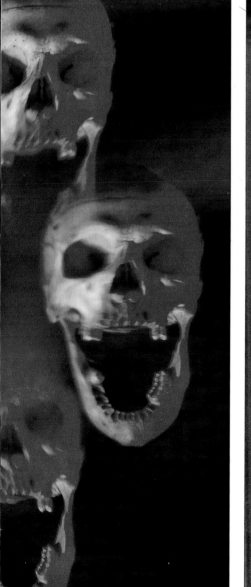

No earthly harbor: ghost ships old and new

Artist Gustave Doré produced this engraving (1873) of one of fiction's most ghastly ghost ships: the ice-bound vessel described in Samuel Taylor Coleridge's *Rime of the Ancient Mariner* (1798).

In 1821 the *Edinburgh Magazine* published an anonymous ghost story: *Vanderdecken's Message Home*. It told of a Dutch sea captain who swore an ungodly oath to round the Cape of Good Hope if it took to all eternity. For his blasphemy he was condemned to sail on forever, bringing bad luck to all who sighted him. The tale inspired Richard Wagner's opera *Der fliegende Holländer* (1843) – and launched the world's most famous ghost ship, the *Flying Dutchman*.

For a specter with its origin in fiction, the *Dutchman* has attracted a surprising number of sightings. Few witnesses to any ghost outrank Britain's King George V (1865-1936), who, as a young naval officer in 1881, saw the ship in her most common haunt off the Cape. The officer who recorded the sighting in the log of the *Bacchante* – "a strange red light . . . a ship all aglow . . . some 200 yards distant" – died mysteriously soon afterwards. Sightings of the *Dutchman* and other ghost ships have been attributed to mirages, a trick of light refraction that can produce a "ghostly" image of a real vessel many miles away. This cannot fully explain the apparition of a 4,300 ton nuclear-powered attack submarine. On April 10, 1963, the U.S. Navy's *Thresher* failed to surface from deep diving trials east of Cape Cod; 129 men died in the worst submarine disaster of all time. In July 1967, cruising the same waters in the yacht *Yorktown Clipper*, Boston businessman John S. Schultz and his family saw a huge submarine surface nearby, briefly rise a few feet above the waves, fold up, and then disappear. From the serial numbers clearly visible, Schultz later identified the ghost ship as the *Thresher*.

Sailors show horror as the *Flying Dutchman* is sighted. The picture dates from the 19th century, when the legend became popular, but tales of ghost ships are old as seamanship itself.

Modern technology provides no protection from the phantoms of the sea: a German World War I U-boat like this is said to have been haunted to its destruction.

The young naval officer later to become Britain's King George V claimed he saw the *Flying Dutchman*. No one suggested he should tell that to the Marines!

❑ An accident at the launching of *U-65*, a German submarine of World War I, killed a dockyard worker. Four crewmen died accidentally during her sea trials – and six more in a torpedo explosion as she armed for her first war patrol. Her captain was killed in an air raid ashore – but was later seen coming aboard. The crew refused to sail until the *U-65* was exorcised by a priest. On July 10, 1918, she was sighted drifting on the surface by a U.S. submarine. As it prepared to attack, the U-boat exploded and sank. There were no survivors.

❑ On June 22, 1893, the British battleship *Victoria* was rammed and sunk by her consort *Camperdown*. Admiral Sir George Tryon (above), whose confused order for a turning maneuver led to the disaster, went down with the *Victoria*. As the warship sank, a crowd of high society members in Lady Tryon's London mansion saw Admiral Tryon's figure walk swiftly and silently through the room.

The haunted White House

I f the sites of great and violent events are those most likely to be haunted, it is no surprise that the White House in Washington, D.C., has its ghosts. Its very name is connected with an act of violence: its gray Virginia stone was painted white to cover scorch marks made by British troops who set it afire in the War of 1812. John Adams (2nd President; 1797-1801) moved in while the mansion was still building. His wife Abigail found the place comfortless and dirty – which is, perhaps, why her ghost has been seen hard at work on laundry in the East Room. Another unquiet First Lady is Dolley Madison (1768-1849). It is said that in 1917, when President Wilson's wife Edith ordered the rose garden Dolley had planned to be moved, Mrs. Madison put in an appearance that scared away the gardeners. But the presence most often felt is that of Abraham Lincoln, whose administrations saw much violence and ended tragically. The Lincolns' 12-year-old son Willie died in the White House, where his ghost was later reported by members of President Grant's family. Lincoln's ghost was often seen near his grave at Oak Ridge Cemetery, Springfield, Ill.; his first appearance (he had earlier been heard and sensed) at the White House was when Grace Coolidge, wife of President Calvin Coolidge (in office 1923-29), saw him standing at a window in the Oval Office. During World War II, Lincoln appeared to Queen Wilhelmina of the Netherlands (a convinced Spiritualist) in her White House bedroom. When she told President Franklin Roosevelt, he calmly replied that Mrs. Roosevelt and many others had seen or heard the ghost in or near the room – and one of his secretaries had seen Lincoln sitting on the bed there, putting on his boots.

Designed by Daniel Chester French and dedicated in 1922, this massive, seated figure at Washington's Lincoln Memorial, is an ever-present reminder of the 16th president, whose spirit walks the White House.

Tranquil under the floodlights: but many inhabitants of the White House – among them Presidents Ulysses S. Grant, Theodore Roosevelt, and Herbert Hoover – reported ghostly happenings there during their terms of office.

❏ Mary Todd Lincoln became a devotee of Spiritualism and held séances in the White House. On one occasion a medium is said to have levitated a grand piano while Lincoln himself and two other men sat on it. After Lincoln's death, a photographer called William Mumler photographed a widow in deep mourning. When the plate was developed it showed the ghostly figure of Lincoln standing behind her (below). The widow then admitted she was Mary Todd Lincoln – which Mumler (who was later ruined by accusations of trickery) claimed he had not known.

Abigail Adams, wife of 2nd President John Adams, was the first First Lady to live in the White House, 1800. She found the new mansion uncomfortable: her spirit, it is said, still tries to clean it up.

Abraham Lincoln's presence is the one most often experienced in the White House. He has been seen in the Lincoln Bedroom, shown here, and looking out a window in the Oval Office.

❏ Hard-headed President Truman once said in a T.V. interview that Lincoln's ghost had knocked on his bedroom door – but later insisted that he had been joking.

Victims of violence

Comparatively few well-attested hauntings are recorded in connection with the Civil War, the most violent era in U.S. history. Of all its battlefields, the only one where ghostly soldiers have often been seen is Shiloh (Pittsburg Landing), Tenn., where more than 20,000 Union and Confederate soldiers died on April 6-7, 1862. But Shiloh's first "ghosts" appeared soon after the War – and were all too real. Ex-Confederates who formed a *Kuklos* (Greek: circle; i.e. club) in Pulaski, Tenn., wore white robes and hoods to hide their identity. Superstitious people murmured that the mystery men were the ghosts of Confederate dead from Shiloh – and *Kuklos* extremists used the legend to launch the terror of the Ku Klux Klan. Other American victims of violence whose ghosts have been heard (but not seen) include 52 passengers from the Mississippi riverboat *Iron Mountain*. New Orleans-bound from Vicksburg, Miss., the 180ft (55m) craft vanished without trace in June 1872. Many believe she was broken up, and all aboard murdered, by river pirates: there are periodic reports from Vicksburg, Natchez, and St. Joseph of agonized cries for help from the river, spoken in the French Creole patois of Iron Mountain's female passengers. Weapons made by the famous Winchester company played a major part in the settlement of the United States. The use of armaments so troubled Sarah L. Winchester (1838-1922) that she spent $20,000,000 in building and maintaining a huge mansion to shelter the spirits of those killed by Winchester arms. The Winchester Mystery House in California's Santa Clara Valley is a maze of 160 rooms (many with 13 windows), connected by 40 stairways (most with 13 steps). Sarah lived there for 36 years (except for a 6-year break when, believing a new Flood was due, she moved to a luxury houseboat), regularly giving banquets for 13: herself and 12 ghostly guests.

Reflecting the state's long, often violent history, many of the colonial mansions of Virginia – such as Edgewood, in Charles City, seen here – are reputed to be haunted.

The sprawling Winchester Mystery House at San Jose, Cal., was built over a period of more than 30 years by Sarah Winchester as a haven for the spirits of those killed by Winchester arms.

In the 19th century psychic Edward Wyllie went looking for America's ghosts with his camera. The results included this photograph of c.1890.

Early victims of their vicious activities were cowed by rumors that Ku Klux Klan members were the ghosts of Confederate soldiers.

Stranger than truth

Tabloid hype made a home on Long Island infamous in the 1970s. But the house seen here in a still from *The Amityville Horror* (1979) was a stand in.

In two of the best-known U.S. supernatural cases of recent years, fiction – aided by media hype – has proved stranger than truth. The movie *The Exorcist* (1973) was "based on reality." In fact, it was originally a minor poltergeist case. In 1949 the Washington, D.C., home of Douglas Deen (14) was plagued by the kind of poltergeist activity associated with high-strung teenagers. After exorcism by a priest, the disturbances ceased. Author William Peter Blatty wove a fine horror tale around the incident – but did not pretend that his possessed girl, levitating and contorting, and her resident demon that mocked the horrified exorcist, were anything but fiction. But many people believe the "true story" – and probably even more credit the Amityville tale. No one denies that on November 13, 1974, at 112 Ocean Avenue, Amityville, L.I., Ronald DeFeo, Jr. (24) shot to death six members of his family. He pleaded insanity, but was given six life sentences. What is questioned is what followed the purchase of the death house by George and Kathy Lutz. They fled after 26 days' residence in December 1975-January 1976, alleging malignant poltergeist activity and attempted "possession." George, they said, had begun to resemble Ronald DeFeo; Kathy had levitated and had been temporarily transformed into an old, hideous crone. Jay Anson's account of their ordeal, *The Amityville Horror*, made a bestselling book and blockbusting movie. The respected American Parapsychological Association declared the tale mostly fiction, but the mystery still grows. Amateur ghost-hunters have "proved" that the Amityville house stands over a Native American burial ground and that an inhabitant of a house on the lot in the 1700s practiced black magic on the spot where Ronald DeFeo established a red-painted "den."

Priests watch in helpless amazement as the body of a young girl possessed by the Devil rises aloft: a scene from *The Exorcist* (1973). Writer William Peter Blatty based his story on a real incident.

If emotionally resonant places are the most likely to be haunted, then Alcatraz Island, San Francisco Bay, site of the most famous U.S. top security prison from 1934 to 1962, should be infested by spooks.

Fear of possession by demons has long haunted humanity. The *Bible* tells us how Jesus himself performed the rite of exorcism, seen here in a 10th century ivory carving.

FACT FILE

❏ The makers of the movie *The Amityville Horror* claimed they "dare not" film at the actual house, but used a similar building in New Jersey. However, occupants of the house since the Lutzes' time have reported no disturbances (except, presumably, from credulous rubberneckers).

❏ Jay Anson did not vouch for the truth of the Amityville story, saying he just wrote down what the Lutzes told him. But both he and actor James Brolin, who starred in the first Amityville movie, claimed to have been affected by the curse. Brolin had several inexplicable accidents while filming; Anson reported a train of sudden deaths and accidents involving those to whom he showed his manuscript. Ronald DeFeo himself, although claiming at his trial that he had heard voices that urged him to kill and that "something had gotten inside him," has always denied any belief in the supernatural. This did not prevent his lawyer, when the Amityville story broke, from seeking a retrial on the grounds of new evidence.

❏ Like homes housing troubled teenagers, prisons are likely sites of psychic disturbance. In April 1908, prisoners in a jail at Asheville, N.C., petitioned for protection against ghosts and demons – and were supported by guards who had heard strange sounds.

SUPERFACTS

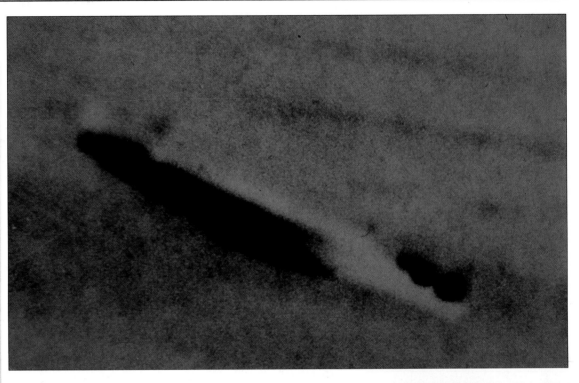

⚠ Beware of hoaxes!

Enthusiastic Ufologists claim medieval chronicles contain many mentions of strange sky craft, or U.F.O.s (above). A famous account, still printed as fact in some books, is said to have been compiled at Ampleforth Abbey, England, in 1290. The monks witnessed "a large round silver thing like a disk, that flew slowly over them and excited the greatest terror. Whereat Abbot Henry cried that it was the fault of Brother Wilfred, an adulterer . . . " Unfortunately this picturesque account, in Latin, was concocted by two British schoolboys, who managed to get it published in *The Times* newspaper in 1953.

Saved by logic

Today we may ascribe paranormal travel to U.F.O. kidnappings or teleportation: earlier people blamed the Devil. In the 9th century four travelers arrived near Lyons, France, in "a cloud-ship." They said they had been hijacked by men with strange powers, including air transport. The locals thought it sounded fishy and decided to stone them to death. But the local archbishop, St. Agobard, turned his logic on the case. Cloud-ships, he said, did not exist – so the strangers must be innocent of the crime of riding in one. They were released.

U.F.O.-gate?

One of the first men to claim to have been taken for a ride in a U.F.O., in 1949, was Daniel Fry, then an engineer at White Sands missile range, N.Mex. In 1968, claims Fry, he acted as an intermediary between an E.T. called "Alan" and President-elect Richard Nixon, passing on Alan's advice about White House staff appointees.

Smoke without fire

Popular accounts of spontaneous human combustion still cite the "triple finger of fire" that struck down three unconnected individuals on April 7, 1938. In

Britain, George Turner burned to ashes in his truck – a can of gasoline beside him was untouched; in Holland, Willem ten Bruik burned up at the wheel of his Volkswagen; at sea, John Greeley went up in flames at the helm of the *Ulrich*. It was an impressive coincidence – until skeptical researchers checked up. There was no record of a ship named *Ulrich*, or of the death of

288

George Turner – and Willem ten Bruik's Volkswagen is equally fictitious: Volkswagen production did not begin until May 1938.

▼ God's broad acres

By the early 19th century Britain's city churchyards were so crowded that corpses often were buried only a few inches deep: an easy target for bodysnatchers as well as a danger to public health. A similar problem in some U.S. cities was solved by Dr. Jacob Bigelow of Boston, who pioneered "garden cemeteries" (below) in the countryside. The first was Mount Auburn Cemetery, Cambridge, Mass., a former picnic ground for Harvard students, opened in 1831.

Batman scam

As late as the 17th century, unscrupulous surgeons profited from an exorcism scam. They diagnosed "demonic possession," curable by a simple operation. As the quack made a small incision in the patient's abdomen, his assistant released a live bat from a bag – and the relieved patient was told to watch the liberated demon fly away.

Man for the job

A few months before the end of the Pacific War in 1945, Lieutenant Hiroo Onoda of the Imperial Japanese Army was given command of a guerrilla force on Lubang Island, Philippines, and ordered to fight "until we return for you." Onoda's war lasted 30 years: he waged a campaign in which all his men died (and some 30 Filipinos were killed) until March 1974, when his former commander was sent back to order him to surrender. In June 1992 the Japanese government funded a survival skills school for teenagers in the Fukushima mountains. Its director was a man uniquely qualified for the task: Hiroo Onoda.

Dirty tricks

In 1953 the American illusionist John Mulholland was asked to write a top secret manual on conjuring tricks. It was intended for the use of C.I.A. agents, who might need to drug drinks, switch documents, or perform other sleight of hand feats during their missions.

▼ Stone magic

Despite protests by the clergy, British locals held to the belief (as some still do) that ancient stone circles had powers of healing and fertility. Parents carried sick children to the stones as a cure; infertile women rubbed themselves against rocks with nicknames such as the Stone Mare in the belief they would become pregnant. Lusty fertility rites persisted at circles such as Avebury Rings (below) into the 18th century: a shocked 16th century antiquarian recorded that "of fortie, three-score or a hundred maidens going there . . . scarcely the third part returned home undefiled."

SUPERFACTS

Cannonball caper ▶
A favorite experiment of Flat Earthists, who also claimed that Earth stood still in space, was to fire a cannon vertically into the air. The ball fell back to Earth at its launching point – thus proving Earth was stationary. Opponents of the astronomer Galileo (1564-1642) (right) used this trick to refute his claim that Earth revolved, scoffing at his explanation that the cannonball itself turned with the turning Earth. The Inquisition ordered Galileo to keep silent or face heresy charges. As late as the 1920s, 200 years after Newton's law of gravity, Britain's Zetetics tried to confound opponents with the cannonball caper.

▼ Genesis in Atlantis
In the 1920s, Karl Zschaetzch combined the legendary lost continent Atlantis (below) and the Biblical Creation story. His Atlantis was an earthly paradise whose people lived in perfect, vegetarian innocence until a woman (Eve) brought them the demon alcohol in the form of hard cider (i.e. apples – The *Bible*'s forbidden fruit). The corrupted

Atlanteans were ''expelled from Eden'' when a comet strike destroyed their home – but a few survivors married into inferior races of other lands to found the modern human race.

Auto-hex
Hexing is an ancient art of African shamans – but some keep their maledictions well up to date. It is reported that a favorite curse against males in modern Ghana is: ''May your sexual organ become as bent as the gearshift of a Mercedes Benz.''

◀Triskaidekaphobics

For the same reason that the Concorde (left) has no Row 13, many hotels in the United States and Europe have no floor or rooms with the unlucky number. The London Hilton, however, has a floor 13 – and reported in 1992 that its room number 1313 is much in demand. At London's famous Savoy Hotel a carved black cat, Kaspar, is always given a place setting at any meal where there are 13 diners. The custom dates from 1898, when South African millionaire Woolf Joel gave a dinner for 13 persons – ignoring the warnings of triskaidekaphobic friends – and was murdered soon afterwards.

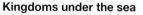

Kingdoms under the sea

Britain claims three legendary drowned kingdoms: Tyno Helig and the Lowland Hundred, off Wales, and Lyonesse, off Cornwall. Tradition says the gods drowned Tyno Helig to punish its ruler's sins; the Lowland Hundred was swamped when a drunken partygoer opened its sluice gates; Lyonesse fell to the sea's wrath. The areas where all three are said to lie were indeed inhabited in ancient times, but the great kingdoms are fiction, perhaps inspired by "drowned palaces" – really natural rock formations – visible at low tide.

The long sleep

Some researchers believe that everyone has extrasensory perception (E.S.P.) potential, but that few have conscious access to it. It may be released in Out of Body Experiences, reported by people who "die" and then revive, or in subjects under hypnosis – and has appeared in coma victims. One was Molly Fancher of Brooklyn, who lay in a coma for 46 years. In 1875 doctors found the unconscious woman could describe the contents of sealed documents and say what people were doing miles away. In 1912 she revived – and her gift vanished. She died in 1915, aged 73.

Waters of forgetfulness

It has been claimed that a disaster zone of Bermuda Triangle type lies along the U.S.-Canada border in the area of the Great Lakes. Since the 19th century, it is said, many ships and, later, aircraft, have inexpicably disappeared there. Unlike its more famous counterpart, the Great Lakes Triangle sometimes gives up survivors of the mysterious wrecks – but they can never remember how their crafts were lost.

Royal understatements

King Louis XVI of France ties with England's George III as history's most incompetent diarist. Louis's entry for July 14, 1789, when the storming of the Bastille prison by Parisians marked the beginning of the revolution that was to cost him his head, was: "Nothing happened." George's entry, "Nothing of importance happened today," was made on July 4, 1776. (It would be weeks before a ship brought the latest news from his American colonies.)

▼ Unlikely tale

An outrageous hoax perpetrated by Britain's *Sunday Sport* tabloid was its 1988 story: "World War II bomber found on Moon." It was followed by "World War II bomber found on Moon vanishes"; and finally by "World War II bomber back from Moon," describing how the U.S. Privateer aircraft, "catapulted to the Moon by a Black Hole above the Bermuda Triangle" (below) had been landed at London's Heathrow airport by a pilot who had been in suspended animation since 1944.

SUPERFACTS

▼ Hot foot
Dr. Jearl Walker, Professor of Physics at Ohio's Cleveland State University, theorized that fire walkers (below) were able to perform unharmed not through faith alone, but because sweat or water on their feet made a protective layer because of the Leidenfrost effect (named for a German scientist who, in 1756, observed that water dropped on a very hot surface dances, taking longer to evaporate than on a cooler surface). In 1980, Dr. Walker tested his belief in a home-made, 5ft (1.5m) fire pit: sometimes it worked – but sometimes, to his sorrow it did not.

Devil's deuce
American gamblers say it is bad luck to receive a $2 dollar bill (deuce) when playing, perhaps because "deuce" is another word for the Devil. To avert the curse, a corner must be torn from the bill; if it already lacks all its corners, it must be destroyed.

Accursed castle ▶
Archduke Franz Ferdinand, killed in a jinxed car in 1914, is said to have courted doom by living in accursed Miramar Castle (right), near Trieste, Italy. The picturesque Habsburg palace was built in 1856 for Archduke Maximilian: his reign as Emperor of Mexico ended in front of a firing squad; his wife went insane. Empress Elizabeth and her son Archduke Rudolf lived there in the 1880s: Elizabeth was assassinated; Rudolf committed suicide. In World War II it was taken over by the British Army, which lost two generals there to sudden, unexpected heart attacks.

By Godfrey!
In 1678, British magistrate Sir Edmund Berry Godfrey, who had recently presided at the trials of Roman Catholics accused of plotting against King Charles II, was found murdered. Suspects under torture named three assassins who (although probably innocent) were executed near the site of the killing, on Greenberry Hill (now Primrose Hill), London. Their names were Green, Berry, and Hill.

Money for old rope
A British newspaper in the 1860s reported that gamblers would pay up to £8 (then about $50, a month's pay for a skilled worker) for a small piece of hangman's rope, a charm to guarantee success at cards.

Unlucky merman
12th century chronicles tell how fishermen in England, caught a naked, shaggy "wild man" in their nets. They took him to be a merman (a man living in the sea, not the fish-tailed version), for he swam like an eel, ate raw fish,

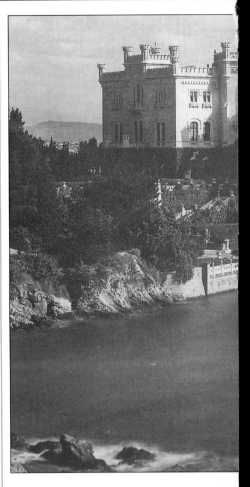

knew nothing of Christianity, and did not speak "even when hung up by his feet and cruelly

before boarding, they met a priest, lawyer, or crosseyed person. Aboard, bad luck was certain if anyone mentioned rabbits or whistled, if a woman was aboard, or if the ship's name ended in "a." Sailors took care never to lend an undamaged article or sew during a storm. They saw it as tempting fate to learn to swim, preferring to wear gold earrings as a charm against drowning.

▼ Pig girl

"Wolf children" (below) are usually said to be found or stolen by their animal foster parents – but a Chinese "pig girl" left her human family by choice. Born on a farm near Canton, Cho-Lee preferred pigs as playmates to her brothers or twin sister, and at the age of three, despite parental protest, moved into the pigsty for good. Until she was five, she lived on sow's milk; later she joined her friends at the trough. Locals who tried to rescue her were driven off by the pigs. An animal behaviorist who studied the odd "family" found Cho-Lee was of normal intelligence and just enjoyed making a pig of herself.

Lady Wonder: equine oracle

In the 1930s-50s crowds flocked to see Lady, or Lady Wonder, the "talking horse" of Richmond, Va., answer questions via a kind of giant typewriter. They were not the usual math problems offered to "educated animals," but requests for predictions. The unusual prophetess accurately forecast election winners and sport results, located lost property, and was even consulted by the police in missing persons cases. Scientists concluded that she had real psychic powers. But a striking feature in contemporary reports is the strong dislike the "loathsome-looking mare" frequently aroused. Often she exposed forgotten scandals and tragedies, and clients left in tears, accusing her owners of trafficking with the Devil.

a kind of fish bearing resemblance to humanity, or an evil spirit lurking in the body of a drowned man." History does not record his eventual fate.

◄ Lucky for some

If tales of a certain Mrs. Murray are true, she may have been a "Jonah," dooming the ships she traveled in, but her own luck was certainly amazing. This legendary lady is said to have survived the *Titanic* disaster (left); the torpedoing and sinking of the liner *Lusitania* in 1915; and the loss of the liner *Celtic*, rammed and sunk in 1927.

Wary sailors

Sailors are more superstitious than most people. Until recently, seamen would not sail on Fridays and were reluctant to do so if,

tortured." His captors kept him for two months, but never decided if he was "mortal man, or

MEN AND MONSTERS

Autobiography after death

Medium Joan Grant believed that she possessed the ability of the priests of ancient Egypt (which she called "far memory") to remember past incarnations and to recall at least 10 former lives. In 1937 she used this skill to write *Winged Pharaoh* – apparently a historical novel, but termed by Grant a "posthumous autobiography": an account of her previous life as Sekeeta, daughter of an Egyptian pharaoh who herself becomes a priest-pharaoh.

Plague of mermaids

The spread of plague baffled most 17th century doctors. But the German scientist and priest Athanasius Kirchner (1601-80), inventor of the "magic lantern," theorized that it was due to contagion from the decaying bodies of dead mermaids.

▲ Houdini's message

Obsessed with desire to prove or disprove an afterlife, Houdini (above) left his wife Beatrice a code message that would let her check if any spirit medium's contact with him after death was genuine. Spiritualists rejoiced when Beatrice said medium Arthur Ford had received a genuine message – but when it was claimed that she was plotting with Ford to make money from the sensational news, she denied her statement. Ford was in the news again in 1967: in a televised séance at Toronto he acted as middleman in a conversation between James L. Pike, former Episcopal Bishop of California, and his son, a recent suicide.

Beast of the Great Beast? ▶

Some writers on the Loch Ness monster have pointed out that around 1901, before modern sightings of the monster, Aleister Crowley (right) spent several months attempting to

"raise demons" at Boleskin House, near Loch Ness. They theorize that Crowley's rituals may have raised up from Hell an unearthly beast that the magician released into the Loch.

were made in long range hypnosis by telepathy), no one knows why hypnotism works. Leading U.S. hypnotist Stanley V. Mitchell was allowed to take part in Soviet experiments in 1964. He reported that he hypnotized a girl and gave her a set of complex instructions that she obeyed perfectly. Only afterwards did the Soviets reveal that the girl understood no English – the language Mitchell had used. He theorized that a kind of psychic translator must have been involved.

The gift of tongues
Most people recalling past lives through hypnotic regression use their native language, though often with the accent and words of earlier periods. But a few respond in a language apparently unknown to them when conscious. An American woman under regression became a Swedish peasant, speaking Swedish in a deep male voice, although research proved she had no knowledge of the language.

Sharada takes over
Researchers into reincarnation differentiate between regression to past lives and possession, when a person is apparently taken over at intervals by another personality, losing awareness of the present self. A classic case was that of an Indian university teacher in 1974-78. When possessed, she dressed, acted, and spoke as an early 19th century Bengali woman, called Sharada. Sharada knew nothing of modern inventions and technology, but, speaking Bengali (a language unknown to the original personality), described in detail her life in Bengal between 1810 and 1830 and her death caused by snakebite.

Talkative statues
France's first Spiritualist circle was founded in 1850 by Baron Ludwig de Güldenstubbé. His enthusiasm discredited the movement when he decided it was possible to communicate with the illustrious dead through their statues. In Paris museums, he left writing materials at statues of such notables as Socrates, St. Paul, and Mary, Queen of Scots – and was delighted later to find messages written in their own languages. He published a collection of some 500 ''spirit messages'' thus received – and would never admit that he might have been, and almost certainly was, hoaxed.

▼ Highly charged
Some scientists say that the auras revealed by Kirlian photography (below) are simply the effects of small electromagnetic charges generated by the cells of all living things. There have been reports of individuals in whom the body's electromagnetic charge became very high, usually after a serious illness or emotional shock. In 1877, Caroline Clare of Ontario, Canada, became a ''human magnet,'' attracting metal objects as large as silverware. In the 1890s it was reported that Jennie Morgan of Missouri generated such a high charge that people who touched her were sometimes knocked senseless.

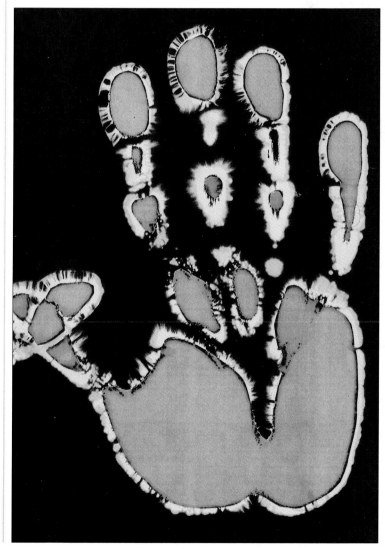

▲ Siberian magic
Two very dissimilar people are said, like the holy terror Rasputin, to have owed their powers to occult lore learned from Siberian shamans (above). One was Genghis Khan, great Mongol war leader of the Middle Ages. The other was the ballet dancer Vaslav Nijinsky (1890-1950), whose miraculous leaps – ''He doesn't just go up higher: he comes down slower!'' – caused many who saw them to believe that he could levitate at will.

Psychic translator
Despite intensive research, especially in the former Soviet Union (where, in the Cold War, reportedly successful experiments

SUPERFACTS

Shakespeare tells all

In the 1940s medium Hester Dowden "solved" the question of the authorship of Shakespeare's plays by automatic writing. Messages from Shakespeare and other Elizabethan dramatists said they were written jointly by Shakespeare, Lord Oxford, Francis Beaumont, and John Fletcher – and edited by Francis Bacon. Oxford, Dowden reported, wrote most of Shakespeare's sonnets – in proof of which he "wrote" three new ones for her.

▼ Hostile witness

The Rev. William Stainton Moses (1839-92) regarded Spiritualism as "dreary twaddle" – until he found he was a medium himself. He received spirit teachings through automatic writing purporting to be by 49 communicators, including Old Testament prophets and Greek philosophers (below). But he continued to distrust the notion of spirit communication, preferring to believe his unconscious mind responsible. Although he dutifully recorded 24 volumes of automatic writing, he was quite prepared to argue with his spirit informants, whom he once accused of being "silly and frivolous, if not mischievous."

Flying saint ▶

St. Joseph of Copertino (1603-63; canonized 1767), a Franciscan friar, often levitated (right). The Church tried to suppress sensational reports, but Joseph's flights were seen by many, among them Pope Urban VIII, who it is said remarked testily: "If he must do this, give him a bucket of whitewash and let him paint the ceiling." Joseph so often disrupted services by floating aloft in religious ecstasy that he was banned from the chapel. He continued to levitate

elsewhere: once, monks had to rescue him by ladder from a tree in which he had landed. In his last days, the doctor found him not on his deathbed, but hovering inches above it.

Snake on a roll

Ancient Greek writers describe the Amphisbaena ("going both ways") as a venomous snake with a head at each end. Gripping one head with the other, it formed itself into a hoop and rolled rapidly along. As late as the 16th century doctors prescribed its flesh as a cure for chilblains. It has a modern parallel in the hoop snake of American folklore.

Tops and bottoms

In the 1960s a British palmist developed "mammarism": predicting women's futures from prints of their breasts. He prospered until a skeptic asked him to interpret prints actually made by two oranges: the seer predicted a brilliant future, but warned of possible Vitamin C deficiency! He then turned to readings based on prints of women's buttocks.

Dead man's hand

Two pair is a promising hand at draw poker. But beware of the "dead man's hand": two aces and two eights. The combination got its unlucky reputation because it was the hand held by Wild Bill Hickok when he was shot in the back by Jack McCall in a saloon in Deadwood, South Dakota, on August 2, 1876.

Monsters crawl among us! ▶

Classical monsters survive in the biological names of modern creepy-crawlies. The Amphisbaena, two-headed snake of myth, is a small, legless lizard: its tail has markings mimicking a second head to confuse predators. The Hydra (right) (antiquity's nine-headed monster) is a tiny, tentacled water creature about 0.5in (13mm) long. The Basilisk is a little crested lizard related to the iguanas – quite unable to kill anyone who confronts it with a glance like its fabulous namesake (below).

works now seem slow and dated, but they are still remarkable both for quantity and for their obscure historical knowledge.

▼ Holy mermaid

The early Christian Church disapproved of mermaids (below) and their like. But when fishermen captured a singing mermaid in Belfast Lough, Northern Ireland, in A.D. 558, locals were unwilling to see her damned. After arguments among local clergy over whose church should receive her, St. Comgall, Bishop of Bangor, baptized her with the name of Murgen ("sea-born"). She died a Christian, and – by the Celtic custom of highly informal canonization – became renowned as St. Murgen. Tradition attributes many miracles to the mermaid saint.

A talkative spirit

Perhaps the most prolific automatic writer was "Patience Worth." From 1913 until her death in 1938, medium Pearl Curran of Missouri received communications from Patience, said to be a 17th century emigrant to America. After initial contact by Ouija board, Patience dictated a huge number of poems, novels, and plays at vast speed via automatic writing. Acclaimed at the time as masterpieces, her

SUPERFACTS

Dragon flight ▷

In 1979, Peter Dickinson explained how dragons flew. Wings were for propulsion and steering only: the dragon was kept aloft by masses of lighter-than-air hydrogen in its body – a sort of animated airship. Dickinson theorized that dragons (right) produced hydrogen by the reaction of hydrochloric acid (present in the digestive system) on calcium from the bone structure (easily replaced by eating limestone). The process was nonstop, so a resting dragon produced a surplus of hydrogen that it disposed of by burning: hence the fiery breath. This explains the absence of dragon remains: the process, continuing after death, would destroy the dragon's body.

First, catch your unicorn

According to medieval lore, boots made of unicorn hide kept the feet and legs healthy – and protected the wearer from plague.

Noisy beast

Medieval romance records the Questing Beast, an unusual creature with serpent's head, leopard's body, lion's haunches, and stag's feet. The knight Sir Palomides devoted his life to its pursuit. Tracking it must have been easy, because its belly continually made the sound of a pack of hounds baying ("questing"), but it is not anywhere recorded that the Questing Beast was ever caught.

Zana the ape-woman

In the mid-19th century, Russian villagers captured a female Alma

(Russian "Yeti"). Zana, as they named her, was heavily built, hairy, with ape-like features. For some years she was untamable, but at last villagers taught her simple chores like grinding corn – and simple pleasures like drinking wine. She had several children, most of whom died under her inexpert care. Later offspring were raised by villagers: unlike their mother, they grew up as humans, able to talk. Zana died in 1890; her last child lived until 1954. Her grandchildren showed their

heritage in dark skins and massive jaws: her grandson Shalikula could pick up a chair, with a grown man sitting on it, with his teeth.

Cards of ill omen

Common to many methods of prediction with playing cards is the belief that spades is an unlucky suit. Ill fortune is associated with the two of spades (coffin) and the nine (death or the Devil.) Other unlucky cards include the nine of diamonds (Curse of Scotland,

perhaps because it resembles the crest of the Earl of Stair, one of the instigators of the massacre at Glencoe, where Campbells murdered MacDonalds in 1692) and the four of clubs (the devil's four-poster bed or devil's bedpost).

▼ See-through monster

A 1977 computer analysis of photographs of the Loch Ness monster (below) – breaking down the pictures into electrical impulses and then reassembling them – gave interesting results. The analysis showed that water ripples could be seen through the monster's neck and suggested that the beast's image was two-dimensional. To skeptics this proved that the pictures were fakes. To believers, it supported the theory that Nessie and other lake beasts are of paranormal origin and not of this world.

Beastly prophet

One of the most peculiar prophets of modern times appeared in Uganda, East Africa, in June 1992. The authoritative British newspaper *The Daily Telegraph* reported that in the village of Kyabagala a goat, speaking in "a loud and terrifying voice," had warned that a great famine was imminent. It went on to say that the worldwide AIDS epidemic was God's punishment on humanity for disobeying the Ten Commandments. Then the prophetic ruminant dropped dead.

◄ Tell-tale name?

Famed British naturalist Sir Peter Scott (1909-89) hailed a photograph of a huge flipper, taken in Loch Ness by M.I.T. scientist Robert R. Rines (left) in 1972 with sonar-linked underwater cameras, as proof of Nessie's existence. But some noted that the name Scott gave Nessie – *Nessiteras rhombopteryx* – was an anagram of "monster hoax by Sir Peter S."

Eastern Zombie

In some parts of China it is believed that corpses must be buried as soon as possible after death. An unburied corpse máy be possessed by a spirit and become a malevolent *Ch'iang-shich*, or Zombie.

Featured creatures

Since World War II, many of the movies' man-made monsters have been presented as by-products of nuclear explosions. Japan's major contribution was *Gojira* (1954): renamed Godzilla, the fire-breathing reptile (very obviously an actor in a monster suit) became a worldwide cult figure. At first the enemy of humanity, he later became its friend, and in *Destroy All Monsters!* (1968) joined with Mothra (giant moth), Rodan (giant pterodactyl), and other featured creatures to save Earth from conquest by alien invaders.

▼ Land of the Werewolf

France, where some 30,000 cases of shape-changing were recorded in 1520-1630 (and one occurred as recently as the 1930s) might claim to be the "land of the Werewolf." In 1764-67 the Beast of Gevaudan (below), widely believed to be a Werewolf, terrorized the Auvergne region, killing 60 people and attacking many more. It defied a mass hunt by 20,000 men, the deployment of King Louis XV's army, and the concerted prayers of the French church. In 1767 elderly hunter Jean Chastel shot a wolf whose stomach was found to contain part of the last victim. It was no supernatural monster, but a smallish, rather unimpressive specimen: some modern zoologists think it may possibly have been a wolf-dog hybrid.

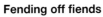
GODS AND DEMONS

Fending off fiends

Since ancient times people have invented various protections against the Devil. Citizens of ancient Babylon kept off demons with a devil trap buried under their homes: an inverted bowl, inscribed with a magical text. A typical example from around 300 B.C. proclaims a bill of divorce to the Devil and all his night monsters and orders them to leave the community. An alternative approach adopts slyness rather than demon-repellants. Even today, some Maltese churches have two clocks, one set to the right time, the other not – to confuse the Devil about the times of church services.

Beating the demon

According to the Apocryphal *Book of Tobit*, Asmodeus – demon of lust, whose task is to stir up trouble between married couples – strangled the first seven husbands of Tobias's wife, Sarah, to prevent the consummation of the marriage. Tobias and Sarah fooled the demon by refraining from intercourse for the first three nights of their marriage. In peasant communities in Europe, this custom of ''Tobias Nights'' was observed until as late as the 19th century.

Heavenly mountains ▶

Many peoples located the home of their gods atop sacred mountains – such as Mount Olympus, where the Greek gods were believed to live, and Mount Fuji (right) in Japan. In India, Mount Meru was the home of sky god Indra; and Mount Kailasa the paradise of Hindu god Shiva. The Chinese long believed they could reach the gods by climbing sacred mountains, and Chinese pilgrims still toil up Mount Taishan. In ancient Sumer, worshipers built artificial mountains, called ziggurats, as homes for their gods.

Not so Good Book

Emperor Menelik II (1844-1913) of Ethiopia did much to modernize his then backward nation, but the progressive ruler had his own superstitions. He believed that he could preserve his health by periodically eating chapters from the *Bible* – and is said to have died when he attempted to counter the effects of a heart attack with an overdose of the *Book of Kings*.

◀ Telling the old, old story

The weightiest version of the *Epic of Gilgamesh* (left), the Assyrian, was written on 12 clay tablets, with about 300 lines on each tablet. Fragments of all 12 survive.

Infernal inspiration

The Italian composer Giuseppe Tartini (1692-1770) incurred the wrath of the Catholic Church when he wed a Cardinal's niece without permission. He hid out, of all places, in a monastery – where one night the Devil appeared to him, picked up his violin, and played a piece of music. When he recovered from the shock of his

◄ Cooler in Hell

Irreverent scientists have pointed out that, on Biblical evidence, Heaven must be hotter than Hell. *Revelations* (Ch.1; v.28) describes Hell (left) as "the lake which burneth with fire and brimstone" – and the boiling point of brimstone (above which it becomes a gas, not a liquid) is 832°F. (445°C.). In Heaven, according to *Isaiah* (Ch.30; v.26), "the light of the sun shall be sevenfold," which it is estimated will give a celestial temperature of about 950°F. (495°C.).

Divine architect

The first pyramid – and Egypt's first great stone building – was the Step Pyramid at Saqqara, built about 2700 B.C. as the tomb of King Zoser. One thousand years later its architect, Imhotep, was declared a god – one of the few people other than pharaohs thus honored in Egypt. Imhotep was learned in medical science as well as architecture, and centuries later the Greeks identified him with Asclepius, god of medicine.

▼ Tracks of tears

Not only images of Christ, the Virgin, and saints have been known to weep, often bloody tears (below). On August 6, 1945, the day of the atomic bombing of Hiroshima, the bronze figure of a Japanese girl owned by Allen Demetrius of Pittsburgh, Pa., shed tears that left green streaks still visible many years later. More recently, skeptical U.S. scientist Shawn Carlson has devised six ways to make images "weep" convincingly.

vision, Tartini wrote down the composition as a sonata, the *Trillo del Diavolo* (Devil's Trill). It is still popular with violin virtuosi.

Onion eyes

To make corpses look their best, ancient Egyptian embalmers replaced missing teeth with false ones of ivory, filled out sparse hair with toupees, and repaired mutilations. A man who had lost his nose was given a wooden one, tied on with leather thongs; the bedsores of an old woman were patched with gazelle skin. Eye sockets were filled with artificial eyes of stone, linen, or, in the case of Ramesses IV, two small, painted onions.

SUPERFACTS

Practical Buddha
Enthusiasts for Eastern mysticism should perhaps consider the ancient legend of Buddha's visit to a yogi who lived by a river. The holy man proudly told Buddha that 25 years of fasting and meditation had given him the power to cross the water by levitating. But Buddha was not impressed. "Surely," he said, "it would have been quicker to build a bridge!"

▼ Marketing Mithra
In the late 4th century A.D. Christianity triumphed over Mithraism – and left suppliers of Mithraic religious images with much unwanted stock on their hands. They simply relabeled their wares: unsalable paintings of Mithra shooting arrows at a rock became Moses striking water from the rock; a minor adjustment transformed Mithra slaying the bull into Samson killing the lion.

The Green Man ▶
Celtic nature worship often used the motif known as the Green Man, or Jack-in-the-Green: a man's face with foliage growing from his ears and mouth, thought to be some Celtic tree god. In the Middle Ages the Green Man became a popular subject in art, even in churches (right), and featured as a fertility symbol in plays, where his part was taken by a young man covered in branches – who was sometimes ducked in the river to ensure rain for the crops. In Britain today many inns bear the name of the Green Man, attesting to local fertility rites long forgotten.

War god in court
War god Mars was a favorite deity of the Romans, who claimed him as the father of Rome's founder Romulus and believed he would always come to the aid of Romulus's descendants. His Greek equivalent, Ares, had no such close relationship with mortals, but was dreaded as violent and cruel. He was said to have been tried for murder by the assembly of gods after he killed one of the sea god's sons for raping his daughter. He was acquitted, but the Greeks remembered this divine court case when they named their homicide court the Areopagus (Hill of Ares).

Menace of the Rosy Cross ▶
In 17th-18th century Europe, the Rosicrucian movement provoked a reaction like the U.S. Red Scares of the 1930s-60s. It was supposedly a mystic brotherhood of ancient times, refounded by Christian Rosencreutz (1378-1484), and was rumored to aim at world revolution led by an Invisible College of master magicians. (Similar stories were told of the Order of Illuminati, founded by a Bavarian lawyer, Adam Weisshaupt, in 1776.) In fact, Rosicrucianism was a harmless cult, partly inspired by the Enochian magic (right) of John Dee. Its major text, *The Chemical Wedding of Christian Rosencreutz* (1616), was written by a clergyman as a literary joke. "Rosy Cross" groups still exist, ranging from

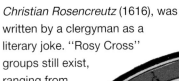

serious students of alchemy to sects offering bogus correspondence courses in occultism.

Prophetic trees ▶

At the center of Norse mythology stood the World Tree, the ash Yggdrasil, which supported the entire universe. On this tree the god Odin (right) hung as a sacrifice to himself in his quest for wisdom Long after the Norse gods were forgotten, the ash was honored in Europe and credited with curative and divinatory powers. The English believed if ash trees failed to produce their seeds in the fall, this heralded the king's death or other national disaster. It was said no ash tree in England bore seed in 1649, the year King Charles I was beheaded.

Miracle drink!

One aspect of an improvement in Sino-American relations in the 1980s was that a famous brand of cola went on sale in China. It is said that an advertising campaign had to be rethought when it was pointed out that the slogan "- - - - adds life" could be read in Chinese to mean: "- - - - brings your ancestors back from the dead."

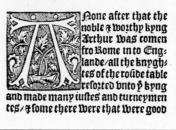

▲ **Jailbird's tale**

The best-known version of King Arthur's story is that of Sir Thomas Malory, completed in 1469. Malory described himself as "a knyght presoner," so scholars believed he had been a noble prisoner of war – until research revealed he had served prison terms for assault, theft, extortion, cattle rustling, and rape. Malory broke jail twice – once swimming a moat; once fighting his way out "armed with swords, daggers, and halberds" – but after his last recorded arrest in 1460, he seems to have stayed behind bars until his death in 1471. The "noble and joyous book entytled *Le Morte Darthur* (*The Death of Arthur*)" (above) was probably written in London's infamous Newgate Prison.

Double header

Supposed relics of King Arthur were a great attraction in 15th-century England: swords, cloaks, or Westminster Abbey's "print of his seal in red wax." Winchester Cathedral still displays a "Round Table" – made in the 14th century and later repainted with Henry VIII's Tudor roses. Dover Castle once boasted the skull of Arthur's knight Sir Gawain. A critic pointed out that another castle also had Gawain's skull – a bigger one. Dover's custodians explained that was the skull of the adult Gawain; theirs was Gawain's skull when he was a boy.

SUPERFACTS

Wimpish witches ▶

Witches are apparently less tough today than in the Middle Ages. Medieval witches were said to rub on flying ointment, so they could be magically transported to Sabbats (right). Modern witches also grease their bodies – but only for weatherproofing when performing "skyclad" (naked) rituals outdoors. Practices in California's Church of Satan include ritual flogging – but it is reported that worshipers are issued protective clothing: padded shorts or panties.

▼ Grammar and glamor

Medieval writers called fairyland "Land of Gramarye" – a mystic word that is actually our prosaic "grammar." Its first meaning, "the art of writing," was corrupted in an age when writing seemed to many a magical skill and came to signify occult knowledge. The

same word gave us *grimoire*, the sorcerer's secret handbook (left) – and "glamor," originally a rather sinister enchantment. Fairies could "cast a glamor" over the eyes of humans – making them mistake a handful of dead leaves for gold, or a hideous monster for a lovely maiden. Cynics might say modern beauty products that promise magical transformation provide the same kind of glamor.

Hairy fairies?

A 16th century British writer made a list of nearly 200 kinds of fairies and spirits. Among the more peculiar names are shellycoats, mumpokers, spoorns, flay-boggarts, gallytrots, gringes, bonelesses, Jinny-burnt-tails, clabbernappers, and – admirers of the works of J.R.R. Tolkien may be surprised to learn – hobbits (but no orcs).

▼ Ancestral guilt

It is said that one of the greatest U.S. writers owed both his name and inspiration for one of his works to the Salem witch trials. Nathaniel Hawthorne (1804-64) (below) was a descendant of John Hathorne, one of the judges who condemned the supposed Salem witches: the "w" may have been added to the family's name in disapproval of their ancestor. Hawthorne's novel *The House of the Seven Gables* (1851) draws on the legend of Nicholas Noyes, a Puritan witch hunter cursed by one of his victims at Salem.

Actor's comeback prevented ▶

Hungarian-American movie actor Peter Lorre (1904-64) (right) was noted for his sinister roles and appeared in several horror films. Soon after his death, police in Oklahoma arrested the leader of a group of Satanists who were alleged to be planning to dig up the actor's corpse and to reanimate it by evil ritual.

Hidden hand

British witches of the 16th-17th centuries were believed to be able to move around unseen by using a Hand of Glory: a hand from the corpse of a hanged man, pickled, and given Satanic baptism. It was said that if a candle were placed in the hand (or wicks attached to its tallowed fingers), anyone in its vicinity would fall into deep sleep for as long as the light burned. Criminals saw this as a useful tool: as late as 1831 a gang of housebreakers in Ireland was caught in possession of a Hand of Glory.

Another haunted White House

The Octagon in Washington, D.C., built in 1800 and now the headquarters of the American Institute of Architects, served as the temporary White House for President Madison when British troops damaged the presidential mansion in 1814. It is said to be haunted by its builder, Colonel John Tayloe, and by his daughter, who jumped to her death from the second floor landing when Tayloe forbade her marriage. Carpeting on the spot where she died is

regularly found rolled aside. The heavy footsteps of sorrowing Colonel Tayloe are often heard. The Octagon is also reputedly haunted by a servant girl who flung herself to death from its balcony to escape the unwelcome advances of a British officer during the War of 1812.

Traveling fairies ▶

Fairies are of European stock, carried abroad by early emigrants like the bemused Irishman (right). In Australia in the 1890s, revenue men arrested a Scottish immigrant family for making bootleg whiskey. The moonshiners were not too surprised by their misfortune: the night before they had forgotten to set out the first "draw" of liquor for the fairies, who naturally were annoyed and withdrew their protection. Settlers also took fairy lore to America, where the only "native" U.S. sprites, the "little people" of some Native American tales, may derive from misunderstandings of the teachings of Jesuit missionaries.

Echoes of World War II

In April 1984 the pilots of two airliners over the Pacific some 180mi (290km) northeast of Japan's Honshu Island witnessed a "nuclear explosion" reminiscent of the atomic destruction of Hiroshima in 1945. They saw a mushroom cloud that within two minutes rose to about 60,000ft (18,290m), reached some 200mi (320 km) in diameter, and then vanished. Investigation revealed no sign of radioactivity: scientists could only suggest meteoric activity. Another echo of World War II was the sighting of ghostly soldiers at Tokyo's Nari Shrine in 1979.

INDEX

CHAPTER 1
STRANGE WORLD

Page numbers in **bold** indicate major references including accompanying photographs. Page numbers in *italics* indicate captions to illustrations. Other entries are in normal type.

A

Abd-ul-Hamid II, Sultan 74, *74*
Adamski, George *23*, 26
Adena culture 56, 57, *57*
Aetherius Society 30
Airship scares 24, 25, *25*
Aliens (see Extraterrestrial)
Alien Liaison 17
Alkemade, Sgt. Nicholas 101
All Souls' Day *86*
Alligators in sewers 104, *104*
Amala (wolf girl) 50, 51
American presidential curse **82-83**
Amulets 86, *87*
Anastasia, Grand Duchess 94, 95, *95*
Anatomists 98, 99, *99*
Andes Candelabrum *18*
Antarctic ozone hole *37*
Ape boys *50*
Apollo 8 mission 30, *30*, *31*
Apollo 11 landing *25*, 79, *79*
Archeological anachronisms **38-39**
Arecibo radio telescope 30, 31, *31*
Arizona medicine wheel *55*
Arli (typing dog) 53
Armageddon 88, *88*, 89
Arnold, Kenneth *16*, 17, 22
Arthur, King 58, 62, 63, 104
Atlantis 19, 32, 56, 58, **68-69**, 290, *290*
Aurora Australis 42, *43*
Aurora Borealis *17*, 36, 42, *43*
Avebury Rings 58, 289, *289*
Aveyron wild boy *50*

B

Ball lightning 28, 42, *42*, 43
Bathurst, Benjamin 92
Batir (talking elephant) 52

Ben-Menahem, Dr. Ari 18
Bentley, Dr. John *44*
Bermuda Triangle 19, **66-67**, 92, 291
Biblical miracles 18
Bierce, Ambrose 92, *93*
Bodysnatchers 89, **98-99**
Brain (human) 102, 103
Braun, Wernher von 37, *37*
Bungee jumping 100, 101
Burke and Hare 98, *99*

C

Callanish stone circle *14-15*
Cannibalism **102-103**
Carnarvon, Lord 76
Carter, Howard 76, 77
Carter, James E. ("Jimmy") 16, 29
Cats (as omens) 87, *87*
Cattle mutilations 27, *27*
Cerne Giant 64 *64*
Chakras *45*
Charles VI (opera) 75
Chikatilo, Andrei *103*
Christian Apostolic Church 34
Churchward, James 68
Clarke, Arthur C. 34
Clever Hans (talking horse) 52, *52*, *53*,
Clifford's Tower, York 85, *85*
Close Encounters **26-27**
Comets 18, **40-41**
Coming of the Saucers, The 16, 17
Concorde airplane 291, *291*
Condon, Dr. Edward U. 23, *23*
Condor I (hot air balloon) 54, 55
Cooper, Gordon 30, *30*
Corpse candles 42, 43, *43*
Cosmic Masters 30
Crop circles 19, *19*, **46-47**
Crying Boy hoax 84
Cursed Seas **66-67**
Curses, jinxes, hexes 19, *19*, **74-75, 76-77, 78-79, 80-81, 82-83, 84-85**, 290, 292
Cyclops, U.S.S. 66, *66*

D

D326 (locomotive) 80, *80*
Dahmer, Jeffrey 102, *102*
Dean, James 80, *81*
De-coo-dah (shaman) 56, *56*
Devil's Arrows 90, *90*
Devil's Bridge 90, *91*
Devil's Den 90
Devil's Dyke 90

Devil's Footprints **90-91**
Devil's Sea 66, 67
Devil's Triangle *66*
Diesel, Rudolf 92
Dinosaur tracks, 38, *39*
Donnelly, Ignatius, 68, *69*
Donner Party 103
Doomsday **88-89**
Dowding, Air Chief Marshall 97
Doyle, Sir Arthur Conan 21, 76
Dragon's bones 38
Druids 58, *59*

E

Earhart, Amelia *93*
Easter Island *18*, 19, **60-61**
Edison, Thomas Alva 24, *37*
Einstein, Albert 21, 37, 96, *97*
Elberfeld horses 52
Eldridge, U.S.S. 96, 97
Entombed toads 38, *38*, 39
Estero (New Jerusalem) 36, *37*
Extraterrestrial intelligences and beings (E.T.I.s and E.T.s) 16, *17*, 22, **26-27 30-31**, 54, 55

F

F-117A stealth fighter *97*
Firewalking **100-101**, 292
Flat Earth beliefs **34-35**, 37, 290
Flight 19 disappearance 66, 67
Foo fighters 29, *29*
Fort, Charles 48, *49*, 92
Four-leaf clover 86
France, Anatole 103, *103*,
Franz Ferdinand, Archduke 80, *81*, 292
Fry, Daniel 69, 288

G

Galileo *35*, 290, *290*
Garfield, James 82
Gazelle boy 51, *51*
Gernon, Bruce, Jr. 67
Ghosts **72-73**
Giants 38, **64-65**
Giants Grave, Penrith 65
Gigantopithecus 64
Glamis Castle 73, *73*
Glastonbury Thorn 62, *63*
Glastonbury Tor **62-63**
Goldstone radio dish 30
Good, Timothy 17
Grayson, Victor 92
Great Eastern **78**

Great Lakes Triangle 291
Great Serpent Mound, Ohio 56, *57*
Great Train Robbery, 80, *80*
Green children 94, *94*
Guinness, Sir Alec 80
Guppy, Mrs. 95, *95*

H

Halley's Comet 18, 36, 40, *41*
Hampton Court 72, *73*
Harding, Warren 82
Harrison, William Henry 82, *82*
Hatfield Barrow 63
Hauser, Kaspar 94, *94*
Heisenberg, Werner Karl 21
Herne the Hunter *72*
Hexes (see Curses)
Heyerdahl, Thor *60*, 61
Hill, Betty and Barney *26*
Hinckley, John W. *82*
Hitler, Adolf 93, *93*
Hollow Earth beliefs 22, **36-37**, 69
Holy Grail 62, *62*
Holyrood Palace *72*
Hope Diamond **74-75**
Hopewell culture 56, 57
Horseshoes (lucky) 86, *87*
Human salamanders 100, 101
Hynek, Dr. J. Allen 26

I

Ignis fatuus 42
Interplanetary Parliament 30

J

Jack o'Lantern 42
James, Jesse 71, *71*
Jehovah's Witnesses 89
Jerusalem 34, *34*
Jessup, Morris 96
Jinxes (see Curses)
Joel (Filipino dog boy) 50
Jones, Jim 89
Jones, Mary 43
Joseph of Arimathea 62, *62*, *63*
Jung, Carl 22, 82

K

Kamala (wolf girl) 50, 51
Kammerer, Paul 82
Kashmir giants *64*
Kataragama ordeals 100
Kennedy, John F. 82, 83, *83*
Kidd, Capt. William 70, *70*, 71, *71*

King, George 30
Koh-i-Noor diamond *74*, 75
Koko (talking gorilla) 53
Koresh (see Teed, Cyrus Reed)
Krem-Akaore giants 64
Kruger, Paul 35

L
Lady Wonder (talking horse) 293
Lawson, Alfred 37
Lemmings 49, 69
Lemuria 68, *68*, 69
Lenticular clouds 28, *29*
Lincoln, Abraham 82, 83, *83*
Little John's grave 65
Living Earth theory 37
Long Man of Wilmington 64, *64*
Lorenzen, Jim and Coral 33
Louis XVI, King 74, *74*, 291
Lowell, Percival 24, *25*
Lowland Hundred 291
Lucky charms 86, 87, *87*, 292, 293
Luther, Martin 34, 35
Lyonesse 69, 291

M
McIver, Dr. Richard 66
McKinley, William 82
Mclean family curse 74, *75*
Macon (airship) 49
Maerth, Oscar Kiss 102
Mahabharata 23
Mantell, Capt. Thomas 28
Mappa Mundi 34
Marconi, Guglielmo 30
Mariner space probes 24, 30
Marlborough Mound 63, *63*
Marocco (talking horse) 52, *52*
Mars (planet) **24-25**, 30, 31
Mary of Agreda 92, 93
Mauna Loa volcano 84, *84*
Meaden, Dr. Terence 46, 47, *47*, 59
Men-an-tol healing stone *20*
Men in Black 26
Mercury spacecraft 30, *30*
Merry Dancers (see *Aurora Borealis*)
Meteors and meteorites 18, **40-41**
Miller, Glenn *92*
Miller, William 88
Miramar Castle 292, *292*
Mississipian culture 56, 57, *57*

Mojave Desert drawings 55
Money pit (see Oak Island)
Monster of Glamis 73
Mort safes 99, *99*
Mound Builders **56-57**
Moundville, Ala. *56*
Mowing Devil *47*
Mu 68
Mysterious appearances **94-95**
Mysterious disappearances **92-93**

N
Napoleon III, Emperor 75, *75*
Natchez (Native Americans) 57
National Aeronautics and Space Administration (N.A.S.A.) 16, *22*, 30, 31, *31*
National Society of Thirteen 87
Nazca Lines **54-55**
Nicholas II, Tsar 94, 95, *95*

O
Oak Island Money Pit **70-71**
Okefenokee Swamp hex 84, *85*
Onishi, Admiral Takijiro 97
Onoda, Hiroo 289
Osten, Wilhelm von 52

P
Parrots 53, *53*
Patagonian giants 64
Patton, General George 97, *97*
Pauli, Wolfgang 82
Pedro Mountains mummy 39, *39*
Pele (volcano goddess) 84, *84*
Persian Gulf wheels 32
Phantom hitchikers 104, *104*
Philadelphia Experiment **96-97**
Poltergeists 45, 47
Poppet (witch doll) 84, *85*
Powys (Wales) standing stone *59*
Presley, Elvis 104, *105*
Prester John *68*
Princess Caraboo 94
Project Blue Book 22, 23, 26

R
Ramu (wolf boy) *51*
Rains of fish, frogs, etc. (see Strange rains)
Reagan, Ronald 82, *82*
Rebel Without a Cause 81
Rectilineator 36
Reeser, Mary 44, *44*

Reiche, Maria 54, 55
Resurrectionists (see Bodysnatchers)
Robertson, Morgan 78, 79, *79*
Rollright Stones 59, *59*
Roosevelt, Franklin D. 82, *83*

S
St. Elmo's fire 42
St. James's Palace 72
Sanderson, Ivan T. 92
Scandinavian ghost rockets 32, *33*
Scarab *87*
Scharnhorst 78
Schiaparelli, Giovanni 24
Seymour, Jane 72, *73*
Showers of blood 48
Silbury Hill **62-63**
Simonton, Pancake Joe *26*
666 (unlucky number) 81
Sodom and Gomorrah 18
Spontaneous human combustion **44-45**, 288
Springheeled Jack 104, 105, *105*
Star of Bethlehem 40
Stead, William T. *79*
Stone circles *14-15*, **58-59**, 289, *289*
Stonehenge 58, *58*, 59, *59*, 64
Strange rains 18-19, **48-49**
Superstitions 81, **86-87**, 292, 293
Symmes, John and Americus 36
Synchronicity 19, 82

T
Talking animals **52-53**, 293
Tamworth Triangle 85
Tecumseh (Shawnee leader) 82, *82*
Teed, Cyrus Reed (Koresh) 36, *37*
Teleportation 92, 93, 288
Tesla, Nikola 30
13 (unlucky number) 86, 87, 291
Time Warps 66, 67, 96, *96*
Titanic **78-79**, 293, *293*
Tower jumping (Pentecost Is.) 100
Tower of London 72
Triangle of the Damned 66
Triskaidekaphobia 86, 87, 291
Tunguska meteor 18, **40-41**
Tutanhkamun, Pharaoh 19, *19*,

76-77
Tyno Helig 291

U
U-boats 96, *96*
Uffington Horse 65, *65*
U.F.O.s *16*, **16-17, 22-23, 26-27, 28-29**, 32, 33, 40, 43, 46, 54, 66, 69, 92, 288, *288*
Uncertainty Principle 21
Unidentified Flying Objects (see U.F.O.s)
Unidentified Submarine Objects (see U.S.O.s)
Urban myths 20, **104-105**, 291
U.S. Air Force 22, 23, *23*, 97
U.S. Navy 96, *96*, 97
U.S. Navy SEALs *33*
U.S.O.s **32-33**

V
Venus (planet) 28, 29, 30
Verne, Jules 79
Vesalius, Andreas 98, *98*
Villa, Pancho 92, *93*
Viking spacecraft *24*, 30
Voliva, Glenn Wilbur 34, 35

W
Wadlow, Robert Pershing 64
War of the Worlds, The 24, *25*
Well dressing *87*
Welles, Orson 24
Wells, H. G. 24
White horses 65, *65*
Whitey (talking cat) 52
Wild children **50-51**, 293, *293*
Will o' the Wisp 42
Witch bottle *85*
Wolf children (see Wild children)
Woodman, Jim 54, 55

Y
Yeti 64

Z
Zamora, Lonnie *27*
Zetetic Society 34, 290
Zion, Ill. 34, 35
Zog I of Albania, King 20, *20*

INDEX

CHAPTER 2
MEN AND MONSTERS

A

Abominable Snowman (see Yeti)
Albertus Magnus, St. **114**
Alchemy **114-115**, *114, 115*
Allison, Dorothy **131**
Alma 178, 298
Amphisbaena 296, *297*
Anita (medium) *145*
Arigó (see de Freitas, José Pedro)
Aristotle **170**
Astrology **152-153**, *152, 153*, 154, *164*
Atti (see Okapi)

B

Baghdad battery 114
Basilisk 166, 167, *297*
Beast of Gevaudan *299*
Bertillon, Alphonse 161, *161*
Besant, Annie *151*
Bessent, Malcolm *133*
Bigfoot 113, *113*, **180-181**, *180*
Boyle, Robert 115
Braid, James 128
Bressanello, Narciso *147*
Brown, Rosemary **146, 147**
Buchanan, Joseph Rhodes 131
Bugbear hypothesis 113
Bunyip 113, 177

C

Cabala *115*
Cambrensis, Giraldus 188
Cartomancy 158
Catherine of Siena, St. 139
Cayce, Edgar 110, **164**, 165
Centaur 166
Chanfray, Richard **116**
Charcot, Jean Martin **129**
Cheiro (see Hamon, Count Louis)
Chimera 166

Clairvoyants 130
Clare, Caroline *295*
Cockatrice (see Basilisk)
Confucius 156
Crandon, Mina (Margery) 118
Croiset, Gerard **130**, *131*
Crowley, Aleister **108, 109, 122-123, 124, 125**, *294*
Ctesias 170
Curran, Pearl 297
Cuvier, Baron 170, 184

D

Dahinden, René *113*
Dalai Lama 150, *151*
Davies, Dr. Morgan 124
de Gasparin, Count Agenor 126
de Loys, Francois 184, *185*
DeSalvo, Albert **130**, *131*
Devi, Shanta 151
Dickinson, Peter 298, *298*
di Grazia, Umberto *137*
Dinosaurs **182-183**
Dixon, Jeane 110, 164
Dominic, St. 139
D'Onston, Dr. Roslyn 124, 125
Dove, Dr. 171
Dowden, Hester 296
Dowsing *111*, **136-137**
Doyle, Sir Arthur Conan 119, *119*, 142
Dracula **190-191**
Dragons *167*, **168-169**, 298, *298*
Druitt, Montague John 125
Dunne, J.W. 148

E

Eddy, Mary Baker 129
Edmund of Canterbury, St. 139
Einstein, Albert 147, 148, *149*
Elixir of Life 114, 117
Evans, Colin *139*
Extrasensory perception (E.S.P.) **132-133**

F

Fox, Catherine **140, 141**
Fox, Leah **140**
Fox, Margaret **140**, *140*

Francis of Assisi, St. 139, 145
Frankenstein **194, 195**

G

Gall, Franz 160
Garrett, Eileen 110, **142, 143**
Gasparetto, Luiz Antonio **146, 147**
Gauquelin, Michel 152

Geller, Uri 108, **126**, 127
Genghis Khan 295, *295*
Germain, Count St. **116-117**
Glauber, Johann Rudolph 115
Goddard, Victor 149
Godzilla 299
Golem 194, *194, 195*
Gottskalk, Bishop 157
Grant, Joan *151*, 294

Earth's oceans may conceal unknown monsters; far larger and more terrifying, perhaps, than the giant squid the crew of the French gunboat *Alecton* tried to capture in the Atlantic in 1861.

Great White Brotherhood 123
Greeley, Horace 140
Griffin 166, 167
Guirdham, Arthur 151
Güldenstubbé, Ludwig de 295
Gull, Sir William 124, *125*
Gunn, Alexander 112

H
Hamon, Count Louis 155
Heidenhaim, Rudolf 129
Helvetius (see Schweitzer, Johann)
Hermann, Alexander 119
Hermetic Order of the Golden Dawn 122, *123*
Heuvelmans, Dr. Bernard 181, *181*
Hibagon 179
Home, Daniel Dunglas 138
Houdin, Robert 118, 119
Houdini, Harry **108**, **118-119**, 294, *294*
Hubbard, L. Ron **123**
Hurkos, Peter **130**, **131**
Hydra 166, 167, 297, *297*
Hypnotherapy 128, *128*, 129, *129*
Hypnotism **128-129**, 295

I
I Ching **156-157**
Irvin, H. Carmichael 142

J
Jack the Ripper **124-125**
James, William 140
Jersey Devil 187, *187*
Joseph of Copertino, St. 139, 296, *296*
Jourdain, Eleanor 148, *149*
Jung, Carl Gustav 158

K
Kirchner, Athanasius 294
Kirlian photography **134-135**, 295, *295*
Kirlian, Semyon **134**
Kirlian, Valentina **134**
Kraken 172
Krivorotov, Alexei 135
Kulagina, Madam 127

L
Lavater, Johann 160, *161*

Le Normand, Mlle M. A. 155
Le Serrec, Robert *173*
Lethbridge, Tom 136, 137
Levitation 110, *111*, **138-139**, 296, *296*
Lista, Ramon 183
Loch Ness Monster 112, *112*, **176**, 294, *294*, 298, *298*, 299, *299*
Lombroso, Cesare 160

M
Magnus, Olaus 172
Magnusson, Eirikur 157
Mammarism 296
Manning, Matthew 146
Manson, Charles 130, *131*
Manticore 166
Marriott, William *110*
Mathers, S. L. McGregor 122
Mermaids *167*, **174-175**, *294*, 297, *297*
Mesmer, Franz Anton **128-129**
Miller, Hamish *137*
Mitchell, Stanley V. 295
Mitla 184
Moberly, Charlotte 148, *149*
Monsters, man-made **194-195**
Morgan, Jennie 295, *295*
Moses, Rev. William Stainton 144, *144*, *145*, 296, *296*
Mothman of West Virginia *112*, 186

N
Nandi Bear 113, 182
Natural Law Party 110, 111
Naylor, R. H. 153
Newton, Isaac 115
Nijinsky, Vaslav 295, *295*
Nostradamus 110, **162-163**

O
Okapi 184, *185*
Ouiji board 144, 145, 297
Owlman of Cornwall 186, *187*

P
Palmistry **154-155**
Paracelsus 114, *115*
Patterson, Roger *181*
Philosopher's Stone 108, *108*, 114, *114*, 115

Phoenix 166, 167
Phrenology **160-161**
Physiognomy 160
Planchette 144, *145*
Polk, Leonidas Lafayette 131
Psychics **130-131**
Psychokinesis 126, *126*, 127, 133
Psychometry 130, 131
Pterodactyl *183*, 186
Pullavar, Subbayah 138

Q
Questing Beast 298

R
R101 (airship) **142-143**, 153
Rasputin **120-121**, 295, *295*
Regardie, Israel 115
Reincarnation **150-151**, 295
Rhine, Dr. Joseph Banks 132, *133*
Rines, Robert R. *299*, 299
Runes 156, *157*

S
Salamander 166, 167, *167*
Sanderson, Ivan *183*
Satyrs 166
Schellenberg, Walter 163
Schuck, Erich *137*
Schweitzer, Johann 115
Scott, Sir Peter 299, *299*
Sea serpents **172-173**
Shelley, Mary Wollstonecraft **194**, **195**, *195*
Shelley, Percy Bysshe 195
Shiels, Anthony "Doc" *139*, *176*
Shipton, Eric 178, *179*
Sphinx 166, *167*
Spinoza, Baruch 115
Spiritualism **140-147**, 295
Stephenson, Robert Donston (see D'Onston, Dr. Roslyn)
Stoker, Bram **190**, *191*
Surrey Puma 184, *185*
Swann, Ingo 133, *133*

T
Tarot 111, *111*, **158-159**, *164*
Tejada, Monica Nieto 127, *127*
Telekinesis (see Psychokinesis)
Tenhaeff, Wilhelm *130*
Teniers, David (the Younger) *106-107*
Teresa of Ávila 139

Thompson, Frederick L. 147
Thunderbird 186, *186*
Thylacine 184, 185, *185*
Tighe, Virginia 150, *150*
Toynbee, Arnold Joseph 149
Transcendental Meditation 111

U
Unicorns 170-171

V
Vampires **190-191**
Vieira, Dr. Waldo 145
von Hohenheim, Bombastus (see Paracelsus)
Voodoo 192, 193, *193*

W
Waite, A. E. 158
Waterton, Charles *185*
Werewolves **188-189**, 299, *299*
Witches *109*

X
Xavier, Chico 144, 145

Y
Yeats, W. B. *123*
Yeti **178-179**
Yogi, Maharishi Mahesh 110, 111
Yokyn 184
Yowie 179
Yusupov, Prince Felix 120, 121

Z
Zana (Alma) 298
Zodiac *114*, 152, *152*, 153, *153*
Zombies **192-193**, 299

INDEX

CHAPTER 3
GODS AND DEMONS

A

Adams, Abigail 282, *283*
African traditional beliefs **250-251**
Ahriman 210, 228, 229
Ahura Mazda 198, **228-229**
Aiello, Sister Elena 214
Akkadia 216
Alcatraz *287*
Alchemy 254, 264
Allah 204, 208, 212
Amaterasu 236, *236*, 237
Amazons 226, 227
American Druidism 231
American Parapsychological
    Association 272, 286
American Society of Psychical
    Research **272-273**
Amityville Horror, The **286-287**
Angels and Archangels *207*, **208-209**, 254, 255, 266
Angels of Mons **208**
Anubis 220, *221*
Aphrodite 204, *204*, 222, *222*
Apis bull 224, *224*, 225
Archangels (see Angels)
Ares 222, 302
Arthur, King **234-235**, 303, *303*
Ashanti *250*, 251
Asmodeus 210, 300
Assassins **248-249**
Astarte (see also Ishtar) 204, *219*
Astrology 254, 255, *255*, 264, 265
Australian Aboriginals **246-247**
Aztecs *201*, 207, 238, *238*, 255

B

Baal 204, *205*
Babylon **198, 216-217**, 218-219, 224
Bastet *220*
Bell Witch 276, 277, *277*
Bentham, Jeremy *279*
Black Madonnas *199, 215*
Black Magic (see also Witchcraft; Satanism) **262-263, 264-265**
Blavatsky, Helena Petrovna 252
Book of the Dead 220-221
Boomerang 247, *247*

Borley Rectory **274-275**
Bubastis *220*
Buddhism 206, 211, 212, 229, 236, *236*, 237, **252-253**, 302
Bull Cults **224-225**
Bull leaping **224-225**
Bull of Heaven 218, *219*
Burton Agnes Hall 278, 279, *279*

C

Cadbury 235, *235*
Camelot 234, *235*
Carrington, Hereward *272*
Cecilia, St. *199*
Celtic beliefs **230-231**, 302, *302*
Central American beliefs **238-239**
Cerberus 226, *226*
Ceres *223*
Cerne Abbas Giant 226, *227*
Chibcha civilization 240, 241, *241*
Chichén Itza *238*, 239, *239*
City X 240
Civil War (U.S.) 284, *285*
Cock Lane ghost (Scratching Fanny) 202, **270-271**
Commodus, Emperor 227
Coolidge, Calvin and Grace 282
Cottingley fairies **268-269**
Coyote 243, *243*
Crete 224, 225, *225*
Crowley, Aleister 262, *262*, 265
Cupid *222*

D

Dagon *217*
Dalai Lama 253, *253*
Day of Judgment *208*, 209
Dee, Dr. John **254-255**, 302, *302*
DeFeo, Ronald, Jr. 286, *286*, 287
Demeter 222, *223*
Demons *210-211*, **212-213**, 300
Devil (see Satan)
Diana of Ephesus 204, 227
Discovery Dance *243*
Doyle, Sir Arthur Conan 268, *268*, 269
Dreamtime **246-247**
Druids **230-231**
Durga *248*

E

Egypt *199*, 206, **220-221**, 224, 225, 301
Eight Immortals *206*
El Dorado **240-241**

Enki 216, 217, 219
Enkidu 218, 219
Enochian language 254, 255, *255*
Epworth Rectory *270*, 271, *271*
Eros *222*
Europa of Tyre *225*
Exorcism *211*, **286-287**
Exorcist, The 286, *287*

F

Fairies **266-267, 268-269**, 304, 305, *305*
Familiars *257*, 258, *258*, 259, *259*
Fawcett, Colonel Percy 240, 241, *241*
Fenrisulfr *207*, 232, 233, *233*
Fetishes 250, *250*
Flying Dutchman 280, *280*, 281
Forman, Simon 255
Freyja 232, *233*
Freyr 232, 233, *233*
Fujiyama *237*, 300, *300*

G

Gabriel, Archangel *208*, 209
Gardner, Gerald 262
Ghost Dance 242, 243
Ghosts **202, 203, 272-273, 274-275**, 278, 279, **282-283, 284-285**, 286, 287, 305
Ghost ships **280-281**
Gilgamesh **218-219**, 300, *300*
God **204-205**, 210
Greek Gods **222-223**, 302
Green Man 262, *302*, *302*
Gremlins 267
Grimoire 304, *304*
Groombridge, Joe 203
Gurney, Edmund 272, 273

H

Hades, 212, 213, 226, *226*
Hand of Glory 305
Hawthorne, Nathaniel 304, *304*
Heaven **206-207**, 208, 266, 301
Hel 213, 233
Hell **199, 206, 210-211, 212-213**, 266, 301, *301*
Hercules (Herakles) **226-227**
Hinduism 206, 212, 248, *248*, 249, *249*
Hitler, Adolf **264-265**
Holy Grail 234, *235*
Holy Lance 264, 265,

Hopkins, Matthew (Witchfinder General) **258-259**

I

Illuminati 302
Inca Empire **240-241**
Incubi and Succubi 211, 257
Inuit shamans 244, 245, *245*
Iron Mountain 284
Ishtar 204, 205, *216*, 219
Islam 204, 206, 212, 248, 289

J

Jackson, Andrew 277, *277*
Jaguar cults 238, 239, *239*
James, William 272, 273, *273*
Japanese religions **236-237**
Jehovah 204, 208
Jesus Christ 208, **214**, *287*
Joad, Dr. Cyril 274, 275, *275*
Johnson, Dr. Samuel 202, **270-271**
Jormungandr (see World Serpent)
Judgment Day (see Day of Judgment)
Jupiter 204, 211, *222*

K

Kali 248, *248*, 249, *249*
Kelley, Edward 254, 255, *255*
Knossos 224, *225*
Ku Klux Klan 284, *285*

L

Labyrinth 224, 225
Lamaism (Tibet) 252, 253, *253*
LaVey, Anton Szandor 262, 263, *263*
Lilitu (Lilith) *198*
Lincoln, Abraham and Mary Todd 282, *282*, 283, *283*, 285, *285*
Loki 232, 233
Long Count calender 238, *239*
Lorre, Peter 305, *305*
Lutz, George and Cathy 286, *286*, 287

M

Machu Picchu *241*
MacLaine, Shirley *201*
Macumba 250
Madison, Dolley 282
Mandela Nelson 251, *251*

Shells, beads, and feathers make up a mask used in traditional ritual magic in Zaïre, Africa

Mani and Manicheanism 228, 229
Marduk **216-217**
Mary (see Virgin Mary)
Mary Celeste 269, *269*
Masham stone circle *231*
Mather, Cotton 260, *260*, 261
Mather, Increase 260
Maya **238-239**
Mazes 225, *225*
Medicine men (see Shamans)
Menelik II, Emperor 300
Mesopotamia **216-217, 218-219**
Messiah War 242
Michael, Archangel 209, *209*, *211*
Minoan civilization **224-225**
Minotaur **224-225**
Mithraism 222, 223, *223*, 224, 302, *302*
Mongols 207, 245
Moses *205*, 302, *302*
Mother Goddess **204-205**, 262
Muhammad 207, *207*, 208, *209*
Mummies 220, 221, *221*, *266*, 301
Murphy-Gibb, Dwina 231
Murray, Margaret 262

N
Native Americans 206, **242-243**, 286
Necromancy (see Witchcraft)

Nemean lion *226*
Neptune *223*
Neumann, Teresa 215
Newspaper Rock, Utah *243*
Norse mythology (see Vikings)

O
Odin 204, 205, 208, 209, 232, 233, *233*, 303, *303*
Olmecs 238, 239
Olympus, Mount 222, 300
Our Lady of Knock 199, 215
Our Lady of Czestochowa *199*

P
Pan 210, *222*
Paradise (see Heaven)
Parsees 228, 229
Pasiphae 224, *225*
Pazuzu *216*
Pedro Mountains mummy *266*
Pentagram *257*
Persian Gods **226-227**
Peyote Road cult 243
Pio, Padre 214-215, *215*
Pointing the Bone 246, 247, *247*
Poltergeists *202*, *270*, 271, 274, 275, *275*, **276-277**, 286, *286*, 287
Poppets *200*, *259*
Poseidon *223*, *225*
Possession 262, 286, 287, *287*
Price, Harry **274-275**

Ptah *199*, 224, *224*
Pyramids **220-221**, 301

Q
Quanah Parker 243
Quetzalcoatl *238*

R
Ragnarok 232, 233, *233*
Raven 242, *242*
Rhine, Professor J. B. 272
Roman Gods **222-223**, 302
Rosicrucianism 302, *302*
Round Table 234, *234*, 303
Ruffini, Antonio *214*
Rupert of the Rhine 259, *259*

S
Sabbat *211*, 256, *256*, 257, 304, *304*
Salem witches **260-261**, 304
Satan 208, **210-211**, 256, *256*, 257, *257*, 300, 304
Satanism 201, 210, 262, 263, 305
Screaming skulls **278-279**
Scrying 254, 255, *255*
Shamans **200**, 237, **242-243**, **244-248**, **250-251**
Shinto **236-237**
Siberian shamans 244, 245, *245*
Sleeman, Sir William 248, 249
Sleipnir 209, 233, *233*
Society for Psychical Research 252, **272-273**, 274, 275
Songlines 246
Sorcery (see Witchcraft)
Sphinx *221*
Spiritualism *203*, 250, 268, *273*, 283
Stigmata **214-215**
Stonehenge 228, 229, *229*
Sumer **216-217, 218-219**, 300
Sunshine Skyway Bridge, Fla. 285
Swastika *264*, 265, *265*

T
Talking Mongoose 274
Tartini, Giuseppe 300
Theseus 224, *225*, 226
Thor 210, 232, *233*
Thresher, U.S.S. 280
Thugs **248-249**
Tiamat 217, *217*

Tibetan beliefs **252-253**
Tintagel Castle 235, *235*
Tobias Nights 300
Totem pole *242*
Trepanation 253
Tryon, Admiral Sir George 281, *281*

U
U-65 (submarine) 281,
Uruk **218-219**

V
Valhalla 206, *207*, 213
Venus *204*, *222*
Vikings 206, *207*, 213, **232-233**, 245, 303, *303*
Virgin Mary 199, *199*, *209*, **214-215**, *234*
Voodoo 250, 251, *251*

W
Weeping Madonnas **214-215**, 301, *301*
Wesley, John *270*, 271, *271*
Wheel of Life 253
White House **282-283**
Wicca (see Witchcraft)
Wicker men 230, *231*
Winchester Mystery House 284, *285*
Wishing wells 230
Witchcraft *200*, 201, *211*, 250, **254-255, 256-257, 258-259, 260-261, 262-263**, 304, *304*, 305
Witch doctors (see Shamans)
World Serpent *207*, 232, 233

Y
Yggdrasil *232*, 303
Yoga *201*, 252

Z
Zarathustra (see Zoroaster)
Zeus 204, 208, 222, 223, 225, 226
Ziggurat 217, *217*, 300
Zoroaster and Zoroastrianism **228-229**
Zulus 250, *251*
Zurvanism 228

PICTURE CREDITS

The publishers wish to thank the following agencies and individuals who have supplied photographs for this book. The photographs have been credited by page number and, where necessary, by position on the page: B(Bottom), T(Top), L(Left), BR(Bottom Right), etc.

PICTURE CREDITS

CHAPTER 2 – MEN AND MONSTERS

Alpha (F.P.G.International): 142-143

Art Resource: 106-107, 118

The Bettmann Archive: 118-119, 119(T), 120, 121(R), 123(TL), 154, 194

B.F.I. Stills, Posters and Designs: 124, 190-191, 192-193(T)

Janet & Colin Bord: 169

F.L.P.A.: 169(R) (C. Carvalho), 171(TL)(J.W.W. Lowman), 171(R)(E. & D. Hosking), 172(E. & D. Hosking), 174(R)(M.B. Withers), 178-179(D. Hall), 182-183(E. & D. Hosking), 183(R)(K. Ghani), 185(TL)(K. Ghani), 186-187(H.D. Brandl), 188 (Curt Ramsmeyer/M. Newman), 191(BR) (Silvestris)

Fortean Picture Library: 112(R), 139(R), 173(T), 176, 177(BL), 181(R), 185(L)(BL)(R), 187(TL)(TR), 187(R), 298, 298-299

Andrew Barker/Fortean Picture Library: 113(L)

Paul Broadhurst/Fortean Picture Library: 137(L)

Loren Coleman/Fortean Picture Library: 112(L)

René Dahinden/Fortean Picture Library: 113(R), 180, 180-181, 181(TL)

Dr. Elmar R. Gruber/Fortean Picture Library: 127(L)(R), 133(TL)(L), 134-135(T), 136-137(T), 144-145, 145(BR), 147(T), 166-167

Lawrence Lawry/Fortean Picture Library: 138-139

Philip Panton/Fortean Picture Library: 111(R), 164-165

Guy Lyon Playfair/Fortean Picture Library: 146-147

Dr. John Thomas Richards/Fortean Picture Library: 111(TL), 126-127

Angus C. Roberts/Fortean Picture Library: 183(BL)

Robert Le Serrec/Fortean Picture Library 173(B)

Shin-ichiro Namiki/Fortean Picture Library: 177(R)

Dennis Stacey/Fortean Picture Library: 127(TL)

Lars Thomas/Fortean Picture Library: 177(TR)

Nicholas Witchell/Fortean Picture Library: 176-177(T)(B), 299(TL)

F.P.G. International: 150-151, 162-163

Giraudon/Art Resource: 170-171

Hammer Film Productions Ltd: 192-193

Images Colour Library: 108(BL), 109(TR)(BL), 111(BL), 114-115, 115(T), 116, 117(L), 122(L), 129(T), 131(TR), 132, 134-135(B), 135(T)(B), 136, 136-137(B), 139(BL), 140-141, 141(R), 150(TR), 152, 152-153, 153(BL)(TR)(BR)(R), 154-155, 155(T), 156, 156-157, 157(L), 158, 158-159, 159(R), 161(TL), 162, 165(B), 167(TL)(BL), 168-169(T)(B), 170, 174(L), 174-175, 184, 187(L), 189(TL)(B), 191(TR), 194-195, 197(R)

J.B. Pictures (Maggie Steber): 192-193(B), 193(L)(R)

Seth Joel: 151

Mary Evans Picture Library: 112(B), 115(B),
117(TR)(BR)(R), 119(L)(R), 120-121, 121(L), 125(T)(B)(R), 128, 130, 132-133, 137(R) 141(T)(B), 142, 143(T)(BL), 148-149, 150(BL), 155(B), 157(BL), 157(R), 159(TL)(BL), 160-161, 161(BL)(R), 163(L)(R), 164, 171(TR), 172-173, 175, 181(BL), 189(BR), 191(TL), 192, 195(TL), 295(L), 296(BL)(TR), 297(T)(BL)(BR), 299(BR)

Mary Evans/The Cutten Collection: 133(R)

Mary Evans/Explorer: 128-129, 129(B), 167(R)

Mary Evans/Guy Lyon Playfair: 126, 146, 147(B)

Mary Evans/Harry Price Coll., Univ. of London: 110, 123(BL)(AR), 138, 294(T)

Mary Evans/Psychic News: 139(BR)

Mary Evans/Sigmund Freud Copyrights: 149(T)

Mary Evans/Society for Psychical Research: 140, 143(R), 148(Inset), 149(B)

Movie Acquisition Corporation Ltd: 190-191, 192-193

National Aeronautics and Space Administration (N.A.S.A.): 165(T)

Amanda O'Neill: 109(BR)

Photofest: 195(R)

Popperfoto: 178, 179(L)(R)

The Rank Organisation: 124(Still from the film, *Hands of the Ripper*, by courtesy of the Rank Organisation Plc)

U.P.I./Bettmann: 108(TR), 122(R), 130-131, 131(BR), 294(B)

Vladimir Krb/Tyrrell Museum of Palaentology: 183(TL)

CHAPTER 3 – GODS AND DEMONS

The Ancient Art & Architecture Collection: 198, 204, 217(L)(R), 218, 223(TL), 225(TL), 228-229(T)(B), 232(TR)(BL), 233(BL)(L)(R), 236, 249(BL), 300

Art Resource: 198-199, 199(BL), 204-205, 208-209, 210-211, 212, 212-213, 214(R), 216, 219(TL), 223(R), 224-225(T)(B), 227(BR), 301(T)

Art Resource/Erich Lessing: 205(L), 209(R), 220

Ashmolean Museum, Oxford: 254(L) (from Images Colour Library)

The Bettmann Archive: 213(R), 244, 250-251, 260(TR), 260-261, 267(T), 273(R), 277(R), 283(TL), 285(R), 304-305, 305(T)

Lee Boltin: 201(BR), 218-219, 219(L), 238, 239(BL)(R), 240, 241(TL)(BL), 244-245, 246-247, 247(TL), 267(R)

Janet & Colin Bord: 205(BL), 235(R)

Dr. G.T. Meaden/Janet & Colin Bord: 227(T)

Bridgeman/Art Resource: 207(T), 235(TL), 255(BL)

British Museum: 249(TL)

Everett Collection, Inc.: 201(TL), 227(BL), 243(R), 261, 286, 287(T)

Fortean Picture Library: 202-203, 215(TL)(R), 234, 241(R), 259(B), 262-263, 273(BL), 301(BR)

Klaus Aarslett/Fortean Picture Library: 263(B)

John Bonar/Fortean Picture Library: 266(L)

Philip Carr-Gomm/Fortean Picture Library: 231(R)

Dr. Elmar R. Gruber/Fortean Picture Library: 202, 214(L), 250, 252, 277(TR)

George Kanigowski/Fortean Picture Library: 203(TL)

Guy Lyon Playfair/Fortean Picture Library: 277(TL)

Lars Thomas/Fortean Picture Library: 284-285

Andreas Trottmann/Fortean Picture Library: 279(B)

Ken Webster/Fortean Picture Library: 276-277

F.P.G. International: 220-221, 236-237, 237(B), 242, 282-283, 283 (BL), 286-287, 300-301

F.P.G. International/Jean Kugler: 253(T)

F.P.G. International/Buddy Mays: 240-241

Giraudon/Art Resource: 208, 209, 226-227, 256-257

Horizon/Douglass Baglin: 246

Horizon/Chun Shih: 253(B)

Images Colour Library: 199(TL)(R), 200(TR), 200-201, 203(BL)(R), 206, 206-207, 207(B), 209(BL), 210, 211(T)(B), 213(TL)(BL), 216-217, 219(R), 221(TL)(BL)(R), 222, 222-223, 224, 225(R), 226, 230, 230-231, 231(BL), 234-355, 235(BL), 238-239, 239(TL), 243(T), 245(B), 246-247(B), 248, 253(L), 254, 254-255, 255(TL)(R), 256, 257(T)(B), 258, 258-259, 259(T), 260(BL), 262, 263(T), 264(T), 265, 266(R), 267(B), 269(TL)(TR), 270(L), 271(TL)(BL)(R), 272(L), 272-273, 273(L), 278, 278-279, 280, 282(R), 283(BL), 285(BL),287(B), 302(BL)(TR), 302-303, 303(L), 304(T)(BL)

Philip Daly/Images Colour Library: 229

J.B. Pictures/Maggie Steber: 251(BL)

Mary Evans Picture Library: 205(R), 214-215, 215(BL), 223(BL), 228, 231(TL), 243(BL), 245(T), 247(BR), 259(R), 269(BL)(BR), 270(R), 276, 279(T), 280-281, 281(BL)(R), 305(B)

Mary Evans/Alfred Pearse: 209(TL)

Mary Evans/Harry Price Coll., Univ. of London: 248-249, 268(T)(B), 272(R), 274, 274-275, 275(BL)(TR)(R)

Mary Evans/Society for Psychical Research: 196-197

North Wind Picture Archives: 217(BL), 303(R)

Photo Researchers, Inc.: 251(TL)

Photo Researchers, Inc./R. Rowan: 200(BL)

Photo Researchers, Inc./Ulrike Welsch: 243(L)

Photri, Inc./Everette Evans: 284

Reuters/Bettmann: 251(R)

Royal Navy Submarine Museum: 281(TL)

Springer/Bettmann Film Archive: 263(R)

U.P.I./Bettmann: 237(TR), 249(R), 253(R), 264(B), 264-265, 285(L)

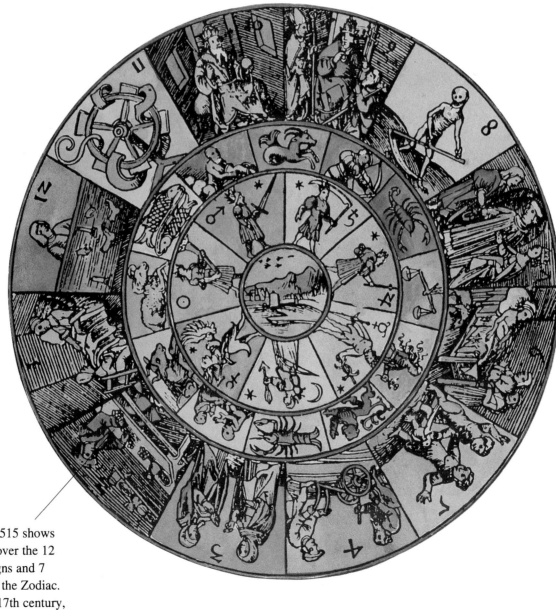

A woodcut of 1515 shows God presiding over the 12 houses, 12 signs and 7 ruling planets of the Zodiac. Until around the 17th century, even learned persons put great trust in astrology.

The "Northern Lights": the natural phenomenon of the *Aurora Borealis*.

A modern pack of Tarot cards – perhaps a key to unlock the future.